Mahatma of New York City

Saurav Pathria

Disclaimer-This is a work of fiction. Names, characters, businesses, places, events and incidents are either the products of the author's imagination or used in a fictitious manner. Any resemblance to actual persons, living or dead, or actual events is purely coincidental.

Photo Credit Front Cover- File' of Yellow Cab by Zitzitoune & Make Art by Mohammad Riza

Cover Design-Saurav Pathria

ISBN: **9781512227338**

DEDICATION

This book is dedicated to all the great souls who walked on this planet.

.

CONTENTS

ACKNOWLEDGMENTS

I thank all the members of my family for their continuous support to help me to continue writing. I also thank my readers for their continuous support.

Chapter 1

Living in a Nest

Every day I woke up, the tireless day started. Go to the restroom, take a bath, brush my teeth, and the list went on. Then the heavy monster was waiting to have a fun ride on my back for the whole day. The weight was heavy, my shoulders were weak. Yes, I am talking about my school bag. Why did my parents give me birth, to carry that heavy bag all day? Anyways, I still had to carry that monster around all day. I wished I was a bag instead of a kid; at least I would have been riding on a back all day. My mom was calling me.

"Jake, come fast, the breakfast is ready", my mom said.

"I will be there in a minute, mom", I said.

"What's in the breakfast?" I asked.

"Orange juice, bread and jam", replied my mom.

"Mom, can I just eat bread and jam, why do I need orange juice. I don't like it", I said.

"It's a very good source of Vitamin C, Jake."

"What is Vita...C?" I asked.

"It is Vitamin C", my mom said.

"Vitamin See....., I see...ha ha....", I laughed.

"Ok, no more jokes, where is your bag?" my mom asked.

"Bag, no, I don't want to carry around that monster all day around", I cried.

"Enough Jake, get your bag, the school bus should be here in few minutes", my mom said.

"I hate my bag", I said.

"I don't care whether you love it or hate it, you need to take it to the school", my mom said.

"But why?" I asked.

"Come on Jake, all of your books and everything else is in the bag", my mom said.

"Yeah, the monster swallows everything", I said.

"Jake, get the bag now", my mom said.

I reluctantly walked towards the bag. I could see the ugly monster laughing at me. I could hardly control my anger and punched the monster in the face. Oh, I felt great, although my hand started to hurt. This monster was one tough monster. Look at it, how happy it looked to climb on my back and take a ride.

"Alright, you ugly thing, come ride on", I said in an extremely angry mood.

"Who are you talking to Jake?" my mom asked.

"No one mom, I just....", I said.

I hung the monster around my shoulders and started to walk out of the house. Other kids were waiting for the bigger monster to arrive, oh yes, the yellow school bus. It was able to swallow up to 40 kids at once. We all stood in line and our parents pushed us ahead. They made sure that the monster does swallow us. We found a seat to sit and placed the monster bags riding on the back to a side, to get a little rest before we had to carry them around again.

"How is it going Jake?" asked Justin.

"Ahhhhh....you know....I hate all this", I said.

"How are you doing Jake", asked Sarah.

"Fine, Sarah, thanks for asking", I said.

We reached the school. I looked at my bag. The bag looked back at me. I could see grin on the monster's face.

"Alright, climb", I said to the bag.

Every bag climbed on each kid's back. I felt as if there were 40 or so monsters looking at me and saying, "What are you going do about it Jake, ha ha ....ha ha...."

I reluctantly walked out of the bus. I soon saw so many other monsters; all climbed onto little kids backs. I felt pity on poor weak kids, who hardly came to this planet, to carry the weight of this, well, you know.

I walked into the school. It sounded like a zoo, with a million voices hitting my eardrums. I walked into my classroom and threw the monster on the ground and said, "What are you gonna do about that, ha ha...ha ha."

Soon, teacher walked into the room.

"Good morning ma'am", all the kids said in one single tone.

"Good morning, you all", said teacher.

"Ok, so we will study about Presidents of our country today, ok", said teacher.

"Yes, ma'am", said kids.

"Ok, so open your book and go to page 25", said teacher.

Kids opened the mouth of the little monsters and took out the books.

"Where is your book Jake?" asked my teacher.

I was too scared to touch my monster bag; I knew I threw it to the ground and I was expecting retaliation.

"Ahhh...", I cried.

"What happened Jake?" asked my teacher.

"Nothing ma'am, I am fine", I said.

The monster trapped my hand inside while I was trying to take out my book. I was able to take the book out after a little struggle.

"I have the book", I said.

"Good.", said my teacher.

"So, you see, President of a country is the leader of all the citizens. He represents our nation. He makes extremely important decisions. These decisions affect us all, directly or indirectly", said my teacher.

I sat there listening to my teacher. I wondered if presidents carried the same big monstrous bags to the school.

"Ma'am, I have a question", I raised my hand and asked.

"Go ahead Jake", the teacher said.

"Did Presidents of our nation carried heavy bags to the school?" I asked.

"Hmm...I am not sure, Jake. I guess it depends", said my teacher.

"Depends?" I asked.

"Yes, it depends Jake", said my teacher.

"Depends on what?" I asked

"Well, I am not really sure how they were brought up, which school they went to, how many textbooks they had to carry to the school etc.", said my teacher.

"But I see that pretty much every child carries huge bags all around", I said.

"Ok, listen Jake; I am not sure what the point of this question is. So, I would suggest that we just learn about our Presidents for now", said my teacher.

"Sure", I replied.

Teacher taught us about our Presidents for another 30 minutes or so. Soon that session was over. There was a 5 minute break and time for next period. It was time for me to put the book back and get another book out of the bag.

"Hello all", said second teacher while she entered the room.

"Hello ma'am", said all the students.

"Ok, get your books out. We will talk about technology today", said our teacher.

I was scared to touch my bag again. I could feel the bag saying, "come on, I am going to eat your hand, ha ha ha".

"Jake, where is your book?" asked my teacher.

"I don't have it", I said.

"What, why not, you should have brought your book", said my teacher.

"I know, I am sorry ma'am", I said.

"Check your bag again, it might be there", said my teacher.

I reached for my bag, I placed previous session's book inside and took out the second one. I was extremely scared.

"There you go Jake, you found the book", said my teacher.

"Yes, ma'am", I said.

"Ok, so we will study about technology today. We will learn how telephones have changed our lives", said my teacher.

She taught us about the inventor and the way telephones impacted our lives.

"Ma'am, I have a question", I asked.

"Sure, go ahead", said my teacher.

"Does tele means far away and phone means sound?" I asked.

"Yes, that it correct Jake".

"Ah, ok, that's how telephone got its name. Sound coming from far away", I said.

All the students in the class started looking at me. Their faces had mixed expressions. Some liked that I knew so much, some were just filled with jealousy.

"Ok, Jake can you tell me how telephone would be beneficial in a commercial set up?" asked my teacher.

"Commercial, you mean like in trade or business?" I asked.

"That is correct", said my teacher.

"Well, if a plane is about to crash, they can telephone the airport", I said.

The whole class was quiet when I said this. My teacher looked a little surprised.

"Yes, that is one way of looking at it", said my teacher.

"I think it is good to have a telephone because you can call an ambulance if you are sick", I said.

"Yes, that would be an excellent use of a telephone, in time of need", said my teacher.

"But, telephone is actually a cell phone now. Everyone has it", I said.

"Yes, that is correct", said my teacher.

"You know ma'am, there is a new name for cell phone too", I said.

"What would be that Jake?" asked my teacher.

"Smartphone", I said.

"Well, that is true", said my teacher.

"What is a smartphone?" asked Sarah.

"Well, I guess Jake could explain that", said my teacher.

"Smartphone...well..it is a very smart device", I said.

All the students in the class started to laugh including the teacher.

"Hold on, it is called a smartphone because it lets you do a lot of things on it", I said.

"Like what?" asked Jatin.

"Ok, Jake, could you answer Jatin's question?" asked my teacher.

"Yes, of course. It has small buttons on the screen. I mean, they are not actual buttons, but, small squares which run different applications. Each application has some specialty. There may be an application to check your e-mail, to book hotels, to rent a car", I said.

"How do you know all this?" asked my teacher.

"Well, I play games on my dad's smartphone and that is how I came to know all this", I said.

"I play games too, but, I never understood the purpose of all those icons on my mom's phone", said Jatin.

"No worries, next time, play around a little with those icons and see what they do", I said.

"Sure, I will", said Jatin.

The teacher taught us about the telephones for another 15-20 minutes and it was time for break.

"Ohhh....", cried Sarah.

We all looked at Sarah.

"What happen Sarah?" my teacher asked as she rushed towards Sarah.

All other students also reached close to Sarah.

"What's going on honey", asked teacher.

"I can't breathe", said Sarah.

"Call the ambulance", said my teacher.

Teacher rushed to another room and brought an injection used in cases of severe allergic reactions. She injected Sarah with the injection. Within 2-3 minutes, Sarah was able to breathe. She told us, she has severe allergies, and probably ate something in the morning, which caused this reaction. After about 10 minutes, I saw some officers with all of their modern gadgets approaching Sarah. They placed a mask on her face and took her for further treatment. Our teacher asked all of us to return back to our seats.

"Alright students, that is very sad. We all need to make sure that we know our allergies", said my teacher.

All the students nod in agreement.

"What was that injection for, ma'am?" I asked.

"It has epinephrine in it", I said.

"Epi...what?" I asked.

"Don't worry about the name, if you grow up to become a doctor, you will know everything about it", said my teacher.

"A doctor, no, I want to be an astronaut", I said.

My teacher smiled.

"Ok, kids read about the telephones in detail when you go home", said my teacher.

She left the classroom.

It was break time. We all headed out of the classroom towards the cafeteria.

"I am worried about Sarah", said Justin when we entered the cafeteria.

"Yes, me too", I said.

We joined the line, picked up our plates and we were given food in our respective plates.

"I am tired of eating this food", said Justin.

"Me too", I said.

"I wish, I had a nice veggie pizza with fresh cheese and juicy tomatoes, olives, hmmmm…", said Justin.

"Ha ha…I would love that too", I said.

"Same burger, fries, cookie and juice, what is wrong with them?" asked Justin in frustration.

"Don't worry, if you grow up to become the mayor of the city, you can change the menu", I said.

"You bet, I will", said Justin.

We stuffed the food down our throats.

"Hey Justy…justy…..justy…come on puppy", said Alwyn, a senior.

Let me tell you about this boy, Alwyn. He is a bully, he scared everyone in the school.

"Go away Alwyn", I said.

"Or else…hmmmm….Jakie…boy..what are you gonna do? You are nothing more than a little puppy to me. I can smash you to the ground and there is nothing you can do about it", said Alwyn.

"Alwyn, you need to stop bullying the kids", I said.

"Or else?" asked Alwyn, while punching on my shoulder.

I stood up and punched Alwyn in the face. He started to bleed from the nose. Everyone was scared. Our teachers came running.

"What is going on in here", asked a teacher.

"He is a bully, Sir", I said.

The teacher ran and got a first aid kit. He placed cotton on Alwyn's nose to stop the bleeding.

After a while, I was in front of principal in his office.

"Alright, Jake, what happened back in the cafeteria?" asked principal.

"Nothing Sir", I replied.

"Nothing, so that boy started to bleed from his nose on his own, right?" asked principal.

"Sir..a..", I said.

"Sir what?" asked principal in a loud voice.

"Sir, he is a bully", I said.

"A bully?" asked principal.

"Yes Sir, a bully...a big bully", I said.

"I never heard that from anybody before Jake", said principal.

"Of course, everyone is scared of him. He punches with his words and hands both", I said.

"And you punch just with your hands", said principal sarcastically.

I kept quiet. Principal picked up the phone.

"Shelly, I need all the students of grade 7 in my office now", said principal.

After about 5 minutes, all the students of my class started entering the room.

"Ok, everyone, I need to know about this boy Alwyn. Jake claims that he is a bully", said principal.

Everyone stayed quiet.

"Ok then I will suspend Jake for a week", said principal.

"Wait", said Justin.

"No Sir", said Jatin.

"What now?" asked Principal.

"Yes Sir, Alwyn is a bully and he bothers everyone", said Justin.

"Yes Sir, I agree", said Jatin.

"Oh, all of you are saying that Alwyn, son of mayor of the city is a bully?" asked Principal.

"Yes Sir", replied Justin.

"I don't believe you all", said principal.

"Ok, all of you go back to your class. Jake you stay here, I need to talk to you", said principal.

All the students of my class went out of the room.

"Jake, I have heard complaints about Alwyn before, but, let me tell you this; I can't do anything if he tries to press charges against you. You see, you can't hit someone. It is a crime, although you are a juvenile", said principal.

"I understand Sir, but, his bullying was just getting to the extreme levels. He would tease fat children; he would call students with different names. He walks around the school, as if he owns the whole school", I said.

"Jake, I will still have to suspend you. I can't allow this kind of behavior in my school", said principal.

"You need to suspend Alwyn too", I said.

"Alwyn, no I can't", said principal.

"You can't, what do you mean Sir?" I asked.

"You can go now Jake. I will e-mail you the suspension notice. I will also mail a hardcopy to your house. I have to call your parents, to let them know about the situation", said principal.

I was extremely angry at all this. I left the room. I went to my classroom and my bag was waiting to be picked up, as if I had less problems already. I picked up the ugly monster and went to the cafeteria. In the meantime, I saw Alwyn's parents entering the cafeteria along with Alwyn.

"There he is", said Alwyn, while pointing towards me.

His parents started walking towards me.

"Who do you think you are?" asked Alwyn's father.

"My name is Jake Sir, in case you don't know", I said.

"Of course, I know your name Jake. How dare you hit my boy?" asked Alwyn's father.

"Sir, he is a bully", I replied.

"A bully, you are calling my son a bully. I have a reputation in this city. I would make sure that you are dismissed from the school", said mayor.

I kept quiet.

"I need to go Sir, I feel a little uncomfortable here", I said.

"Wait, apologize to Alwyn", said Alwyn's father.

"I refuse to do that Sir. Your son is a bully, he got what he deserved", I said.

Alwyn's father held me from my arm and said "Apologize now Jake."

I hit Alwyn's father in the leg with my shoes.

"How dare you?" he said while holding my arm more strongly and twisting it.

"You have to let the kid go", said principal in a bold voice.

"You know what he did?" asked Alwyn's father.

"I do, and I am the one who will decide his punishment, not you", said principal.

"He needs to apologize to my son. You listen to me principal, I run this city. I own this city. This city is my domain and you are just a small part of that domain", said Alwyn's father.

Principal's name was Jacob. He looked extremely angry. He took out his cell phone and called the school security.

"I need you in cafeteria right now, I want Mr. Mayor out of my school", said principal.

"Are you serious Jacobs, you are in big trouble", said Alwyn's father.

"Listen Mr. Mayor, I would do the same to you, that Jake did to your son, if you don't shut up now", said principal.

Alwyn's father, mother and Alwyn looked at principal with their mouth opened. Everyone else in the cafeteria was quiet now. There was a pin drop silence in the hall.

"Ok, listen Mr. Mayor, you need to apologize to Jake for holding his arm", said principal.

"Apologize, are you out of your mind", said Alwyn's father.

"If you don't apologize Mr. Mayor then I will call POLICE and have you arrested for assault on a minor", said principal.

"Assault on a minor, I hardly touched him", said Alwyn's father.

Principal pulled my shirt up; there were red marks on my arms from the strong hold of Alwyn's father.

"You see that, apologize or go to jail, your option", said principal.

"Alright, I am sorry Jake", said Alwyn's father.

"Did everybody hear what Mr. Mayor just said", asked principal.

Principal looked around cafeteria. There were some who moved their head across, in disagreement.

"You see, no one heard the apology Mr. Mayor, louder this time", said principal.

"I am sorry, sorry, sorry", said Alwyn's father in a loud tone.

"Ok, I guess everyone heard it now", said principal.

"Are we done here?" asked Alwyn's father.

"Yes Mr. Mayor, oh one more thing, your son is suspended for a week. I have sufficient student complaints for him bullying other students", said principal.

Alwyn's father asked principal to come to a side, to which principal refused.

"Alright then, we should be going now", said Alwyn's father in an arrogant tone.

Alwyn's parents left along with Alwyn.

A huge clap followed their departure from staff members of the cafeteria.

I was extremely happy at what Principal Jacobs just did.

"Thank you Sir", I said.

"No worries, Jake, I am just doing my job. I am the principal of this school. It is my job to make sure that everyone in this school is safe", said principal.

"That is great Sir. When would I receive my letter of suspension Sir?" I asked.

"Never", said principal.

"I beg your pardon Sir", I asked.

"You heard me right Jake. If I was a kid getting bullied by a student like Alwyn, I would have probably done the same", said principal.

"Well, ok Sir", I said.

"You can go back to your class Jake; you are not going to be suspended. I will call your parents and let them know that I have reverted my decision. But, you need to make sure that you will not hit anyone again", said principal.

"You have my word Sir", I said.

I was filled with deep respect for the principal. I went back to my class. Everyone was extremely happy to see me back. I told teacher that the principal was not going to suspend me. I heard a huge clap and cheers from my classmates.

"That is awesome Jake", said Justin.

It was getting close to the end of the school timings.

"Alright students, you should finish this homework by tomorrow and I will have your assignments graded by Thursday", said teacher in the class.

This day was hardly over, even at home we had to go through the agony of reading the same books again. So, the school was over. It was time for me to pick up my bag, yes the same bag. We walked across the hallway to get outside the school. We were waiting for the bus to arrive.

"Hey Jake, so your parents know about the fight?" asked Justin.

"Yes, principal called them, although he called them again to inform them that he has reverted his decision to suspend me", I said.

"But, how did you convince the principal?" asked Justin.

"Well, I did not convince him. He saw Alwyn's father attitude, and I guess from there he may have got an idea as to how Alwyn might have been behaving. Oh, by the way thank you for standing by me in principal's office", I said.

"No worries Jake that is what friends are for", said Justin.

"Hey Jatin, thanks for standing by me", I said this while Jatin was about to board the bus.

We talked as we walked up the stairs of the bus.

"No problem Jake. So, the school is over now. What are you going to do at home?" asked Jatin.

"First I have to go through the agony of listening to my mom's long lecture and then I have to do the homework. Life is just awesome", I said.

"Oh boy, yes I can see the storm of words heading your way. Can't you just go home and pretend as if you are extremely sick?" asked Justin.

"So you think that my mom is going to buy that excuse?" I asked.

"Well, you gotta try Jake. Otherwise, it will be a mess, I bet", said Jatin.

By now all the students boarded the bus and it was time for the bus to drop every kid to their respective homes. Bus stopped many times before Justin's home approached.

"Alright, Jake good luck buddy, hopefully it would not go too bad", said Justin.

"Thanks Justin, have a good one", I said.

"Oh yes, you too Jake", said Justin.

Justin picked up his bag and started moving towards the exit. He went outside and waved us bye. I and Jatin waved back. Bus was reaching close to my house. My heart started to pound.

"Good luck Jake", said Jatin.

"Thanks Jatin", I said.

I picked up my heavy bag and hung it around my shoulders. I was very tired by now. The day had sucked all the energy out of me. I walked down the steps of the bus and approached my house. I rang the bell and out came my mom. She was talking to my dad. My dad and my mom divorced last year. He lived separately with his girlfriend now. I threw my bag on a side and went to my room. I laid on the bed quiet. I heard a knock on my door.

"Jake", my mom said.

"Yes mom", I said.

"Open this door", my mom said.

I opened the door and she walked into my room.

"Ok Jake, what happened in the school today?" asked my mom.

"Nothing", I replied.

"Nothing, I got a call from the principal of the school that you punched a boy in the face and he started to bleed", my mom said.

"He is a bully, he has been bothering everyone for so long now", I said.

"Listen Jake, no more of this. I don't want any complaints from the school about this in the future, ever", my mom said.

"If he bullies the kids again then I will punch him again mom", I said.

"No you won't", my mom said.

"Will see", I said.

"What did you say Jake? I hope I am clear about this. I don't want any more complaints from your school regarding this", my mom said.

"Do your homework now", my mom said.

I sat on the chair and looked outside the window. I looked up in the sky. Looking at the sky, I felt as if there was nothing around. I felt as if I was flying in the air like a free bird. No rules, no homework, no bullies, no mom yelling at me, no father who had a girlfriend and the list went on.

I looked at my bag. The bag looked back at me. I went outside the room.

"Mom, can I go outside in the park to play?" I asked my mom.

"Not until you have finished your homework Jake", my mom said.

"But, it would be dark by then", I said.

"I don't care", my mom said.

I reluctantly walked towards my room. I reached my bag and opened the book. I started working on my homework. It was a long assignment. It took me 2 hours to finish the whole homework. It was dark by now. I was extremely frustrated. I looked up the sky and I could see the stars now.

"Jake, come out for dinner", my mom said.

"Ok", I said.

"Did you finish your homework?", my mom asked.

"You didn't ask, if I went to play in the ground. All you are concerned about is homework", I said sarcastically.

"Jake, this is all for your good. This knowledge will pave your way for the future", my mom said.

"I know ma but there is no balance in this whole system", I said.

"What balance?" asked my mom.

"A balanced schedule, where there is time for everything, from studies to play and fun time. It seems like this balance is all, you know", I said.

"It is a competitive world Jake. If you don't stand out then you will perish. That is how this world works", my mom said.

"Then why did you bring me into this world mom, if you knew that I will have to carry this burden everyday?" I started to cry.

My mom reached close to me and comforted me.

"Oh my poor baby, I am sorry if I hurt you", she said.

"It's ok mom", I said while rubbing my tears.

I sat on the dining table and ate the pasta that my mom had cooked.

"I am not thankless mom. I do thank you for working hard and bringing the food to the table. Dad did not care about us and....", I said.

"Don't talk about your dad Jake, he has his own life and we are no one to comment on that", my mom said.

"You are right mom. I am sorry about that", I said.

"Don't be, eat your meal", my mom said.

I finished the delicious pasta that my mother had cooked.

"Mom, I will try not to punch anyone in the future", I said while hugging my mom.

"I trust you Jake, you are my wonderful baby", said my mom while moving her soft hands on my face.

"Ok enough drama now", said my mom while rubbing her tears.

I laughed and so did my mom.

"You know, I love you Jake. You are my only reason for living. I want to see you successful in your life", my mom said.

"Of course mom, I will try to become a successful person", I said.

"You sure will, one day", my mom said.

"Thanks ma", I said.

I went back to my room and slept after 15 minutes.

"Jake, wake up", I heard my mom calling.

"Coming mom", I said while rubbing my eyes. I was feeling extremely tired. I had no desire to go to school. But still, I got out of my bed and went to take a shower. I was ready in about 30 minutes. I picked up my heavy bag. Today, interestingly, bag wasn't laughing at me. I felt as if my bag had some sympathy for me today. I picked the monster and it hung around my shoulders nicely today, although I still had to bear its weight.

"Good morning mom", I said.

"Good morning Jake", my mom said.

"So, what's in the breakfast?" I asked.

"I made some pancakes today", my mom said.

"Yeah", I said while getting excited.

"Ok, enjoy these", my mom said.

I ate pancakes in no time. My mom was surprised to see that.

"Well, you were craving for these, weren't you?" asked my mom.

"Oh yes mom, those were absolutely delicious", I said.

"Ok, you have your bag?" asked my mom.

"Yes, there it is, the monster waiting to have a fun ride on my back, ha ha", I laughed.

"You are a naughty boy Jake; this poor bag carries your books all day long. You should thank it, rather than cursing all day", my mom said.

"Thank this guy, it takes a free ride on my back", I said.

"Ok, let's go out, your bus will be arriving soon", my mom said.

"Yes sure mom", I said.

I went out of my house and soon the bigger monster arrived. I was soon swallowed by it. I waived my mom bye.

"Hey Jake, how is it going?" asked Justin.

"I survived", I said.

"Ha ha ha...of course you did. So, your mom did not give you a big lecture?" asked Justin.

"She wanted to, but, I did a little drama", I said.

"What drama ha ha...?" asked Justin.

"I told her that our lives are like birds trapped in a cage", I said.

"Hmmm..birds trapped in a cage, that is exactly how I feel sometimes", said Justin.

"Hey Sarah, how are you doing?" I asked.

"I am fine Jake, no more allergies, hopefully. They did a complete allergy profile check on me. I now know what I am allergic to", said Sarah.

"That is great, Sarah, you need to be very careful in the future", I said.

The bus stopped in front of Jatin's house. He touched his mom's feet and then boarded the bus.

"Hey Jatin, what's up with that feet touching", I asked.

"You see our ancestors used to respect their elders by touching their feet. I have been trying to learn more and more about my Indian ancestry. I don't want it to just vanish away, in the cloud of modernization. My mom does not want me to touch her feet, it is me who is learning new things, ha ha...", Jatin laughed.

"Hey, that is great buddy, I wish I could also learn something about my ancestry", I said.

Soon our bus reached the school. We were all prepared to pick our heavy bags. After picking the bags, we headed straight to the school. We reached our classroom and the same schedule started again.

During the lunch break, we lined up to get our food at the cafeteria.

"Where is Alwyn?" asked Justin.

"Principal suspended him for a week", I said.

"What, no way", said Justin.

"That is awesome Jake, how did that happen?" asked Justin.

"Alwyn's father grabbed me by the arm, here in cafeteria and principal saw it", I said.

"Ok", said Justin.

In the meantime Jatin and Sarah also joined us.

"Ok, listen, Alwyn got suspended for a week", said Justin.

"Really", said Jatin.

"How did that happen?" asked Sarah.

I told them about the whole incidence.

"Isn't that fantastic? Why didn't you tell us earlier?" asked Justin.

"Surprise", I said.

"It is. I have even more respect for our principal", said Sarah.

"Absolutely, me too", said Jatin.

We soon ate the same boring lunch and headed to our classrooms. The sessions went on and on, till it was time to head home. We were handed out long sheets of, of course you know by now, "HOMEWORK", yes. Our lives were just fascinating. We used to wake up at 6 and work till 6 or 7 in the evening. Ok, enough bickering. So, we headed towards ambulance, aa...I mean school bus. Yes, ambulance would have been awesome at this stage. We were stuffed into the yellow box to be taken away to another jail. Yes, first jail was school. Anyways, so everyone left for their homes.

Finally, came my stop and I moved myself out of the bus with that 100 pound bag on my shoulders. Yes, I know, I am exaggerating, but for a kid the weight of that bag was no less than a 100 pound for an adult.

So, I reached my home. My mom was waiting for me.

"Here comes my star", my mom said.

"Thanks mom, how are you doing?" I asked.

"I am fine, I am going to make a nice sandwich for you", my mom said.

"That would be great mom", I said.

In the meantime, I opened my bag and took out my books to do homework. I sat there, a little sad.

"What happened Jake?", my mom asked.

"Nothing, I am fine", I said.

"Oh poor soul, too much homework", my mom said.

"This has been ongoing from your time mom?" I asked.

"What ongoing?" asked my mom.

"This, the daily painful never ending slaughter of study, study and study?" I asked.

"That is how one learns", my mom said.

"I should be getting to my homework now", I said.

"Sure, no problem", my mom said.

I started working on my homework. I did not look anywhere else and focused completely on my homework. I finished my homework and again it was dark by the time I finished. I went to see my mom, who was in the kitchen.

"Mom, can I finish my homework after I play in the ground from tomorrow?" I asked.

"Do you think you could finish it on time and then get up early in the morning to go to school?" my mom asked.

"Certainly", I replied.

"Ok, I don't mind as long as you finish your homework", my mom said.

I was extremely happy and hugged my mom.

"Can I play a game on my computer?", I asked.

"Sure, but don't play those zombie games. Racing car games are fine", my mom said.

"Sure ma, thanks, I love you", I said this and ran towards my room to play a game.

I played game for an hour or so and it was time for dinner again. I ate delicious dinner and went to bed.

Again, the same routine followed.

"Jake, how are you this morning?" asked Justin while in bus.

"Fine, Justin", I said.

"You don't look very happy today, what happened?" asked Justin.

"Na, nothing serious, I am just bored of this routine", I said.

"Bored, you have got years of the same routine ahead of us, before we could be worth earning something", said Justin.

"Yes, I know it is all about competition and survival. It seems like the more like us come to this planet, the more severe would be the competition", I said.

"More like us?" asked Justin while raising his eyebrow.

"I mean population Justin. Look how fast the cities are growing, within next 50-60 years there would be hardly any resources left on this planet", I said.

"Wow, what are you, environment guy now?" asked Justin.

"Nope, just a school going boy ha ha", I said.

"Hey, why do you worry so much about this competition? We all have to go through this and this will be over once we have achieved something in life", said Sarah.

"I hope this would be over as soon as possible", I said.

"Seed sown in soil, takes years to grow into a huge tree and yes hard work always pay back", said Jatin.

"Yes, Guru", said Justin.

Everyone laughed and Jatin pretended like a guru, with his hand held above. We all laughed.

"I totally agree with what Jatin just said. Everything comes with patience. But, where do I go do find this, patience guy", I laughed.

"Inside", said Jatin.

"Yes, inside your pocket", said Justin.

"Come on now, we all know what Jatin meant. He is talking about patience inside our hearts. Right Jatin?" asked Sarah.

"Absolutely, you got it", said Jatin.

We arrived at the school. The same schedule followed. I arrived home in the evening. After having some snacks, I asked my mom if I could go to play in the ground. My mom gave me the permission. I arrived in the playground. There were many children playing in the ground. Some children were accompanied by their parents. I waited for 15 minutes before I got a turn to use the swing. I was going as high as possible. I was enjoying the ride. I was a little aggressive in taking the swing extremely high. Suddenly, the chain holding the swing broke from the left side and I went flying in the air and was thrown 10-15 feet away. I was injured, I could tell. Soon, I saw ambulance arriving at the ground. I was taken in the ambulance and was injected with some medicines. I guess I slept for a while.

Chapter 2

First Flight from the Nest

"Mom", I said as I saw my mom in front me.

"Jake, my baby", said my mom while moving her hand very gently on my head.

"What happened to me?" I asked my mom.

"Nothing, you are fine", my mom said.

"Ahhh", I said as I felt pain in my left arm. I saw a huge plaster on my left arm.

I saw a doctor and a nurse entering my room.

"Hey strong guy", said doctor.

"What happened to me?" I asked.

"Nothing major, your arm, well, never mind, you would be fine soon", said doctor.

"What happened to my arm mom?" I asked my mom.

"It is fractured Jake", my mom said.

"Fractured?" I asked.

"It will get better with time", said doctor.

"But, I have to go to school every day. I have to finish so much homework", I said.

"Don't worry about the homework, I will call your school to let them know, that you are injured", my mom said.

"Jake, you need to take care of your health. You should not be worried about school or homework. That is all secondary", said doctor.

Doctor took my mom to a side and talked to her for 2-3 minutes.

In the meantime, nurse injected something in my vein. I felt dizzy and slept for, I don't know how long.

"Jake, wake up", said a nurse.

I opened my eyes and I saw her with a plate of fruits and a sandwich.

"Where is my mom?" I asked.

"She had to go to job, but your dad will be coming here soon", said nurse.

"My dad, well, as if he has time for all this", I said sarcastically.

The nurse kept quiet. I ate the food; thankfully my right hand was still working. After eating the food I went to sleep.

"Jake", said my dad.

I opened my eyes and saw my dad standing there with his girlfriend.

"Hi", I said in a low voice.

"Hey strong man, what happened to you?" asked my dad while getting close to me.

I was certainly not happy to see my dad come to the hospital with his girlfriend.

"Survived", I said sarcastically.

"Oh come on, you would be fine", said my dad while rubbing his hand on my right shoulder.

"Thanks dad", I said.

"Hello Jake", said Julie, my dad's girlfriend.

"Hello", I replied.

"How are you feeling?" asked Julie.

"Well, I certainly feel the pain but hopefully in a few days, I would be headed home", I said.

"So, what exactly happened?" asked my dad.

"I was on the swing in the park and going pretty high. I guess the swing could not handle that much force and broke", I said.

"But, that is unacceptable. I am going to sue the city for negligence", said my dad.

"I was negligent too, dad", I said.

"But the swing should not break just like that", my dad said.

"I agree, something has to be done to make sure no one else is injured", I said.

"Yes, Jake. You don't worry about it. I will talk to my attorney today", said my dad.

"If you need anything, let us know Jake", said Julie.

"Thank you, I guess I have pretty much what I need", I said.

"Well, you take care of yourself young man, we should be going now", said my dad.

"Oh yes, sure, thanks for coming ", I said.

"Don't be Jake, I am your dad and this is what dads do. So, no thanks for it", said my dad.

"Ok", I said.

My dad and Julie left the room.

I felt some pain in my left arm. I guess the medicines were making the pain go away. It was getting close to the evening and I was expecting to see my mom.

"Hey Jake", the doctor said while entering my room.

"Hello Sir", I said.

"How are you feeling?" he asked.

"I feel pain once in a while", I said.

He wrote something on his notepad.

"Ok, what else?" he asked.

"I feel dizzy, sad and you know.....", I said.

"Don't be sad, you will be fine soon", said doctor.

"Na, it is not this pain, well, anyways", I said.

"What is it?" he asked.

"Never mind Sir, I trust you and I will out of here soon", I said.

"Sure you will be. We are giving you the best treatment available Jake", said doctor.

"Thank you Sir", I replied.

In the meantime a nurse also entered the room. She checked the level of bottle, which was hooked to my vein and replaced it with a new bottle. Doctor gave nurse some instructions.

"Ok Jake, you take care of yourself", said doctor.

"Yes Sir, thanks again", I said.

"You are very welcome", doctor said and left the room.

"Ok Jake, you need to take these pills", said nurse while giving me a glass of water and some pills. I took the pills.

"Thank you", I said.

"You are very welcome", said nurse.

"When would my mom come", I asked.

"She should be here soon. Maybe she got stuck in traffic or something", she said.

"Maybe", I said.

"Jake, I will let you rest now. Take care and don't worry about anything", nurse said while leaving the room.

"Thank you", I said.

The pills made me dizzy and I went to sleep for I don't know how long.

"Jake", I heard.

"Jake", I heard again.

"Hmmm...what? I slowly opened my eyes and my mom was standing in front of me.

"Hey Jake", my mom said.

"Hello mom, how are you doing?" I asked my mom.

"I am fine, I am sorry I got late", my mom said.

"What happened mom?", I asked.

"Nothing, just some office stuff that I had to finish today", my mom said.

"No worries mom", I said.

"So, how are you doing?" asked my mom.

"I still feel pain once in a while", I said.

"Did they not give you painkillers?" my mom asked.

"They are taking very good care of me, mom", I said.

"Ok, that is good to know. If you feel the pain, I can call the nurse to give you more medicine", my mom said.

"I can bear that much pain", I said.

"I know you are strong boy", my mom said.

"Dad came with his girlfriend today", I said.

"Oh, Ok, he came with his girlfriend", my mom asked while looking a little surprised.

"Yes, she was trying to be very nice to me", I said.

"They have their own life Jake. It's good your dad came to meet you", my mom said.

"Yes, he could at least do this much", I said.

My mom and I sat quiet for 5 minutes.

"So Jake, you need something?" asked my mom.

My mom looked extremely tired.

"No, mom. You should go home and take rest", I said.

"Are you sure, you don't need anything?" my mom asked.

"No ma, I am fine", I said.

My mom kissed me on my check and left the room. I wasn't feeling sleepy anymore. I laid in my room with my eyes opened. After a little while, it was time for dinner. I ate the dinner and slept.

I opened my eyes and it was morning. Nurse entered my room.

"Hello Jake. How are you feeling?" she asked.

"I am fine. Could you please move the curtain to a side", I said.

"No problem", she said, while removing the curtain.

I could see sunrays entering my room, the birds flying. It was a beautiful morning. I kept looking outside the window.

"So, are you ready for breakfast?" the nurse asked.

"Yes, after I have gone to the restroom", I said.

"Sure", I will be back in 5-10 minutes with your breakfast", she said.

I came back from restroom. I stood close to the window and started looking outside. It was very beautiful. The sun was changing from orange to yellow. Birds were flying in huge flocks. I was on a pretty high floor of the building. I saw people walking down on the street. I saw school buses. I saw people rushing to wherever they were heading to.

"Jake", someone called my name from back. The nurse was standing there with breakfast.

"Oh, yes", I said.

"You are enjoying looking outside?" asked the nurse. Oh, by the way her name was Cindy.

"Yes, I don't remember when was the last time I was able to enjoy the sunrise", I said.

"Oh yes, our lives are so busy now", she said.

"Yes, of course", I said.

"Ok, enjoy your breakfast" she said.

"Sure, thank you", I said.

I ate the breakfast with my right hand. Hopefully, it was still functional. Once the breakfast was finished, I stood close to the window again. The sun was much higher now, with a strong light entering my room. The streets below looked much busier. People were walking very fast here and there. In the midst of all this, I could see some people sitting alone with shopping carts in front of them. They had a lot of stuff in those carts.

"Hey Jake", I heard someone calling my name.

"Oh, hello doctor", I said.

"How are you feeling today?" he asked.

"I am feeling much better today", I replied.

"Enjoying the view?" asked doctor. Doctor's name was John.

"Yes Sir, it is wonderful over here", I said.

John held my right hand and started checking my pulse. Then he took out a thermometer and asked me to hold it under my tongue for a minute.

"Ok, everything seems normal", said John.

"Thank you", I said.

"Well, you should not stand here for long. You should take rest as much as possible", said doctor.

"Who are those people?" I asked.

"Who?" asked John.

"Those right there, on the bench", I said while pointing down at individuals sitting on the bench.

"They are probably homeless folks", said John.

"Homeless?" I asked.

"Yes, they probably don't have a home to live in", said John.

"But why?" I asked.

"Well, some of them have addiction problems and they end up losing their jobs", said John.

"But, where are their families?" I asked.

"They are usually deserted by their family members", said John.

"But why?" I asked.

"You see Jake; society does not like people with addiction to drugs and other substances. There are people for whom all forms of counselling fails. They are finally left alone, with no member of even their family to support them", said John.

"That is sad", I said.

"Yes, it is. Well, I guess, I better be going now to see other patients", said John.

"Of course Sir, thank you for stopping by", I said.

John moved out of the room while I stood near the window. I kept looking down. I saw one guy standing on the bench approach a trash can. He took out something from it and started eating from it. I was in shock. Some people drove in their luxury cars and stopped by in front of luxury restaurants and some finding food in the trash cans. I lived my life in a little cocoon. From my childhood, I was carrying my bag to school, learning stuff at school and eating, playing and sleeping in that pampered environment. I guess, this was the first time I saw what life really meant. It wasn't a fairytale to me anymore. I felt extremely sad and went back to my bed. I stayed awake while lying in the bed and staring at the sky from the window. I had lunch just like routine and it was evening by now and I was expecting to see my mom.

"Jake", I heard.

"Mom", I said.

"Hey sweetheart, how are you doing?" she asked.

"I am fine mom, the pain was less today. When are they going to send me home? I have missed some days at school and I would have a lot to catch up", I said.

"Don't worry about all that. You need to get better", my mom said.

My mom's name is Sheela and my dad's name is Andy. Sorry about that. I just call them mom and dad.

"Mom, how many more days do I have to stay here?" I asked.

"I will talk to the doctor and see when they plan to relieve you", my mom said.

My mom went out and returned after about 10-15 minutes.

"Ok, Jake, they are going to let you go home a day after tomorrow, so that is a great new", my mom said.

"That is great", I said.

My mom stayed for another 30 minutes or so and then she left. Nurse Cindy served me the dinner and I went to bed.

I woke up early in the morning and moved the curtain from the window. It was still a bit dark. I could see a little bit of light from the sunrise. It was extremely beautiful and peaceful. I looked down and could see a homeless man sleeping on the bench. The street light was well lit for me to see around the street from one end to another. There was another huge building in the front on the right side. The street ran between the hospital's building and building on the right. There was a huge lake on the left and that is where I saw the sun coming out. It felt as if the sun came right out of the lake. From this height, I wished I was a bird. I could fly wherever I liked. No more going to school, homework, dad and mom fighting and the list went on.

"Oh, you woke up", I heard a female voice.

It was Cindy, the nurse.

"Yes, Cindy. How are you this morning?" I asked.

"I am fine, Jake. How about yourself?" she asked.

"I am feeling better", I said.

"You are ready for breakfast?" she asked.

"Yes, of course", I replied.

Soon Cindy brought me the breakfast.

"Cindy, where do homeless people eat breakfast?" I asked.

"What? Say that again", asked Cindy.

"The homeless, where do they eat breakfast?" I asked.

"Well, hmmm...don't worry about them. You have enough going on with yourself right now", said Cindy.

"No, I am just curious", I said.

"Government must be doing something for them", said Cindy.

"If government is doing something for them, then why do they sleep outside in the cold?" I asked.

"I really don't know sweetie", she replied.

"I see so many rich people passing by them, pretending they never even see a guy sleeping out in the cold", I said.

"We can't do anything for them. Most of them suffer from drug addiction, Jake", said Cindy.

"What kind of drug addiction?" I asked.

"Don't worry about it; you will know everything, once you grow up. I should be going by now", said Cindy.

"Oh yes, of course. Thank you for the breakfast", I said.

"You are very welcome", she said.

Cindy went outside the room. I looked down and there were two men sitting close to the trash can and taking something out of it. They went to a side and shared whatever they took out of trash can. In a while, I saw three policemen, approaching the two men. They stood next to them and it seemed like they were asking them something. Soon, one of those men stood up, the policeman took something out from his right side and pointed this gadget at the man. The homeless man fell on the ground and was shaking pretty bad. A police car came and they put the man in the back seat.

Then police officers started questioning the second man. He was telling them something and was waving his hand here and there. Soon, police officers left that place and that man went back to the trash can and took something else out of there and started eating it. I saw him shaking his hand while he took something out of the can. He looked at his hand and put the finger in his mouth. I am guessing something must have poked him. He sat on the bench and looked up. He looked up to the sky and then started looking up the building and that is when my eyes met his eyes. I moved myself to the side. After a while, I peeked and he was still looking up towards the window of my room.

"Jake", I heard someone calling my name.

"Doctor John", I said.

"How are you feeling? You seem to be enjoying looking out of that window", said John.

"Oh no, I am just...you know", I said.

"Don't worry about that", he said.

"Ok, let me check your pulse and other stats", said John.

"So, John, are all homeless people taken to jail, sooner or later?" I asked.

"Homeless people, what?" John asked while looking extremely surprised.

"Yes, the people who have no home", I said.

"You have been looking quite a lot down that window, haven't you?" asked John.

"Na, it is just...", I said.

"You see there are lots of things going out in this world. We can't fix everything. I would ask you to take rest as much as possible and stop worrying about other things. You should be worried about your own health at this point", said doctor.

Cindy entered the room while John was talking to me.

"Cindy, could you please give Jake these medicines in 2 hours", said John while pointing to his notepad.

"Absolutely", she said.

"Well, Jake, you take care of yourself now. Don't worry what goes in the streets of this city. You will see different types of people every day. Rest is most important for your recovery", said John and left the room.

"Alright, sweetie, you take rest now", said Cindy as she left the room too.

I was back in front of the window. The homeless man was not there anymore. I saw the city trash pickup truck, taking out trash from the can. I could see so many boats in the lake by now. Many people were jogging alongside the lake. I looked down the street, I saw a man walking on the side. Suddenly, I saw a car coming that way at a very high speed. The car hit the man, stopped for a while and then fled at a much higher speed. I was shocked. I tried to run out of the room but there was still a needle in my vein which was attached to a bottle with a long tube.

I shouted from my room "help, help." Then I realized there was a button to press that led to the nursing station. I pressed that button 10-15 times in panic.

Nurse Cindy came to my room in 2-3 minutes.

"Help, help", I said.

"What happened Jake?" Cindy asked.

I went to the window and said "there there".

"What Jake?" asked Cindy.

"That man lying on the side of the street", I said.

"Ok, he looks like a homeless drunk man to me", said Cindy.

"No Cindy, I saw a car hit him", I said.

"What, are you sure?" she asked.

"Absolutely, hurry up, he needs help. He maybe still alive", I said.

Cindy ran out of the room. I stood at the window, looking downwards. After about 5 minutes or so, I saw an ambulance approaching. I saw two police cars approaching too. They placed him in the ambulance. Soon, ambulance left and police cars followed the ambulance. I kept looking out the window. After the lunch, I felt asleep.

"Jake", I heard a voice.

I opened my eyes and I saw two police officers with Cindy, standing in my room.

"Hello", I said.

"Jake, my name is Officer Randal and this is Officer Trevino. We were wondering if you don't mind talking to us for a while", said officer Randal.

"Sure", I said.

"By the way, if you feel that you are not in a position to talk to us, then we can come later on", said Officer Randal.

"Oh no, I am fine", I said.

"Jake, I am going to go and see some patients, while you talk to Officers", said Cindy.

"Sure Cindy", I said.

"So, young man, you saved a life today", said Trevino.

"That man is alive?" I asked.

"Yes, he is alive. In fact, he is just 1 floor below you, in the Intensive Care Unit of this hospital", said Officer Trevino.

"Has he sustained major injuries?" I asked.

"Yes, he sustained some injury to his brain, right arm and some to the leg", said Officer Randal.

"Did you catch the guy who hit him?" I asked.

"No, we have not. We need your help in that regard", said Officer Trevino.

"Ok", I said.

"So tell me what you saw", asked Officer Randal.

"I saw this man walking on the side and this car came at a very high speed. This car hit him, stopped for a while and then fled the place", I said.

"From which direction the car came?" asked officer Randal while writing something on his notepad.

"It came from the right side", I said.

"By right side, you mean", asked Officer Randal.

"Wait, I can show you exactly", I said.

I got up from my bed and started walking towards the window. Both officers followed me.

"Ok, so the car came from that side", I pointed with my hand.

"Ok", he said.

"The man was walking over there", I said.

"You remember the color of the car?" asked Officer Trevino.

"It was a red car", I said.

"Do you remember what kind of a car it was, did you see number plate by any chance. I know it is high from here but we still need to ask you these questions", said Officer Randal.

"Well, it was a type of car that I have seen in some movies. You know those that go fast. Whoooom...... you know. To answer your second question, no I did not see the number plate", I said.

"That's fine Jake", said Officer Randal.

"If I show you some pictures on my phone, would you be able to tell which is the closest car?" asked Officer Randal.

"Yes, I can try", I said.

Officer Randal showed some pictures of different types of cars. There was one car which looked exactly like the one I saw, "There, that one", I said.

"Are you sure?" asked Officer Randal.

"Yes Sir, I am sure. That car looked exactly like this car", I said.

"Good, thank you", said Officer Randal.

Soon my mom entered the room. She looked a little scared when she saw two police officers in my room.

"Jake, is everything alright?" she asked.

"Oh yes mom, these officers are here to ask me about the car who hit the homeless man", I said.

"Car, homeless.." my mom said.

"Hello ma'am, my name is Officer Randal and this is Officer Trevino. We received a call this afternoon that a man was hit by a car. It was your son who saw the car hitting the man. So, we thought that he might be of great help to us in finding the person involved in this hit and run", said Officer Randal.

"Jake", my mom said while looking at me.

"Yes ma'am, it was Jake", said Officer Trevino.

"But he is himself sick, I don't think he should be looking out of that window and then be involved in giving a statement to the police", my mom said.

"Don't worry ma'am, Jake would remain completely anonymous during this investigation", said Officer Trevino.

"Don't worry mom, I should be fine", I said.

"Ok Jake, take care of yourself and thanks for your help", said Officer Randal while shaking my right hand.

"Thanks for your help Jake", said Officer Trevino and he also shook my hand.

"You have a good evening ma'am", said Officer Randal to my mom. Officers Randal and Trevino left the room.

"Jake, come sit on the bed now", my mom said.

I sat on the bed while my mom took my right hand in her hand.

"You should be taking care of yourself", my mom said.

"I am fine mom, you don't have to worry", I said.

"So, how was your day?" I asked.

"You know, it is a job, you have to obey the orders of your boss and blah blah", my mom said.

"What happened? Did your boss say anything wrong to you?" I asked.

"Na, just regular stress at work", my mom said.

"Regular stress", I asked.

"Yes, this is regular at any job, nowadays. The world is extremely competitive", my mom said.

"Sorry about that mom", I said.

"No worries Jake", my mom said.

Soon Cindy came to the room.

"Hey hello, Sheela and Jake", said Cindy.

"How are your feeling Jake?" asked Cindy.

"I am feeling much better, the pain is also bearable now", I said.

"That is good", said Cindy.

"When could I take Jake home?" asked my mom.

"Well, I need to talk to Doctor John again. He will have to examine Jake, before we can discharge him", said Cindy.

"I understand", my mom said.

"Your son saved a life today", said Cindy.

"Yes, I came to know about it", my mom replied.

"That homeless man is in stable condition now", said Cindy.

"That is great", I said.

"Can I meet with him?" I asked.

"No, Jake", my mom said.

"I guess, not right now, maybe after a week or so. He had some serious head injury", said Cindy.

"Poor guy", I said.

Cindy smiled. My mom went towards the window and stood there.

"So, this is your little window to the world, I mean to the city", my mom said.

"Well, why don't you both talk and I should be going now", said Cindy.

"Oh sure Cindy, thanks", my mom said.

I walked towards the window. The sun was setting. It was going down into the lake.

"You see those people fishing", I said.

"Where?" asked my mom.

"Mom, there, where those cars are parked by the lake", I said.

"You must have got an eagle eye Jake. I don't see a thing", my mom said.

"Forget about that, look how the sun is going into the lake", I said.

"Sun is setting Jake, it is not going into the lake", my mom said while smiling.

"Oh come on, mom, it does feel like that, no?" I asked.

"Sure it does. Whatever, it is nice view from up here", my mom said.

"Jake", someone called my name.

"Doctor John", my mom said.

"Hi Sheela", said John.

"Hey Jake, how are you feeling now?" asked John.

"I am feeling better", I said.

John removed the long cloth by which my arm was hanging.

"Ahhh", I said.

"Oh sorry, does it hurt?" asked John.

"Yes", I said.

"Ok, come and sit on the bed", John said while holding my left arm.

He pressed the button for calling someone from the nursing station.

"Yes Doctor", said Cindy while entering the room.

"Could you please give Jake this medicine now", said John.

"Sure", said Cindy. She left the room and came back with a pill. I took the pill with water.

"Ok Jake, that should take care of the pain", said John.

"Thank you", I said.

My mom looked concerned while she watched standing on the side. Soon, I saw tears coming down her eyes. John placed the cloth back.

"Mom", I said.

"Yes, Sweetie", my mom said while wiping her tears.

"Don't cry, I am fine", I said.

Cindy approached my mom and placed hand on my mom's left shoulder to comfort her.

"No need to worry Sheela, he is fine. This pain would stay for a while", said John.

"Cindy, can I talk to you for a second", said John.

John took Cindy out of the room. They returned back in 3-4 minutes.

"Ok, Sheela, we can't let Jake go home by tomorrow", said John.

"Oh ok, I will have to check with my insurance company if they will cover this extended stay", my mom said.

"Please do that, in my opinion, he will receive much better care here. You need to take care of your job, and it would be cumbersome for you to take care of Jake at the same time", said John.

"No, I understand that", my mom said.

"Please give me 5 minutes", she went out with the phone in her hand. John and Cindy followed her. My mom came back after 5 minutes or so.

"Hey Sweetie, so everything is all set, you will stay here for 4-5 more days", my mom said.

"Will insurance cover it?" I asked.

"Absolutely", my mom replied.

"That is good, mom", I said.

My mom stayed in the room for another 30 minutes or so and then left for home. I went to sleep. I woke up early in the morning. I rushed to the window and removed the curtain to a side. Sun was coming out of the lake. Birds were ready for the day. I could hear some honks from the cars. The street was picking up rush. I saw a man sleeping on the bench. I could see a cart behind him. The cart was filled with clothes, shoes and some boxes. He wore a camel colored jacket, had long hair and beard. He was wearing high ankle boots and dark blue jeans. His left arm was placed under his head, which probably worked as a pillow. His face looked dirty. His hands looked injured. I could see a cardboard with something written on it, coming from side of his jacket. There were few people walking by him. Most of them moved aside as they approached this man. He was in deep sleep. I kept looking at the guy. After a while Cindy brought me the breakfast.

"Jake, I figured out that you would be awake by now, so I brought you the breakfast", said Cindy.

"Thanks Cindy", I said.

"What happened to you? Why are you crying? Are you in pain?" asked Cindy.

"I am fine Cindy", I said.

"Are you sure, you don't need medicine?" asked Cindy.

"No, I am fine, don't worry Cindy", I said.

"Ok, you enjoy your breakfast and I should be going by now", said Cindy.

"Sure, thanks", I said.

I did not eat my breakfast and moved close to the window. I saw this homeless man sitting on the bench now. He looked extremely weak and tired. He looked at people passing by. Most of them took out their cell phones, once they approached this man. I am guessing they were pretending that they were busy on their cell phones and never saw the man.

"Jake", Doctor John called my name.

"Hey Doctor", I said.

"How are you this morning?" asked John.

"I am fine Sir", I said.

He checked my vitals, just like routine and left the room. I looked outside the window and the homeless man was gone. His cart, which I assume was his, was still by the wall, behind the bench.

After a while, I saw a man running from the left extreme of the street towards the right side. It was that homeless man. Soon I saw a police car behind the man. Police car stopped and two police officers came out of the car. They pointed their guns at that homeless man. He threw a can at the police officers and suddenly I heard pop, pop pop. I saw the homeless man hit the ground. I saw officers approaching the man. They turned the man around. He had fallen with his face down. He was not moving. I saw an ambulance approach the scene in a while. Some individuals came out of the ambulance. They approached the man, started pressing his chest and placed the man on a stretcher. They placed the homeless man in the ambulance and left the place. The police car followed the ambulance.

"Jake", I heard someone calling my name.

"Officer Randal", I said.

"Hello Jake, how is it going, why are you crying?" he asked.

"Did they kill him?" I asked.

"Who killed who?" asked Officer Randal.

"Did the police officers kill the homeless man?" I asked while pointing down.

"I have no idea, what you are talking about Jake", he said.

"I saw that a homeless man was running and these two police officers shoot at him, I guess", I said.

"What?" asked officer Randal as he looked surprised.

"Yes, Sir, I saw this homeless man running and those two officers shooting at him", I said.

Officer Randal presses a button on a gadget that hung through his right shoulder. He starts talking to someone through that gadget.

"Ok, you are right, an armed homeless man was shot today a little while ago at Crossroads street, where he died at the scene", said officer Randal.

"What do you mean by armed?" I asked.

"Well, armed means, he had a gun", said officer Randal.

"No way, that man had a can of beer or soda in his hand. I saw no gun", I said.

"Well, it is hard to see from here", said Officer Randal.

"Trust me; I could see everything from right here. That man had no gun", I said.

"Jake, I am here to show you some pictures of the cars matching the description that you provided. Do you mind telling me, which car you think matches the description of the car that hit that man. I ask you to focus on these pictures and stop worrying about the homeless man that was shot today", said Officer Randal.

"No problem", I said.

Officer Randal showed me some pictures of the cars. I looked at the pictures for a while.

"None of these", I said.

"What?" asked Officer Randal.

"Yes Sir, none of these pictures is the picture of the car that hit that homeless man", I said.

"Are you sure Jake?" asked Officer Randal.

"Yes Sir, I am. You need to tell the police that he had no gun", I said.

"Is this the reason you are not telling me about the car Jake?" asked Officer Randal.

"That man had no gun, you police officers are cowards to shoot at an unarmed person", I said while raising my voice.

"Jake, I need you to calm down", said Officer Randal.

I started crying very loud by now. After about a minute Cindy walked into the room.

"What happened Jake?" asked Cindy.

"These cowards shot him", I said.

"Who shot whom?" asked Cindy.

"Well, there was a shootout today. There was an armed homeless man who was shot by the police", said Officer Randal.

"He was not armed", I said this with utmost intensity in my voice and while my tears were falling down my cheek.

"Well, Officer Randal, can I talk to you for a minute?" asked Cindy.

Cindy took Officer Randal out of the room and returned alone.

"Ok Jake, Officer Randal is gone, he will not bother you, ok", said Cindy.

"How could someone kill an innocent man?" I asked.

"Well, they are claiming he was armed, but I trust what you say. He might have robbed someone or something else might have happened, we just don't know Jake", said Cindy.

"We need to inform the police that the man had no gun", I said.

"Ok, let me see what I can do Jake", said Cindy.

Cindy goes out of the room. I kept looking out of the window and I saw 2 men sitting on the bench and 3 more men who stood around the bench. They all were talking to each other. Other people were just moving here and there. The cars and buses were moving through the street by now. They blocked the street, when they shot that homeless man. The street seemed busy gain. Most of the people walking by would have never known, what just happened on that street a little ago.

"Jake", I heard Cindy calling my name.

"Yes, Cindy", I said.

"I called 911 and told them what you saw on the street today", said Cindy.

"That is great Cindy. Are they going to come to talk to me?" I asked.

"I would hope so. Why don't you have your lunch?" asked Cindy.

"Sure", I said.

Cindy brought my lunch and after the lunch I felt tired and sleepy.

I slept for, I don't know how long.

"Jake", I heard.

"Jake, these detectives are here to talk to you about the shootout this morning", said Cindy.

"Oh yes, nice to see you", I said while rubbing my eyes.

"Are you in a position to talk to us?" asked one detective.

"Oh yes Sir. Please have a seat and I will be back from the restroom soon", I said.

I returned from the room. One detective was looking down the window and one was sitting on the chair next to my bed.

"There you are", said one detective.

"We are not bothering you, are we?" asked detective sitting on the chair.

"Not at all Sir, in fact I wanted to talk to someone about what I saw this morning", I said.

"Ok, by the way, I am detective Jim Garcia and this is my colleague detective James Bush", said detective Garcia.

I shook my right hand with both detectives.

"What happened to your arm?" asked detective Garcia while staring down the window and then looking back at me.

"Oh, nothing major, I fell off the swing. It broke, I mean the swing broke first and then my arm", I said.

"It broke, I mean the swing?" asked detective Bush, while looking extremely surprised.

"Yes Sir", I said.

"Hey Jim, my kids go to the city park and they do use the swing. I have to ask them, not to use these swings anymore", said detective Bush.

"We can found out the company which makes these swings and do a little investigation. All we need is a complaint which Jake can write for us. Right Jake", said detective Garcia.

"Of course Sir, I would be more than happy to provide you with a complaint", I said.

"Ok, let us focus on what you saw today from the beginning", said detective Garcia while taking out a notepad and a pen from his pocket.

"Ok, so, I was standing right here", I moved towards the window as detective Garcia moved back a little bit. He stood behind me.

"Ok, go on", said detective Garcia.

"I saw this homeless man running from that side", I said while pointing down towards the left extreme of the street.

"Wait, how did you know that the man was homeless?" asked detective Bush, who was also standing behind me by now, alongside detective Garcia.

"Well, I saw that man sleeping on that bench", I pointed down towards the bench, where few homeless men were gathered.

"Ok, continue", said detective Garcia.

"I saw him sleeping there. I also saw him waking up. Then I had my breakfast. When I came back to the window, he was not there. After a while I saw a man running from that side, he was the same homeless man that was sleeping on the bench", I said while pointing to the left side of the street again.

"Ok, what next?" asked detective Garcia.

"I saw a police car following him, after a while I saw two officers coming out of the car. This homeless man looked scared. He threw a can of soda or maybe beer at the officers and that is when I heard pop, pop, pop....I saw the homeless man fell to the ground with his face down. The officers approached him, turned him around. He was not moving. After a while, I saw an ambulance approaching and they took the man in the ambulance", I said.

"Are you sure that he had a can of soda or beer in his hand?" asked detective Bush from behind.

"Yes Sir, I am hundred percent sure", I said.

"Ok Jake, give us a minute", said detective Garcia while taking detective Bush out of the room.

After about 5 minutes, detective Garcia entered the room.

"Jake", he said.

"Yes Sir", I replied.

"I have asked detective Bush to go to the left end of the street. He will show us something from there. I want you to identify what he is showing us from there", said detective Garcia.

"Yes Sir, no problem", I said.

After about 5 minutes, I saw a car approaching the left end of the street. Soon I saw the car turning on its flash lights.

"Who is that coming out of the car with flashing light?" asked detective Garcia.

"He is detective Bush", I replied.

"Good", said detective Garcia.

"He is going to take out something from his pocket. Please tell me what you see", said detective Garcia while holding a binocular to his eyes.

Soon detective Bush took something out of his pocket.

"It is a banana", I said.

"A banana, what?" asked detective Garcia.

"No Sir, I am just kidding, it looks like a cell phone to me", I said.

"Very nice Jake", said detective Garcia.

"Ok, what now?" asked detective Garcia while detective Bush took something out of his pocket.

"It is a can", I said.

"Are you sure, it is a can", asked detective Garcia.

Detective Garcia took his cell phone out, dialed a number and said "Jamie, show the thing".

"Ok, what is it now?" asked detective Garcia.

"It looks like a can again", I said.

"Are you sure, it is a can again?" asked detective Garcia.

"Yes, Sir", I said.

Detective Garcia placed the phone on his ear again and said "alright, show the can again".

"What is that thing which detective Bush is showing Jake?" asked detective Garcia.

"It looks like a gun Sir", I said.

"Ok, which hand is the gun in?" asked detective Garcia.

"It is in his right hand Sir", I said.

Soon detective Bush placed the gun back in his holster. Detective Garcia said "Alright Jamie, back to Houston."

"Great Jake, you have got an eagle eye", said detective Garcia.

"Thank you Sir", I said.

"So you really saw a can in the homeless guy's hand...hmmmm", said detective Garcia while he sat on the chair next to my bed.

I also went back to sit on my bed. Detective Garcia sat on the chair with his hand on his head.

"What happened detective?" I asked.

"Nothing much, Jake", said detective Garcia.

He sat there quiet for about 5 minutes and then detective James Bush entered the room.

"Hey Jim", said detective Bush.

"Hey Jamie", said detective Garcia.

"How did it go?" asked detective Bush.

"This boy has eye of an eagle. I sometimes had to use binoculars to see clearly", said detective Garcia.

"Ok, that is great Jake", said detective Bush.

"Thank you Sir", I replied.

"So Jim, what now?" he asked.

"Well, so Jake, what is your impression of the shooting today. In your opinion do you think it was justified?" asked detective Garcia.

"Justified? No way. The officers came out of the car like raging bulls. There guns were out in no time. That man probably got scared and therefore threw his can at them", I said.

"Hmm...", said detective Bush.

"If you were in the shoes of police officers, what would have you done? I know you are too small to judge that but since you saw everything, live, I guess you can shed more light on this issue?" asked detective Garcia.

"I would have not shot the man. What did he do to deserve to die?" I asked.

"Well, he stole something from a nearby convenient store. That is when officers followed him", said detective Bush.

"Oh, he may have stolen a can of soda or beer", I said.

"Jamie, can you find out, what exactly he stole from the store?" asked detective Garcia.

"Of course", said detective Bush as he called someone on the phone. After he hung up.

"Where is the gun that the officers claim they saw in the hand of that guy?" asked detective Garcia.

"It is in the Police station", said detective Bush.

"So he had a gun on him. But, Jake is claiming that he threw a can at them and he never saw that man pointing a gun at the officers", said detective Garcia.

"Maybe, he did not pull out his weapon and just wanted to scare the police with that can", said detective Bush.

"Hmmm.... that is a possibility. If he really threw a can at them, they could have just tazed him", said detective Garcia.

"Thank you so much for your help Jake. Hey, can you say all this in front of a judge in the court?" asked detective Garcia.

"Yes, of course", I said.

"Ok Jake, we should be going now", said detective Garcia while shaking my right hand. Detective Bush also shook my hand and both left the room.

I laid on the bed with my eyes closed. After about 15 minutes, I heard a voice calling my name. I opened my eyes and Cindy was standing there with some medicines and a new plaster like thing.

"Hi Cindy", I said.

"Hello Jake. I need to check your plaster, in the meantime you should take these pills", said Cindy.

I took the pills. Cindy started looking at the plaster.

"Hmmm, we would need to replace it Jake, seems like it is all soggy. It may not be good and could actually cause infection", said Cindy.

"Ok", I said.

Cindy left the room. She entered the room with another nurse.

Cindy started cutting the plaster with a pair of scissors.

"Ahhh", I screamed.

"Sorry hon", said Cindy.

She stopped for a while.

"Are you okay, do you think you can handle this?" she asked.

"It is very painful", I said.

"Maybe we should wait for 15-20 minutes for those painkillers to kick in", said Cindy.

Cindy and nurse left the room.

After about 10 minutes my mom entered the room.

"Jake, how are you sweetheart?" she asked.

"I am fine mom. Nice to see you", I said.

"So, how was your day?" she asked.

"It was fine mom. I had complete rest today", I said. I did not tell her about the shoot out and the detectives.

"That is good", my mom said while she sat on the chair next to my bed.

"Jake, oh hello Sheela", said Cindy while entering my room.

"Hello Cindy", my mom said.

"We need to change Jake's plaster as it is getting soggy and that may cause infection", said Cindy.

"Ok..." my mom said.

"If you want to leave Sheela then please do so now. It is a little painful process and you may want to avoid seeing the procedure", said Cindy.

"Yes mom, you should leave", I said.

"Don't be crazy Jake, I will stay right here with you", my mom said.

"Alright, Jake, we will try again", said Cindy.

Cindy and the second nurse cut my plaster off. I somehow managed to bear the excruciating pain. A new plaster was wrapped around my arm. My arm looked twisted and very weird, it was yellowish in color. My mom held my right hand while Cindy and other nurse finished the whole procedure.

"Brave boy", said Cindy.

I smiled, despite the pain I was feeling. After about 5 minutes Cindy and other nurse wrapped up the old plaster and some other stuff.

"Ok Jake, you should be resting now", said Cindy while leaving the room.

"Thank you", I smiled back.

My mom stayed in the room for 30-40 more minutes. We talked about the weather. It had started to snow outside.

"Oh, I forgot, your friends Justin and Jatin came to see you last evening. They did not know where you were? I told them about you. They may be coming to see you tomorrow", my mom said.

"Tomorrow, don't they have to go to school?" I asked.

"Tomorrow is Saturday sweetheart", my mom said.

"Oh ok. How are they going to get to the hospital?" I asked.

"They are going to come to our house and I will drive them here", my mom said.

"That would be great", I said.

"You should go and take rest now", I said.

My mom got up from the chair kissed me on my cheek and said "Ok, have a sound sleep."

"Thanks ma", I said.

My mom left the room. I slowly got off the bed. I could still feel the pain from my left arm. I walked towards the window. It was dark by now. It was extremely beautiful; the snow was covering up the street below. The street's color changed from black to white. People were walking across the street while wearing long coats. I could see some trucks spraying salt on the street. There was a man sitting on the bench. He had an umbrella over him. I could see only his legs. He was wearing black pants and brown shoes. His pants were torn. His shoes were also in a pretty bad shape. After about 2-3 minutes, he got up and started walking towards the right side of the street. He crossed one street which ran across the crossroads street. He kept on walking. He took a cardboard out from his pocket and started to walk back while holding the cardboard with his both hands. He kept looking inside the cars which were stopped at the red light. He waived his right hand at the cars once in a while.

Soon he walked in front of a car to reach another car that was stopped in the right lane. I saw a hand coming out of the car and handing this man something, like a paper. It could have been money, I guess. He bowed his head and walked back to the street. He kept on moving in front of the cars. Soon, I saw a police car driving in the extreme left lane. The police car stopped behind the left most car. The cars started to move as it was green signal now. The police car did not move. Suddenly car's lights started to flash. Then I heard a string of two short sirens like toooo... toooo. I saw the man approaching the police car. I saw this man take out something from his pocket and handing it over to the driver in the police car. It looked like money to me. The police car left. The man looked very disappointed. He shook his head. He started walking back to the bench slowly and slowly. He sat on the bench with umbrella over his head. Soon, he went from a sitting position to sleeping position. He placed his hand below his head and placed the umbrella over his head. The umbrella was hardly covering half of his body. The snow started to pile on half of his body, below the waist. He removed the snow few times but it kept coming back.

"Jake, are you ready for dinner?" asked Cindy while I turned my face away from the window.

"Look at him", I said.

"Look at whom?" asked Cindy.

"That guy on the bench", I said.

Cindy came towards the window and looked down.

"Jake, you really shouldn't worry about him", said Cindy.

"Do you believe in God Cindy?" I asked.

"Yes, I do believe in God", replied Cindy.

"Are we all his kids?" I asked.

"Yes, we are", said Cindy.

"Then why does he let some of his kids sleep in those big hotels and some of his kids on a bench?" I said.

"I don't really know", said Cindy.

"Then why do you trust in God?" I asked.

"Well, I guess hmmm...don't worry about all this Jake. I am going to bring you the dinner", said Cindy.

"Has God turned his back towards some of his kids?" I asked.

"I don't really know Jake. I am sorry", said Cindy.

"No worries Cindy, is there anyone who could help this guy?" I asked.

"He must have been removed from the homeless shelter", said Cindy.

"What if no one knows that he is here? What if he never ever went to a homeless shelter?" I asked.

"Ya, that is possible", said Cindy.

"Can't you call the police? Wait, don't call the police, they take money from him", I said.

"What? Police takes money from a homeless guy?" Cindy asked while she looked extremely displeased.

"Yes, I saw this man giving money to someone in a police car", I said.

"I don't believe this", said Cindy while placing her hand over her mouth.

"I don't think we should call the police", I said.

"Let me see what I could do", Cindy left the room.

After about 5 minutes, she came back to the room. I was standing in front of the window looking down. Cindy came and stood next to me.

"Look the snow is covering half of his body", I said.

"Oh boy", said Cindy.

"Did you call someone?" I asked.

"Yes, I called the homeless shelter and they said they were full", said Cindy.

"What?" I said.

"Yes, I am sorry. There is nothing we can do to help him", said Cindy.

"So we should let him sleep in the snow", I said.

"I don't know what can we do Jake?" asked Cindy.

"No, no, no..." I said.

"Jake, I have to attend other patients, I will get you your dinner now", said Cindy as she left the room.

I looked up in the sky and said, "Dude, are you going to let this guy sleep on a bench with snow all around him?"

Soon Cindy came back to the room.

"Who are you talking to Jake", asked Cindy.

"No one Cindy", I replied.

"Ok, have your dinner on time and yes don't look out that window anymore. You should take rest and sleep on time", said Cindy.

"Alright Cindy, thank you", I said.

Cindy left the room.

I looked up the sky and said, "Come on you deaf. If you are really out there, or you even exist, help this poor guy."

I stood in front of the window. The snow was getting higher on his pants. It was hard to even see his black pants now. After about 15-20 minutes, I went back to my bed, as I was getting tired of standing. I was hungry too. I started eating the food despite the fact that I was extremely sad. I finished eating the food in about 15 minutes. My energy was back. I stood up from the bed and went to the window to see the man again. He was lying on the bench with a huge pile of snow covering him from waist below.

I was getting extremely irritated at this world. People were driving in these big cars. No one, I mean, not even a single grown up man could care to stop and help this guy. I was ashamed to be a human.

I looked up the sky and said, "Screw you moron, is this your world? If it is, then guess what, I don't like it and I don't like you", I said.

I placed my head on the window, it was extremely cold. I had to move my head back immediately. I wondered how that guy on the bench must be feeling.

"You know, from today on, I don't believe in you and I don't think you even exist", I said.

I went back to my bed. I turned off the light from a button on the right side of the bed and laid on the bed with my eyes open and staring at the right side, looking up the sky through my window. After a while, I started to see the stars. I got up from my bed to realize that the snowfall had stopped. I moved towards the window to see that the man was still sleeping on the bench but snow was falling off from his pants due to the wind. His umbrella was waving in all directions. In the midst of all this, I could see a glimpse of his face. He was asleep. His hands looked blue, I am not sure if he was alive or not.

I came close to my bed and pressed the nursing station button.

After 2-3 minutes, Cindy came to my room.

"Yes, Jake, are you ok?" she asked.

"I am fine Cindy. Look that man's hands are turning blue. He may be dead", I said.

Cindy looked down the window and saw the man. She was able to see the face of the man because his umbrella was displaced because of the heavy wind.

"Oh no, you are right, he looks blue", said Cindy.

"We need to help him", I said.

"Oh my god", said Cindy while leaving the room.

I kept looking down the window and to my surprise; I saw an ambulance approaching him in few minutes. The two doctors came out of the ambulance and removed this man's umbrella to a side. They started touching his face and then one doctor touched side of his neck. I was getting extremely nervous by now. They placed the man on a stretcher and placed him in the ambulance. They closed back door of the ambulance. I could still see through the small windows of the ambulance. They started to press his chest. The doctor was literally on this guy with full force. After about 2-3 minutes, I saw something came out of this homeless man's mouth. He looked confused. The ambulance started to move now. Doctors cleaned something from his face. The ambulance came from the left side of the street and turned right from the first street that ran across Crossroads Street.

"Jake", I heard.

"Oh, Cindy", I said.

"I called the ambulance, have they taken him?" she asked.

"Yes, Cindy. He was taken in the ambulance", I said.

"That is great, Jake", said Cindy.

"Thank you so much Cindy. You are an awesome nurse", I said.

"No worries Jake, I am just doing my job", said Cindy.

"Oh no, that was more than just job", I said.

"Thanks, Jake. You should sleep now", said Cindy.

"Yes, of course", I said.

Cindy left the room.

I went back to my bed and turned off the light. I kept staring at the stars from the window and I don't remember when I slept.

I opened my eyes and it was still dark outside. I went to the restroom and came back. I stood next to the window again. I looked down at the bench and there was someone else sleeping on the bench under the umbrella. The man was wearing a grey trouser with what looked like running shoes. He had a black jacket on him. I could not see his face because of the umbrella covering his face. There was no snow on the street, so that means that it did not snow again.

The sun was coming out of the lake. I could see the crossroads street getting filled with cars and buses. Pedestrians' number was also increasing. I started to hear car honks after a while. The sun managed to look above the lake now. It was at my level. I could see number of joggers increasing by the side of the lake.

A man approached this homeless man sleeping on the bench. He held him from his arm and shook him. The guy woke up. He placed the umbrella on a side and started to walk. The other man laid on the bench and placed umbrella over his head. It seemed like he went to sleep. I saw this first man walk to the extreme left of the crossroads street and turn left after he crossed the crossroads street.

"Jake", I heard.

"Cindy, good morning", I said.

"How are you feeling?" asked Cindy.

"Great Cindy", I said.

"Any pain today?" asked Cindy.

"No pain", I said.

"Ok, Doctor John will be here in 5 minutes, till then let me grab you the breakfast", said Cindy.

"Sure, thanks", I said.

I was still standing at the window. The light from the sun was getting very strong now. Street was getting filled with cars and buses. So many people were walking fast with their phones in their hands and their eyes fixed on the screens of their phones. They were completely unaware of the world around them. Restaurants were placing chairs outside. Some people were smoking on the street. Some people were drinking something wrapped in a brown paper. Cars were stopping and then moving on the lights. A lot of cars were moving across the crossroads street.

"Jake", said Doctor John while he entered the room along with Cindy.

"Doctor John", I said.

"How are you young man?" asked Doctor John.

"I am feeling fine", I replied.

Doctor John monitored me while Cindy placed the breakfast on the table next to my bed.

"Alright, everything looks fine", he said while writing something on his notepad.

He showed the notepad to Cindy and she noded her head and left the room.

"Alright Jake, based on my observation, I am going to discharge you today", said Doctor John.

"Really", I said while getting extremely excited.

"Oh yes, I will call your mom now", said Doctor John.

"Thank you so much Doctor John", I said.

Doctor John left the room. I ate my breakfast and went back to the window. There was no one sleeping on the bench. The umbrella was still there. The sun was very high by now. I could see very few joggers by the lake. The street below was filled with cars, buses and people. Many people were eating food on tables outside the restrooms. From the extreme left side of the street, I saw a man walking towards the bench. He was the homeless guy who was sleeping earlier on the bench. He walked very slowly, almost limping.

I saw a car stopping close to the homeless guy and giving something to this man. It looked like a burger from far away. I was shocked to find that the burger was already half eaten. How disgusting? Someone gave this man, a half-eaten burger. The homeless man started eating the burger. I nearly vomited. The man kept eating the burger slowly, as he reached the bench. He stopped close to the trash can. He took a can out of the trash can and started drinking from it.

He sat on the bench, looked around the street. He was finished with his burger. He got up threw the paper in the trash can. He was still holding on to the can and drinking from it. He went back and sat on the bench. He looked around the street, from right side to left. He started looking up. Soon, he was looking up at the sky. He looked down at the street again. The next moment he looked up straight at me. I had no time to move. His eyes were staring right back at me. I was frozen for a while. I also kept looking into his eyes. There was extreme sadness in his eyes. It was filled with hopelessness. I waived my right hand at him. He did not plunge but kept looking at me. I moved my hand down. After a while, he brought his right hand up and waived back at me. It is at this moment, I saw a smile on his face. He kept waving back at me with smile on his face. It seemed like he caught someone's attention after a long time. I could now see his teeth, as his smile got bigger. His teeth were extremely dirty, yellowish like the inside of an egg.

He had a huge beard. He wore a torn black cap on his head. He moved his right hand down and raised his left hand with can in it. He showed me the can as a way of saying cheers. I waived him back as in a way to ask him to stop where he was. I moved into the room to where my breakfast was. There was a can of orange juice on the table. I picked up the can, went back to the window. I opened the can. The homeless man was still looking up. He was happy to see me back. I raised the orange juice can up with my right hand. He saw me doing this and raised his can too. He made a gesture of cheers and so did I. I and he started to drink from our respective cans. His smile was even bigger now, as if he was almost laughing. I saw tears coming out of his eyes while he still had a smile on his face. I placed the can of orange juice on a side and waived him back. I pointed towards my eyes and then waived back at him in a way to ask him not to cry.

He rubbed his tears. He waived me back. He got up and threw his can in the trash can. He started moving to the left side of the street. He reached to the extreme left side of the street and waived in a way to say bye. I waived back. He moved to the street that ran across the crossroads street to the left.

I kept looking down.

"Jake", I heard a voice.

"Mom, Justin, hey Jatin...", I said.

"Hey Jake, how are you sweetheart?" asked my mom while reaching close to me and hugging me.

"I am fine", I said.

"Hey Jake. How are you?" asked Jatin.

"Fine, how are you guys?" I asked.

"We are good", said Justin.

"How is your arm now?" asked Jatin.

"I feel better now", I said.

"That is good to know", my mom said.

"Doctor said I can go home now", I said.

"Of course, you could. He called me this morning and told me that you are doing much better now and I could take you home today", my mom said.

"Isn't that awesome Jake?" asked Justin.

"Yes, it is", I said.

"Ok, I need to go and talk to the doctor now and why don't you boys chat till I come back", said my mom while leaving the room.

"Sure, thanks ma", I said.

"So dude", said Jatin.

"Dude, so how was your stay here?" asked Justin.

"Don't use this word 'dude' here, my mom hates this word", I said.

"Ha ha, no worries", said Justin.

"Hey stand here, next to the window", I said.

"Wow, it's an awesome view", said Jatin.

"Ya", said Justin.

"A lot goes in this street everyday", I said.

"Of course, it is a street..ha ha..", Justin laughed.

"A lot like buses, cars, trucks ha ha..." Jatin laughed.

"No, I mean other stuff", I said.

"What other stuff?" asked Justin.

"Homeless people sleep on this street", I said.

"You mean the robbers", said Justin.

"No, not robbers you fool", I said.

"Who are homeless people?" asked Jatin.

"People who don't have a house to live in", I said.

"Everyone that I know has a house", said Justin.

Soon I saw the man who waived me earlier.

"There is one", I said.

"Who?" asked Justin.

"One homeless man", I said.

"How do you know he is homeless?" asked Jatin.

"I know because he was sleeping on that bench below", I said.

"Sleeping on the bench? How could someone sleep on a bench?" askedJatin.

"I saw other men too, they also slept on that bench", I said.

"I don't believe you", said Jatin.

"Everyone has a house. Government provides houses to everyone", said Justin.

"If government provided houses to everyone, then why would they be sleeping on the bench", I said.

"I don't know. They must have forgotten where there house was and must have slept here", said Justin.

"They have no house. Trust me. That is what John and Cindy told me. They are homeless folks", I said.

While we were talking the homeless man reached close to the trash can. He started looking inside the trash can.

"Why is he looking into the trash can?" asked Justin.

"He is looking for food", I said.

"You are kidding, right?" asked Jatin.

"No, I am not. See what he does", I said.

The man turned and looked upwards. He looked straight at us. I waived at him. He did not waive back and started to move towards the bench. He sat on the bench, looked up towards us again. He then started looking down towards the cars. He then laid on the bench and moved the umbrella above his face.

"See, he is sleeping there", I said.

"He did not take food out of the trash can, as you were suggesting", said Jatin.

"He may have felt embarrassed, since we were looking at him", I said.

"Jake", I heard a voice.

"Hello Doctor John", I said.

"Your friends and mom is here to take you home, hmmm..", said Doctor John.

"Oh yes, they are here", I said while I placed my right arm around Jatin's shoulders.

"Great, so you are good to go. I have told your mom the medicines that you are going to need for next few days. Also, you can go to school if you feel better. You just need to be a little careful. I will see you back in the hospital after a week. Alright, young man", said Doctor John while shaking my right hand.

"Yes Sir, absolutely, thank you so much for everything", I said.

"No worries, it is our job", said Doctor John as he left the room.

"Jake, you can change your clothes. You can now wear the clothes that your mother has brought", said Cindy.

I went close to Cindy and hugged her.

"Thank you so much Cindy", I said.

"You are most welcome", said Cindy.

"I guess, I will see you in a week then", I said.

"Oh yes sure, hopefully by next week you will be feeling even better", said Cindy.

"Thank you", I said as Cindy left the room.

My mom gave me bag of clothes.

"Ok boys, you wait outside while I change Jake's clothes", my mom said.

"Yes ma'am, of course", said Jatin.

Both Justin and Jatin moved out of the room. My mom changed my clothes. We were about to leave when I said "One minute mom".

"What Jake?" my mom asked.

"Give me a minute", I said as I walked towards the window.

The homeless man was probably sleeping on the bench with umbrella covering his face. I could tell it was the same guy by looking at his shoes and trousers. I waited on the window.

"Jake", my mom called as she opened the door of the room.

I kept looking down.

"Jake, we need to go home", said my mom again.

"Wait, I am coming mom", I said.

A little blow of wind moved the homeless man's umbrella from his face. His eyes were closed. I waived but it was of no use. He was sleeping. I moved towards my bed and opened a drawer by the side of the bed. There was a small mirror in it. I approached the window again. The sun was extremely bright by now. I held the mirror high, the reflection from the mirror was going down the street. I adjusted the mirror till the reflection from the mirror started hitting the homeless guy's eyes. He did not move. After a while, he opened his eyes and placed his right hand in front of his eyes. I lowered the mirror. He looked up straight into my eyes. I looked back and smiled. I waived him a gesture of bye. He sat and looked up again. He waived as if asking a question? I waived back in way to tell him that I was leaving. He gave me a big smile. He raised his right hand and gave me thumbs up and then waived me bye. I smiled back and left the room with my mom.

I, Justin, Jatin and my mom reached where my mom had parked the car.

I sat on the front seat. My mom moved my arm and placed the seat belt underneath. Jatin and Justin sat on the back seat.

"Mom, can we go through the crossroads street?" I asked.

"Why crossroads?" asked my mom.

"I have been looking at the crossroads street from a height. I want to feel it up close", I said.

"Sure, we can drive through cross roads street", my mom said.

Chapter 3

The Birds of the Concrete Jungle

My mom entered the crossroads street from the extreme left, yes the same extreme left. My mom kept on driving and we reached the bench where the homeless guys used to sit. I looked to my left and there was no one sitting on the bench. My mom kept driving through the street.

"Are you boys hungry?" asked my mom.

"Oh yes, I am hungry mom and so would be Justin and Jatin", I said.

My mom looked through the rear mirror and saw their expressions.

"Alright, we will have lunch, right here, in this Italian restaurant", my mom said.

"Nice mom, Justin loves a veggie pizza", I said.

"Oh that is great, you boys could enjoy that", my mom said.

My mom parked the car and came to the right side to un-hook my seat belt.

Once we all were out, my mom started to walk inside the restaurant.

"Wait mom, we can eat here outside on these chairs. They have nice fire out here, so we don't have to worry about the cold", I said.

"Whatever you like sweetheart", my mom said.

We sat on chairs. I picked a chair through which I could look straight towards my hospital room's window. I also looked across and the bench was in my sight of vision now. The homeless man was not there.

We placed an order and were waiting for the pizza to arrive.

"Mom, do you mind if I walk a little bit. I have been sitting in that room for days. I feel like walking", I said.

"I can come with you", said Jatin.

"Ok, don't go far away, just stay in this street", my mom said.

"Thanks mom", I said.

I and Jatin started to walk towards the left side of the street. Well, it was actually right side now, because the restaurant was across the street. The street looked huge. From the hospital's room window, everything looked very small. We crossed some shops, when we reached the street that ran across the crossroads street.

"You want to go to that side?" asked Jatin.

"Desperately", I said.

We pressed the button to cross the street. Soon the signal for walk flashed. We crossed this street and were back on crossroads street. We walked close to the bench. No one was there. I looked around the bench. There were blood stains on the bench. I looked at the cart which was full of stuff and then I went and looked inside the trashcan. I and Jatin kept on walking all the way to the end of the crossroads street. We reached the end; well it wasn't the end actually. The street just curved left.

"We should go back now", said Jatin.

As we walked back towards the street, I saw detective Garcia talking to this homeless guy whom I waived this morning. They both were standing close to the bench. We approached them.

"Jake", said detective Garcia.

"Hello Sir", I said.

"How are you doing? Seems like you are fine now, walking on the street, hmmm..", said detective Garcia.

I saw detective Bush walking towards us.

"Has this man been bothering you?" asked detective Bush while pointing towards the homeless man.

"No, of course not", I said.

"Ok, so you guys are here with your parents?" asked detective Garcia.

"Yes, my mother is waiting for us at the restaurant", I said while pointing towards the restaurant.

"Oh good", said detective Garcia.

"We are investigating the shootout. You know the one you saw, with the homeless guy. Remember?" asked detective Bush.

"Yes, of course, I remember", I said.

"We should be going now and stop bothering this guy", I said.

"Wait, what did you say?" asked Officer Garcia.

"I said, do not bother this guy. He is a good man".

"Wait, we are not bothering him? It is our duty to question them", said detective Bush.

"Sorry Sir, but you did not come to ask anybody eating in that restaurant any question. These homeless guys are the scapegoat of every crime, aren't they?" I asked.

"Don't be crazy, Jake", said detective Bush.

"I hope that is not the case. I have lost my faith in police from the moment I saw that man shot by police", I said.

"Trust us Jake, we are working on the same case diligently", said Officer Garcia.

"We were inquiring about that homeless guy from this homeless guy", said detective Bush.

"He must have a name other than homeless", I said.

"Yeah sure, what's your name buddy?" asked detective Garcia.

"Nobody", he replied.

"Nobody, that's your name?" asked detective Bush.

"Yes, my name is Mr. Nobody", he said.

"See Jake, these people do not co-operate. They are way over their head", said detective Bush.

"You need to ask nicely", I said.

"You wanna be my guest", said detective Bush.

I reached close to the man and offered my right hand for shaking. He did not move.

"Where's your can?" I asked.

"Can, how do you know, I had a can kid?" asked the homeless man.

"You probably don't recognize me. My clothes are different and I am down here in front of you", I said.

"Wait, you are that boy from that window up there. How did you get down?" he asked.

"I was relieved from hospital", I said.

"What happened to your arm?" he asked.

"Oh, I fell from a swing", I said.

"My name is Jake", I said while offering my hand for a handshake.

He rubbed is hand across his pants in order to clean it and shook my hand and said, "Thank you, my name David".

"Thank you for what?" I asked.

"Never mind", he said.

"Ok, David, I guess you are good to go", said detective Garcia.

David leaves while waving me bye. He goes and sits on the bench. He turned his head left and looks at me. He smiles and so do I.

"We should be going now detective Garcia", I said.

"Of course Jake and yes we might be contacting you about the testimony that you may be required to give in the court. We will talk to your parents about this", he said.

"Sure, no problem", I said, while I and Jatin started to walk back to the restaurant.

We reached at the restaurant.

"Wow, there you are. Your pizza has been sitting here from 5 minutes", my mom said.

"Oh no problem", I said.

We sat at the table and started eating the pizza.

"Who were you talking to?" asked my mom.

"Oh they are just detectives ", I said.

"Wait detectives", my mom said.

"Yes, they were investigating the case in which that car hit the homeless guy and ran away", I said. I did not tell my mom that I also saw a man getting shot by the police and I was helping detectives in their investigation.

Eating pizza with my right hand was not a big issue. We sat at the restaurant for 30-45 minutes.

"Jake take 2 slices for David", said Jatin slowly in my ear.

"What is going on boys?" asked my mom.

"Nothing mom", I said.

"Mom, can I ask you something?" I said.

"Sure", my mom said.

"Can I have another pizza for a friend?" I asked.

"Pizza for a friend", said my mom while she looked confused.

"Yes", he lives on that bench, while I pointed in that direction.

"He lives on a bench. Are you crazy? No, we are not talking to a homeless man", my mom said.

"Ok, then I will go and give him my share of pizza", I said.

"No you would not", I said.

"Would you expect someone to give me a pizza, if I was a homeless boy sitting on that bench right now?" I asked.

My mom smiled. She called the waiter and ordered a large size margarita pizza with a cup of coffee to go. I stood up and kissed my mom on the cheek. The waiter brought the pizza in about 20 minutes in a big bag.

"Ok, we will be back soon", I said while holding Jatin's hand in order to take him with me.

We walked fast towards the bench. As we approached close, David was gone. We looked around but we could not find him. We looked around the street that was running across. I saw David approaching a trash can on the right side of the street that ran across. I gave the bag to Jatin and asked him to run towards David and give the bag to him. Jatin ran towards David. I saw Jatin arriving close to David and talking to him. Jatin looked back and pointed towards me. I waived with my right hand. Jatin tried to give the bag to David. He did not take the bag. Jatin started walking towards me with the bag in his hand.

I started to walk towards Jatin.

"What happened?" I asked when I reached close to Jatin.

"He refused to take it", said Jatin.

"I know, but why?" I asked.

"He said he does not need charity", said Jatin.

I took the bag in my right hand and started to walk towards David who had his hand in the trash can by now.

"David, how are you doing?" I asked.

"Hey Jake", he said.

"Is there something in that trash can?" I asked.

He took out a can from the trash can. It was can of beans. He placed his fingers inside the can and started eating from the can.

"Hmm..it seems like there is really incredible stuff in that trash can", I said.

I placed the bag of pizza on a side and started walking towards the trash can. I looked inside and moved my right hand inside the trash can.

David held my hand and said, "What the hell are you doing?"

"I am trying to find the food for which you declined one of the best pizzas in the city", I said.

"Go away, you don't belong here", said David.

"Do you own this trash can?" I asked.

"No", replied David.

"Then I have as much right as you to take food out of this trash can", I said.

I moved my hand into the trash can.

"Don't you get it", said David while holding my right hand and moving me away from the trash can.

"I will call the police if you touch me again, I have my life and I can choose to take food out of this trash can. You are nobody to stop me", I said.

"What do you want from me? What does he want?" asked David while looking at Jatin.

"I think he wants you to eat the pizza", said Jatin.

"Ok, I can eat the pizza today. But, what about tomorrow, a day after tomorrow, tomorrow after tomorrow, I will have to eat from this trash can boy", said David while shaking his head and throwing the can of bean from his hand back into the trash can.

"Please eat this. Don't think it as a charity. Think that I am your friend and I just want to share my food with you", I said.

I picked up the bag and gave to David. He took the bag and offered his right hand for a handshake. I also moved my hand forward and shook his hand.

"Wait", said David while I and Jatin were moving back towards the crossroads street.

David gave the coffee cup to Jatin to hold and opened the box. He closed the box and came close to me. He placed his right over my head and said, "This pizza is worth a million dollars to me."

I looked closely and there were tears in David's eyes. He started walking with us towards the crossroads street. We reached the crossroads street.

"Jatin", I said.

"Oh yes", said Jatin while giving David the cup of coffee.

David took the cup and said, "Thanks".

"You are very welcome David", said Jatin.

"Alright, Jake, thanks for the lunch", said David.

"No problem", I said while I and Jatin waived David bye.

We started moving towards the restaurant and David towards the bench. I saw David go and sit on the bench after he crossed the street. He sat on the bench with pizza box in his lap. He opened the box and started eating the pizza, he paused for a second. Looked up the sky and then he looked in my direction. He was eating the pizza and waived at me one more time with the slice of pizza in his hand. I waived back and we arrived at the restaurant.

"So, you gave the pizza to your friend?" asked my mom.

"Yes, you deserve the credit for it mom", I said.

My mom smiled while I and Jatin sat on the chairs.

"Ready for dessert?" my mom asked.

"Sure", I said.

"So Justin told me a lot of interesting things about you", said my mom while looking at the menu card.

"Really, like what?" I asked.

"Don't worry, let us order the dessert", my mom said.

We enjoyed our lunch and got back into the car. My mom dropped Jatin and Justin to their respective houses. I reached home and went to bed. I slept for 3-4 hours.

"Jake", I heard.

"Yes, ma", I said.

"Sweetheart, how are you feeling?" she asked.

"Much better ma", I said.

"Good. Would you like to have a sandwich?" asked my mom.

"Sure, absolutely", I said.

I got up from bed, looked outside the window and it was getting close to evening. I could hardly see the sun. The view from my home was very narrow as compared to the view; I had from the hospital room. I went to the restroom. I came out and went straight to the kitchen where my mom had made a nice sandwich.

"It seems like it will snow tonight", my mom said.

"Really", I said.

"Yes, it is in the news that a heavy storm is heading towards our city and it is expected to snow heavily tonight", my mom said.

I picked up the sandwich and said, "Poor homeless folks, these storms are like angels of death for them."

"Angels of death, where did you learn all that?" asked my mom.

"I am a grown man now", I said.

"Yes, you are a grown man of 7th grade", my mom said.

"Don't get confused by my size", I said.

"Oh yes, I know inside you are no less than the size of a Dinosaur, right?" my mom laughed.

"No, not a Dinosaur", I said.

My mom smiled.

"So what were you saying about the homeless folks?" asked my mom.

"David will freeze tonight", I said.

"David, now who is David?" asked my mom.

"The homeless guy for whom I took the pizza", I said.

"Stop worrying about them Jake and start worrying about your own self", my mom said.

"Ok", I said.

The phone rang. My mom went to attend the phone. She came back with tears in her eyes.

"What happened mom?" I asked.

"My dad passed away", she said.

"Oh no, you mean grandpa?" I asked.

"Yes", my mom said.

"We need to go", my mom said.

"Sorry ma", I said while hugging my mom.

"Thanks, let us go. Get your jacket", my mom said.

"Ok", I said.

Chapter 4

Flight over the Barn

My grandpa lived 15 miles from the city on a ranch. He had a lot of land. We arrived at his house in about 30 minutes. There was an ambulance outside. I and my mom got out of the car and went inside the house. My grandpa was lying on a bed. My maternal grandma died few years back and my grandpa lived alone.

"Sorry for you loss ma'am, my name is Doctor Daniel."

"How did all this happen?" my mom asked while getting close to my grandpa with tears in her eyes.

"Well, we got a call 1 hour back. When we arrived here, he had already passed away", said Doctor Daniel.

"Did he call you?" I asked.

"No he has an emergency alert system, which he used to wear around his neck. He must have pressed this button and then we were called to attend to the emergency", said Doctor Daniel.

"Ok", my mom said while she took a seat on the chair next to a bed where my grandpa laid.

"Ma'am, we have to have the police come and take some samples to rule out any foul play", said Doctor Daniel.

"Foul play?" my mom asked.

"Yes, ma'am, this is a standard procedure. If he had died in a hospital then it was probably not required. But, since he lived far away, we need to follow the standard protocol", said Doctor Daniel.

Doctor Daniel called someone on the phone. After about 30 minutes or so some police officers came to the house. They took hair and skin samples of my grandpa. They also searched the whole house.

My mom received a phone call from someone.

"Who was that?" I asked after she hung up.

"He was our family attorney. He told me that dad left this whole house and all the land in my name", my mom said.

"Wow, he really loved you", I said.

"Yes, but what are we going to do with all this land?" my mom said.

"No clue ma", I said.

The officers moved my grandpa into the ambulance.

"Ma'am we need some more time to examine your father's body and we will release him to you in 2-3 hours. Don't worry we will bring him back in the ambulance. In the meantime, you can start preparing for his funeral", said Doctor Daniel.

"Sure", my mom said.

"I just found out that your father wished his organs to be donated, so we have to hurry up to preserve his vital organs and made those available for donation", said Doctor Daniel.

"He signed up for organ donation program?" asked my mom.

"Yes, ma'am", replied Doctor Daniel.

"Ok", my mom said.

Doctor Daniel and others took my grandpa in the ambulance. My mom stood up from the chair and started walking towards the kitchen.

"I guess, I will have to prepare your dinner here", my mom said.

"Don't worry about the dinner ma, I am fine", I said.

"Jake, you are still recovering", my mom said.

"Alright ma", I said.

My mom started to cook something in the kitchen. I opened the front door of the house and moved down the small wooden stairs. I moved even further. I saw to the left and then to the right. There was huge land to my left and to my right; I guess it all belonged to grandpa. There were huge trees on the end of each side. I saw nearly 20-30 cows grazing grass in the fields. There was a barn at a distance on the left. I started walking towards it. I reached close to the barn and there were calves inside. They were cute. I reached close to the calves and I saw an old man cleaning the area.

"Hey boy", he yelled at me.

"Yes Sir", I said.

"Who are you? What are doing here?" he asked.

"Nothing Sir, I was just curious to see what was in this building", I said.

"How did you get here? Where are your parents he asked?" he asked while getting very close to me.

"I came here with my mom. My grandpa used to live here", I said.

"Your grandpa used to live here, hmmm...is Ron your grandpa?" he asked.

"He was", I said.

"He was, what do you mean boy?" he asked while he looked very confused.

"Yes, he died", I said.

"What the hell?" he said as he moved outside the barn.

He started walking towards the house.

"Trust me, he died. That is why we are here?" I said while following him.

"Shut up boy", he said.

He walked all the way to the house.

"Ron", he said in a loud voice.

"Ron, Ron", he said while knocking at the door.

He then opened the door and started to walk inside.

"Where is Ron?" he asked my mom.

"Hi, I am Sheela, Ron's daughter", my mom said.

"Where the hell is Ron, lady", said the old man while he looked completely irritated.

"He passed away", my mom said.

"Passed away, when? We had the damn lunch together", he said.

"Maybe you were in that barn and you did not realize that he died", I said.

"Ok, I am calling 911. How do I know you are not intruders or something like that", said the old man.

He went towards the phone and dialed 911. He talked to someone on the phone and told the person the whole story.

"What? Are you sure it was Ron?" he said.

He heard something from the phone and phone fell off his hands.

"No, no, no", he said as he dropped to his knees. The next moment he had his face on the ground. I could see his tears on the floor. He cried out loud, "Ron, you can't leave me alone here. You son of a", he said.

My mom and I started to cry as well. I reached this man and placed my right hand on his back. He was crying like a small baby.

He moved back towards the wall with his face upwards facing the ceiling.

My mom went to the kitchen brought a glass of water for him. He moved my mother's hand to a side. He moved outside the house. I and my mom followed him. Soon we saw him come out with a gun. I and my mom got very scared. He started shooting at a tree close by; he kept on shooting till all the bullets in the gun were fired. He then started kicking the tree.

"Why is he doing that?" I asked my mom.

"I have no idea, Jake", my mom said.

"Should we call ambulance, he needs help", I said.

"I think that would be a good idea", said my mom as we started to walk towards the house.

"Where are you both going?" he asked.

"Well, we were just going inside the house", I said.

"Why were you shooting at the tree?" I asked.

"I don't know", he said.

"How long have you been working for my dad?" my mom asked.

"Well, 2 months now. Therefore, you don't know me", he said.

"Yes, I visited him 3 months back", my mom said.

"I was living like a dog on the street and he gave me a new life", said the old man.

"What is your name?" I asked.

"My name is Clay", he said.

"Nice to meet you clay, my name is Jake", I said.

"Hi", he said.

It was almost dark now.

"So, I am going to cook the food, you are most welcome to join us", my mom said.

"Oh no, you guys carry on, I am going to go back to the barn now", said Clay.

I and my mom walked back to the house. My mom started cooking the food. I went outside and sat on the stairs. I looked up the sky; I could not see the stars. It was probably going to snow as the forecast said.

"Jake", I heard my mom calling me.

I went inside and my mom had cooked a huge meal.

"Wow, so much food", I said.

Soon the phone rang.

"Can I take it?" I asked.

"Sure", my mom said.

I attended the phone and someone from the hospital said that my grandpa won't be released tonight as some further investigation was pending. I hung up the phone.

"Who was that Jake?" my mom asked.

"It was from hospital, they will have to keep grandpa in the hospital for tonight", I said.

"Ok", my mom said while she looked a little confused.

"Maybe they are investigating something", I said.

"For sure", my mom said.

"Should I go and give food to Clay?" I asked.

"Yes, of course, that is why I cooked plenty", my mom said.

My mom placed the food in a plate and covered it with an aluminum foil.

"Wait, you won't be able to carry it over there", my mom said.

"Come on, give it to me, my right hand is strong enough", I said.

"Are you sure? I can come with you", my mom said.

"Na, I got this. Trust me", I said while picking up the plate with my right hand. My mom opened the door and I started to walk towards the barn.

It started to snow. I was a little wet by the time I reached the barn. I entered the barn and started to look for Clay. He had a small room in the back. I saw him lying on the bed with his eyes opened looking straight towards the ceiling.

"Clay", I said.

"Yes", he said while turning his head towards me.

"I have got dinner for you", I said.

"I am not hungry", he said in a sad voice.

I placed the plate on a small table he had in his room. I could hear noise of cows in the back. Clay probably brought all the cows back to the barn.

"Well, you need to eat the food or who else will take care of these poor cows", I said.

Clay got up and went outside the room. I followed him. There were 20-30 cows in the barn by now. He picked up a huge stack of hay and started placing it in front of cows. Little calves were hiding themselves under cows' bellies. I could see them because I was short in height.

Clay went all the way back to the barn picking and placing hay in front of the cows. He then closed the main gate to the barn.

"It is cold, calves are very sensitive", he said.

"They look cute", I said.

"Yes, I know", said Clay.

"Can I touch them?" I asked.

"Not a good idea right now. You got to know them well enough to gain their confidence. They don't appreciate strangers around them", said Clay while we walked back to his room.

I sat on a chair next to the table.

"So, your mom cooked this meal?" he asked.

"Yes, she did", I said.

Clay removed the foil. There was pasta, some long green beans and salad in his plate. He smelled the food by bringing it close to the nose.

"Smells good", he said.

He took the spoon and picked some pasta and placed the spoon in his mouth. He took 3-4 bites and then paused and said, "Man".

"What happened, you didn't like it?" I asked.

"Are you kidding me boy? This is the one of the best pastas, I have tasted in years", he said.

Clay finished the pasta in no time.

"Sorry, I didn't ask you", he said.

"No worries, I will go and eat now", I said.

I started to walk out of Clay's room. He said, "wait".

I stopped and looked back. He picked up the plate and started walking by my side.

"I am gonna go and check how much pasta your mom made. If she has a lot, I am going to ask her for some more", he said.

I smiled and said, "Yes, she made plenty, come you can have more", I said.

We started to walk and reached the front of the house. I opened the door.

"Mom", I said, while I held the door for Clay to enter in.

She was not around. I looked around and figured out that she was in the restroom.

"Come to the kitchen", I said to Clay.

We walked towards the kitchen. The food was on this huge counter next to the kitchen. Clay stopped for a while and said, "Wow that is a lot of food."

"Didn't I tell you?" I said.

I removed the foil from the pasta bowl and started to serve Clay more pasta.

"That's enough", he said.

"Come on take more, you work so much", I said.

I gave good portion of pasta to Clay. I also gave him more beans and salad. His plate was full again.

"You should eat also", said Clay.

"Yes, sure", I said and picked one plate. I added pasta, beans and salad to my plate.

"Let us go and sit in the dining room", I said.

"Na, I have to go and work. I will eat in the barn", said Clay.

"Wait, give me a minute", I said.

"Sure", said Clay.

I went to the other room. My mom was still the restroom.

"Ma, I am going back to the barn with Clay", I said.

"Ok, sweetie, be back in 10-15 minutes", she said.

"Sure ma, I am taking my food with me. I will eat over there", I said.

"No problem, enjoy", she said.

"Let's go", I said to Clay as I came out of the room.

Clay was already standing next to the door. We started to walk out and it was snowing heavily now.

"Wait, let me get the foil, hold my plate", I said to Clay.

Clay held both plates as I went inside the house.

"Hold on, I am coming too", said Clay.

We came back, Clay placed foil on both mine and his plate and we started to walk back towards the barn again. We reached the barn. Both of us were a little wet. We reached Clay's room. Both of us placed the plates on the table and sat on the chairs. I and clay, both removed foils from our plates.

"Hmm..this is really good", I said while eating the pasta.

"I told you", said Clay.

"So you said earlier today that you were on street", I said.

"Yes, I was on street for more than 5 years", said Clay.

"By street you mean, you were homeless?" I asked.

"Yes", said Clay.

"How did you become homeless?" I asked.

"It's a long story, some other day", said Clay.

"No, I want to hear", I said.

"Ok, so I worked for a company. I was honest in my dealings. The company members did not like my being honest. They wanted me to take the bribe and pass certain contracts", said Clay.

"Pass contracts for what?" I asked.

"Well, you know contracts for re-building bridges", said Clay.

"Ok, then what happened?" I asked.

"They changed the material that was to be used in making the bridge. The bridge collapsed after six months and I was arrested. I was later acquitted. But, the arrest record started to pop up in my background check and I was unable to get any job because I was seen as a criminal. I had some savings which perished soon. My wife died 10 years back. I have a daughter who is married and has two kids", said Clay.

"Your daughter did not help you?" I asked.

"I did not want to take money from my daughter. I was getting un-employment benefits for a while until they stopped paying me that also. I had to sell my car, house and pretty much everything I had in my belongings. I was on street in no time. I used to beg money. I got robbed many times. I was also stabbed twice. Sometimes, I would get food and sometimes I would just go hungry. Police did not let us stay anywhere. They demanded money from us, so that we could live in few un-known corners of the city. I had few belongings which were robbed from me as well", said Clay while he stopped eating.

"Oh no", I said.

"Yep", said Clay.

"One day I was sleeping on a bench in the city. Ron, your grandpa came to me. He offered me a sandwich which he bought from a nearby shop. I took the sandwich and said 'God-Bless'. He started to walk back towards his truck. I saw vegetables in his truck. I figured out that he was a farmer. I approached Ron again and asked, "Is there a way for me to earn this sandwich Sir? He replied, "It is yours, you earned it". I said, "No Sir, I have not provided you anything in return for this sandwich".

He looked at me and said, "Ok, help me unload these buckets of vegetables". I was very happy. After I unloaded few buckets, he asked, "You look like a hardworking man, why don't you do a job?" I said I have been trying to get a job for years now, every time my criminal history comes in between. They do a background check on every employee these days", I said.

"Oh boy, you could have opened a business", said Ron. The business lease requires a background check too. It is all messed up; the excess of everything is bad. These laws were supposed to protect us but in my case too much legal monitoring harmed me", I said. "Well, it is sad, how long have you been here?" he asked. "5 years", I said. "5 years", he said with his eyes wide opened. I helped your grandpa with placing all the vegetable baskets inside the grocery store. He asked, "Do you want a job?" I said, "Yes, Sir, I would love to have a job". He asked me to sit on the right side of the truck. He drove me here; there are 4 more individuals who work here. He introduced me to all of them and gave me this small room in the barn to live. I have lived here ever since. I have worked and earned my bread and butter. Your grandpa gave me few months of life of dignity", said Clay.

"That is very sweet of grandpa. I have a friend who is homeless", I said.

"What?" asked Clay as he looked very surprised.

"Yes", I said.

"Your friend, how long has he been homeless?" asked Clay.

"I don't know", I said.

"How old is he and how did he become your friend?" asked Clay.

"Well, I was staying at the hospital and he slept on the bench below, something like that", I said.

"Ok", said Clay.

"I am thinking that he would be sleeping out in the snow cold", I said.

"Yes, I know, I spent hundreds of nights out in the cold", said Clay.

"I thought government provided homes to everyone", I said.

"Don't be fooled by this system. If you are earning, you are fine. The moment you stop earning, you are in trouble. If you have some arrest record on your history, think that you are screwed up for life. Hospitals throw you out, if you don't have health insurance. It is a rich nation, but only for the rich. Poor people sleep on the streets. They are either shot or arrested by the police if they are out on the street for long. Some parasites will rob homeless. Some cops will demand money from homeless. It is a devil's paradise out there", said Clay.

"What are all the charities for? I know we receive many brochures at home", I asked.

"Charities, I know what charities are doing out there. Ultimately, one is responsible for one's own fate. No charity or government organization is able to cope up with the real problem", said Clay.

"What is the real problem?" I asked.

"Everyone thinks that homeless people need probably a dollar or one time meal. No, they need an opportunity to stand on their feet. Well, some do get addicted to drugs and alcohol but they have to take those or they will die of depression", said Clay.

"I understand. Yes, if government and these charities were playing their part well, then no one would be sleeping on the streets", I said.

"Exactly", said Clay.

We finished our meal.

"I feel sad for David", I said.

"Yes, I know it is worse when it snows", said Clay.

"Do you have space for one more individual here?" I asked.

"No, you should not sleep in the barn, you should go back to the house", said Clay.

"I was not talking about myself", I said.

"Wait, say that again", said Clay.

"I was talking about David. Can we bring him here?" I asked.

"You want to bring David into this barn, now?" asked Clay.

"Yes, now", I said.

"Do you know him well enough?" asked Clay.

"My grandpa hardly knew you, but he did give you a chance, didn't he?" I asked.

"Yes, he did", said Clay.

"So, what is the problem? There is ample space in the barn where he could sleep and he maybe he could assist you for so many other things", I said.

"You want him to come here for tonight or forever?" asked Clay.

"Till he is able to stand on his feet, I mean till he earns bread of respect", I said.

"You have to ask your mother about this, I think she is the new boss now", said Clay.

"Don't worry about it, I will be back in 5 minutes", I said and moved out of the barn and started to walk towards the house.

I entered the house and saw my mother in the kitchen again.

"Did you eat dinner, ma?" I asked.

"Yes, sweetheart, I did", my mom said.

"Hey mom, can we bring David here, he could live in the barn with Clay", I said.

"What?" my mom asked.

"Yes, David you know the homeless guy for whom I took the pizza", I said.

"No Jake, we cannot bring anyone from the street to our house", my mom said.

"He could help Clay in work, I mean take care of cows and so much other stuff", I said.

"How do you know he will help Clay and not rob or kill us all", my mom said.

"Well, I don't know ma, I guess everyone thinks that way and these people just stay on the streets forever", I said.

"Listen Jake, I can't allow anyone to be in our house, Ok", my mom said.

"But..", I said.

"No ifs and buts, I have made a decision that we are not going to bring anyone to our place, whom we don't know well enough", my mom said.

"Alright, ma", I said as I walked out of the house and started to walk back towards the barn.

I reached Clay's room.

"So, what did she say?" asked Clay.

"She said, of course, we can bring David here. She said grandpa brought you here and why not David", I said.

"Ok", said Clay.

"So, should we go now?" I asked.

"You mean, right now?" asked Clay.

"Yes, right now. It is snowing bad outside", I said.

"Ok, let me get the keys to the truck", said Clay as he walked towards the back of the barn.

He brought the keys to the truck. We went outside; there were two ways to the road outside, one through the front of the house and one through the back.

"So which way are we going?" I asked.

"Well, I usually go this way, it is shorter", said Clay while pointing towards the back way.

"That is perfect", I said. I did not want him to take the front path as my mom would have heard the noise of the truck.

"Ok, let me help you buckle up", said Clay.

"Thanks Clay", I said.

He went to the driving seat. He turned the truck on and boy did it make noise. For a moment I thought I was standing near an airplane.

"Wow that is a lot of noise. Mom's car is very quiet", I said.

"Yes, this is a hardworking truck", said Clay.

"Ha ha ha...", I laughed.

We drove towards the city.

"So, where does your friend live?" asked Clay.

"He lives on Crossroads Street, on a bench", I said.

"What? Crossroads street", said Clay while he looked very surprised.

"Yes, on Crossroads street", I said.

Clay kept quiet and continued driving. Soon we reached Crossroads street.

"We need to go to that end of the street", I said.

"I know this street very well, Jake", said Clay.

"Really, how come?" I asked.

"This is the area where I spent 5 years of hell", said Clay while his eyes got wet and his throat choked.

"What?" I asked.

"Yes, Jake. I can't believe that I am driving a truck on this street, full stomach. I have nice warm jacket on me. I am wearing shoes with no holes in it", said Clay as he drove truck on the crossroads street.

We approached close to the bench were I saw David last time.

"Stop the truck next to the bench", I said.

Clay slowed the truck next to the bench. The snowfall was heavy by now. I looked from the window of the truck and saw, which looked like David, sleeping on the bench with umbrella covering half of his body.

"There he is", I said.

"He looks like a new entry in this area, maybe he used to live on some other street before", said Clay while carefully trying to look at David.

"I don't know if I can park here", said Clay.

"It will be 2 minutes", I said.

"Ok, let me turn on the parking lights. I hope no police car comes this way", said Clay while opening his side of the door.

He came to my side and un-buckled my seat belt. I came out of the truck. David's half body was covered with snow. I moved his umbrella to a side. He was fast asleep. He had bent his knees towards his stomach to avoid snow, as much as possible.

"Oh boy, this is a heart-less world. If God appeared in front of me, I would shoot the mother f...well, sorry about that Jake", said Clay.

"God is blind Clay, just like all these people who sleep warm in their luxurious hotel rooms", I said.

"David", I said.

"David, hey buddy", said Clay.

"Wake up David", I said.

David opened his eyes slowly, he looked at us. He then moved up and sat.

"Hey boy, what are you doing here, this late?" asked David.

"We came here to take you to our barn", I said.

"Take me", he said.

"Yes, we want you to come with us", I said.

"Wait what?" asked David.

"Hey, David, you see Jake wants to take you to his grandpa's barn", said Clay.

"Who are you?" asked David.

"His name is Clay; he used to live on this street also. He lived here for 5 years", I said.

"5 years, wo, I came to this street 2 months back. I got robbed in the other part of the city and police officers were bothering me non-stop there", said David.

"Yes, I know, the robbers in uniform", said Clay.

"Come with us David", I said.

"I don't know boy", said David.

"Trust me bro, his grandpa was a great man, I have a new life now, just because of him", said Clay.

"Was a great man", said David.

"Yes, he passed away today", I said.

"He passed away today, really, and both of you are here to pick me up", said David.

"Well, he is in the hospital right now, so no funeral proceedings could be started until his body is given back to us", I said.

"Aren't you sad?" asked David.

"Of course, I am. We all have to die someday, but life has to go on", I said.

"You talk like a grown up man", said David.

"I think we should get going before a police car comes", said Clay.

"Na, you guys carry on, I am fine where I am. I don't have much left in me anyways. It is a matter of time before I am a free bird again", said David.

"Free bird?" I asked.

"Yes, I will die soon and then my soul will fly like a free bird", said David.

"Don't be crazy man, you could still do something productive", said Clay.

"You know what; I have heard enough from you. Why don't you both leave me alone now", said David.

"We could help", I said.

"I wish to be alone", said David.

I and Clay started to walk back towards our truck. I opened the door and sat inside. Clay hooked the seat belt for me. Clay got back on the steering wheel and started driving the car. We reached close to the end of the street when Clay saw something from his rear mirror.

"What the hell?" he said.

"What happened Clay?" I asked.

"They are removing his jacket and shoes", said Clay.

"Who is removing what?" I asked while trying to look back.

Clay immediately made a U-turn. We reached close to the bench and there were three men, one had David's jacket in his hand. Other guy was removing his shoes and one man had a knife in his hand.

Clay lowered his side of the mirror and said, "You are dead".

He took out a pistol from the glove compartment and pointed it out of the window. The three men started to run. He then picked up his phone and dialed 911.

After about 2-3 minutes, 2 police cars arrived at the scene. They started questioning David, Clay and me. Clay gave complete description of the three men.

"You know someone in the city?" asked one officer from David.

"I know myself", said David.

"I mean, do you know someone else except your own self. Someone with whom you could stay for the night?" asked officer again.

"Sir, we know him", I said to the officer.

"Do you know this boy?" asked officer from David.

"Yes", he said.

"Ok, can you stay with them for tonight, just to be sure you are not mugged again", said officer to David.

David did not say anything this time.

"Yes, of course, we will take him with us. We have a barn, where I live and there is ample space where he could stay for the night", said Clay.

"Would you?" asked officer from David.

David looked very sad.

"Why don't you just shoot me and get me out of my misery", said David.

"Shoot you, now why would we do that?" asked officer.

"Because I am breaking all types of laws, I guess", said David.

"We are not going to shoot you. Courts decide the punishment, not we", said officer.

"Can I talk to him alone?" I asked officer.

"Sure, go ahead", said officer.

"We are trying to help you David", I said.

"I don't need help", said David.

I moved towards the officer and said, "Sir may I?" I took the officer to a side and said, "I and Clay could stay here for a while to make sure no one harms him."

"I would not advise that", said officer.

"Officer, I have lived on this street for 5 years, I know what goes here", said Clay.

"You Sir, you lived here for 5 years", said officer as he looked very surprised.

"Yes", said Clay.

"Well, we can take him to jail, at least no one would harm him there", said officer.

"That's the only thing you guys know" said Clay.

"I am sorry Sir, what did you say?" asked officer.

"Never mind Sir", I said while trying to calm down the situation.

"Ok, we need to go now. He is on his own. We gave him all the options, to which he declined", said officer while he started to write on his notepad. He removed a page from his notepad and gave it to David.

"What is that?" asked David.

"It is a citation for littering", said officer.

"You got to be me kidding me", said Clay.

"Sir", said officer while pointing at Clay.

"How the hell is he supposed to pay for that citation? You know, take away whatever is left on his body, vultures", said Clay.

"Sir, I am going to arrest you for obstruction of justice", said officer to Clay.

"Clay, oh no officer, he did not mean it", I said.

"Alright, you all have a good night now", said officer and left.

"Can I see that?" asked Clay from David.

Clay started looking at the citation.

"Man, you got to get out of this place", said Clay to David.

"Alright", said David.

"Awesome", I said.

David had no shoes as they were stolen. He had no jacket either. Clay removed his jacket and gave it to David. The sidewalk was all wet with snow. David only had socks in his feet. The truck was parked on the other side. Clay went back to the truck; he moved it forward and made a U-turn to bring the truck close to the bench. He then came towards David and said, "Alright bud let's go".

Clay bent and picked up David by placing his left arm over his shoulder. He then moved David towards the truck. He made him sit in the middle of the truck. The truck had one long seat, it was old style.

He placed seat belt around David. He then asked me to sit in the truck. Once he buckled me up, he closed my door and moved towards the driving seat.

He started the truck and we drove.

"Long time", said David.

"Long time?" asked Clay.

"I have been inside a truck", said David while placing his hands near the air vent.

"I bet", said Clay.

"Oh man", said David while he placed his hands on the air vent.

"Man, you were freezing out there", said Clay.

David kept quiet.

"You can move your feet up, if you wish", said Clay.

David immediately moved his feet above and placed them below his knees. He basically sat in meditation posture. David kept looking left and right. Within 15 minutes we arrived at the barn.

"Hold on there", said Clay as he parked the truck in front of the barn.

"Ok", said David.

"Hold on, let me grab a pair of shoes", said Clay.

David walked inside the barn and brought two pairs of shoes.

"Ok try these", he said to David.

David picked up the shoes and tried on. After wearing first pair of shoes he said, "These are fine."

"Are you sure?" I asked.

"Yes", said David. Clay came to my side, un-buckled me and David. We both were out of the truck. I saw my mom standing outside the door of the house. There were some lights outside the house, so I could see her.

"Jake...Jake", I heard my mom calling my name loud.

"I will be back", I said as Clay took David inside the barn.

I came close to my mom.

"Where were you?" asked my mom.

"Oh mom, Clay had to pick some medicines from the pharmacy. I just accompanied him", I said.

"Ok, come inside now, it is getting extremely cold", my mom said.

I thought my mom saw David but I guess she did not because it was dark on our side.

"Mom, if you don't mind, can I sleep at the barn. There is ample of space back there", I said.

"No Jake", my mom said.

"Ok, give me 15 minutes, I will back", I said.

"For what?" asked my mom.

"Clay was telling me a story, I just want him to finish", I said.

"Alright, be back soon", my mom said.

I hugged my mom and started walking towards the barn again. The snow literally covered my whole jacket. I entered the barn and went to Clay's room.

"Where is he?" I asked.

"In the shower", replied Clay.

"That is great. So, where are his clothes, we need to get those washed", I said.

"Washed, they need to be burned. No detergent in the world could wash a homeless man's clothes. Who could know better than me", said Clay.

"I am sorry, I did not realize that", I said.

"I have given him a nice pajama and a shirt. I have also given him a warm woolen sweater that Ron gave me", said Clay.

"That is great Clay", I said.

"Should I bring food for him?" I asked.

"Yes, sure", said Clay.

I walked towards the house, moved towards the kitchen. My mom was sitting on a chair with her eyes closed. She looked sad, probably because of grandpa's passing away.

"Ma", I said.

She opened her eyes and said, "You are back in just 5 minutes", she said while looking at her watch.

"Ma, I need to take some food for Clay", I said.

"Food, you already took food for him, didn't you?" my mom asked.

"Yes, but he absolutely loved it. Can I take some more for him?" I asked.

"Yes dear, come", my mom said.

"Oh, sorry ma, did you eat?" I asked.

"I had some chamomile tea, to relax myself", my mom said.

"So, you are not having food?" I asked.

"No dear, I just had few biscuits with the tea", my mom said.

"Don't be sad ma", I said.

My mom smiled and placed food in a plate. She added good portion to the plate and then covered it with foil.

"Oh ma, you are so generous", I said.

My mom smiled and I picked plate with my right hand.

"Jake, how is your arm?" my mom asked.

"Absolutely great", I said.

"Are you sure, I can carry that plate to the barn", my mom asked.

"Oh no, don't worry, I got this", I said.

"You are a solid boy", my mom said.

"Ha ha", I laughed.

My mom opened the door and I started to walk towards the barn. The snow covered the whole plate. I reached Clay's room. Clay and David were sitting on the chairs next to the table and chatting.

"There you are", said Clay.

"Hey David, you look great", I said.

"Yes, a bath after 7 months", said David.

"Yes, I can understand that. I brought food for you", I said.

I placed the plate in front of David and removed the foil.

"Wo", he said.

"What?" I asked.

"Nothing", he said while taking a long breath. He then looked at Clay and me.

"Thank you guys", said David.

"No worries", said Clay.

"Enjoy the meal", I said.

David placed the fork and spoon on a side. He moved his right hand into the plate and I stopped him.

"Wait, why don't you use the fork?" I asked.

"Fork, hmmm..., I guess I am used to eat with hand", said David.

"David, you should use the fork and spoon. You are not on the street anymore", I said.

David kept quiet and used his right hand to eat pasta, beans and salad.

"I can't believe this", said David.

"You like it, don't you?" I asked.

David started crying. He rubbed his tears with the side of the sweater.

"Oh come on now, you are a grown man, do not cry", I said.

"Stop crying man", said Clay.

David started eating the food. He was totally lost in eating. I and Clay looked at each other and smiled.

"How is your arm boy?" asked David.

"I am fine", I said.

"Have a seat", said David while pointing to a chair close by.

"Na, I have to go. My mom is waiting for me", I said.

"Oh yes, you should be going now", said Clay.

"So, David would sleep...", I said.

"Don't worry; I am going to move a bed to this room. This room is big enough for 20 beds", said Clay.

"20, oh sure, even more, I could play football in here", I said.

David and Clay laughed.

"I should be going now", I said.

"Thank you so much", said David while offering his hand for a hand-shake.

"You are most welcome", I said as I shook David's hand.

I moved out of the barn and walked towards the house. I went inside.

"Did you give the food to Clay?" my mom asked.

"Yes, ma", he enjoyed it.

"I am also going to eat a little bit more, I am hungry again", I said.

"That is great, I can eat some too", my mom said.

I and my mom enjoyed the food. My mom took out some pills from her bag and said, "There are your pills."

"Sure", I took the pills in my hand and swallowed all at once.

"Easy there", my mom said.

"What?" I asked while smiling.

"You should be careful. You swallowed 5 pills, all at once", my mom said.

"Ha ha", I laughed.

"Don't laugh now", my mom said.

My mom took my plate and hers to the kitchen.

I went to the restroom. After I came back, my mom was standing outside with a glass of milk.

"No", I said.

"Jake, you need to drink this milk. All those medicines will otherwise burn your stomach", my mom said.

"I don't want to drink it, my stomach is full", I said.

"Jake, no more excuses. You have to drink this", my mom said.

"Ok, give me 5 minutes, please", I said.

"Alright, I will come back after 5 minutes", said my mom and left the room. Grandpa's house was huge. There were probably 10 rooms in it. I walked from one room to another. Some rooms were very scary.

"Jake", I heard my mom calling me.

"Yes, ma", I said.

"You will sleep here", my mom said while pointing towards a room.

"Here, no way", I said.

"Why not?" my mom asked.

"It looks scary, come on mom", I said.

"Ok, then choose whichever room you like", my mom said. I moved from room to room. I went in front of the room where my mom was resting and said, "this one."

"What?" my mom said.

"Yes, ma, please let us get a small bed from another room. This room is big enough for two beds", I said.

My mom moved out of the room. She looked around and said, "There, let me move this mattress to my room."

She moved the mattress to her room and said, "Happy".

"Love you ma", I said. After a while I was on the mattress, ready to sleep. There was a window just behind my face. I bent by head to look through the window, yes, I know my usual habit of looking outside the window. The snow was still falling; the tree leaves were getting covered by the snow. I kept looking outside the window and don't know when I fell asleep.

"Jake", I heard my mom calling me.

"Jake", she said again.

"Ahmmm...," I said while slowly opening my eyes.

"Wake up, your breakfast is ready", my mom said.

I got up, went to the restroom and there was again a lot of food that my mom had cooked.

"Wow, so much food", I said.

"Yes, sweetie, I am expecting some of my friends to come by today. Also, our relatives will start pouring in slowly and slowly. I have also called the funeral services, although, I have not given them a date, since we don't know when they will be releasing dad", my mom said.

"Ok, did Clay come in?" I asked.

"Clay, no", my mom said. I asked my mom to get my jacket on. I had to wear the jacket through one arm only. The other arm went inside the jacket folded inwards.

"Ok, ma, I have to go and see Clay", I said.

"Wait, eat your breakfast first and then take some for Clay also", my mom said.

"Ok", I said. I ate my breakfast. Ma, "put some more", I said. I had to take both Clay's and David's breakfast in one plate.

"Ok", my mom said as she added more to the plate. "Ok, there, it won't hold more than this", my mom said. She then covered the plate with a foil.

"Thanks ma", I said. "Wait where my hug is?" my mom asked. I went towards her and hugged her with my right arm. My mom opened the door and for a second, I just froze. There was snow all around. Last evening, I was able to see the green fields and now all the fields were white. Trees were covered with snow. The whole scene was spectacular. I moved out slowly, the stairs were a little slippery.

"Jake, be careful, are you sure you don't need my help?" my mom asked.

"Oh no, I am good, thanks ma", I said.

I moved towards the barn. The door was closed. I hit the door with my feet to make a noise. Clay opened the door.

"Hello young man", he said.

"Hello Clay", I said.

"Where is David?" I asked.

"He is out there", said Clay.

"Where, in the back?" I asked.

I went inside Clay's room and placed the plate on his table. I then moved out and followed Clay. David was attaching milking machines to the cows.

"David", I said.

"Hey there", said David.

"What are you doing?" I asked.

"My boss gave me the orders to attach the milking machine to the cows", said David.

"Your Boss?" I asked.

"Clay", said David.

"Oh Clay, ha ha", I laughed.

Clay also smiled.

"I brought breakfast for you both", I said.

"Breakfast, we had breakfast 2 hours back", said Clay.

"2 hours back?" I asked.

"Yes, we got up early, I made some pancakes and coffee", said Clay.

"Where?" I asked.

"Come, let me show you", said Clay.

He took me inside his room and opened a door. I placed plate on the table. There was a small room and after the small room there was a kitchen. The kitchen had huge windows. I saw huge land covered with snow though the window.

"Wow, what a sight?" I said.

"So, you have never been here before?" asked Clay.

"No, I have never been here before. No one showed me around like you do", I said.

"So, this is the place where I cooked mine and Ron's meal. Sometimes, Ron would make nice Chinese food. Oh man, he knew all the great sauces", said Clay.

"So, how did you make David work?" I asked.

"Well, he got up early than me; I guess a homeless man could never sleep for more than 2-3 hours at a stretch, because of fear, cold, hunger and so many other factors", said Clay.

"Ok", I said.

"He was sitting on the bed, when I woke up. He asked me, if he could be of some help. I made breakfast and told him to attach the milking machine to the cows. He looked very desperate for work. I called two other guys, who usually come early in the morning to take a day off. They have been asking for a day off from long time", said Clay.

"You mean David hooked all the cows to the machine?" I asked.

"Yes, he did. He looks like a very smart guy. Although, I found him a little shy, as he speaks very less", said Clay.

"No worries, he will open up slowly. Maybe, he is having tough time believing that he has found some work to do", I said.

"Yes, I feel that he wants to earn every meal", said Clay.

"He is just like you", I said.

"Na, he is better than me", said Clay.

"You are trying to be way too modest", I said.

"How's your arm?" asked Clay.

"Oh, I am great", I said.

We started walking out. We reached Clay's room.

"So, what should I do with this food?" I asked.

"Don't worry, I am hungry again and so would be David", said Clay.

"Did David tell you anything about his background?" I asked Clay.

"Yes, he had been homeless for few months. His wife divorced him and his two kids live with his wife now. He told me, he has AIDS", said Clay.

"AIDS, what is that?" I asked.

"Well, it is a very serious disease. It has no cure. He said he had no money for the treatment and ended up on the street after selling everything", said Clay.

"So, government does nothing about it?" I asked.

"Nope", said Clay.

We walked outside and towards the back of the barn. David was busy removing the milking machine from some cows.

"How is it going David?" asked Clay.

"It is great", said David.

"Hungry?" asked Clay.

"Na", said David.

"Don't hesitate man, Jake got some more food for us", said Clay.

David moved towards a sink for washing hands. After washing hands, he said, "What a great feeling."

"Great feeling?" I asked.

"Yes, to work and earn your food", said David.

"Sure, it must be", I said.

All three of us started to walk towards Clay's room which was on the right side.

We entered the room, Clay removed the foil and said, "Wo."

"Ha ha", I laughed.

"Did everybody get to eat or you brought all for us", said Clay.

"Oh no, mom made plenty", I said.

Clay moved back to the room and went to the kitchen. He brought plates and spoons and forks.

"Ok, there you are", he said while giving a fork and a spoon to me and David.

"Oh no, I ate", I said.

"Are you sure?" asked Clay.

"Yes, I ate before coming here", I said.

"Ok", said David and divided the portion on the plate in half.

"There you go bud", he said to David.

They both started eating the food.

"Nice", said Clay.

"Yes, really good", said David.

"So, when did you get this disease, AIDS?" I asked David.

David looked at Clay in surprise.

"Don't worry buddy, we are not like others. I have seen the worst myself. We are not going to despise you because of your disease. I know if Ron was here, he would not have cared a single percent about this", said Clay.

"Well, I was diagnosed few months back", said David.

"If you had a bad disease then why were you not in a hospital?" I asked.

"The world is not the way as it looks. Don't be fooled by big cars, restaurants, nice houses etc. We are a developed nation but a nation only for the rich. Poor people have no place in this society. You may not believe, me neither, until I myself was homeless", said Clay.

"Really", I said.

"Yes, I agree with Clay. No one gives a damn about you, sorry", said David.

"Hey, we give a damn about you, right Clay", I said.

We all laughed. Clay and David finished their food.

"Can I stay here for one more day, if that is not too much of a burden?" asked David in a very low voice.

"I guess, Jake and his mom are the boss here", said Clay.

"Of course, you can stay here", I said.

"I will work", said David.

"Don't worry man", said Clay while placing his right hand over David's left shoulder.

"Yes, you don't have to worry about anything", I said.

"Thanks", said David.

David picked his and Clay's plate. "Wait", said Clay.

"Give that plate to me", said Clay.

"I got this" said David and took both his and Clay's plate to the kitchen. He then returned with two glasses of water. He gave one to Clay and offered me the second. "I am fine", I said.

"Ok", said David and started drinking the water from the glass.

"I will have to keep my glass separate, although HIV does not spread through saliva. Many people are scared that they would get AIDS just by touching or looking at a person with AIDS" said David.

"Is it a very dangerous disease?" I asked.

"Yes, it is", said David.

"So, why don't you get treatment?" I asked.

"Where do I get the treatment, it is so expensive. They throw you out of the hospital if you can't pay the bills", said David.

"That is not good. What is the government doing? We are taught so many things about the government in the school. They make the bridges, schools, hospitals etc.", I said.

"Yes, they do all that", said David while sitting on the chair again.

"So, that means if I get AIDS, I would have to live on that bench too", I said.

David and Clay laughed.

"No, why would you get AIDS at first place?" asked Clay.

"Oh, I should not stay here, you both could get this from me", said David.

"Don't be a fool, nothing is going to happen", said Clay.

"No, I am serious", said David.

"David, if one of your fingers gets a little infection. Do you treat the infection or cut the hand?" I asked.

"Wo, big words out of that small mouth", said Clay and then he laughed.

"Yes, where did you learn all those examples?" asked David.

"Don't be fooled by my size David. A lot cooks in my brain everyday", I said.

"Oh boy, ha ha...", David laughed.

We started to walk towards the back.

"So you don't take any medicine for your disease?" I asked David.

"No", replied David.

We kept on walking. Clay opened the back door. He then opened a small gate, which kept all the cows inside. It was a beautiful sunny day. To my surprise, there was no snow in the back of the barn; it was just a small area though. Cows moved outside. Some cows did not move out, they were with their calves.

"Haaa haa....haaa", said Clay as the cows moved out. David closed the small gate. We three walked outside.

"Where did the snow go?" I asked Clay.

"I removed it with the help of David", said Clay.

"So cows don't feel cold in here?" I asked Clay.

"They like sun, I am going to take them back in 20-30 minutes", said David.

I heard a honk.

"Who is that?" I asked.

"Must be the milk-van", said Clay.

I ran from inside the barn to see the milk-van. It was parked closed to the front gate. It was a white van.

"Hey there", said the driver of the vehicle after seeing me standing there.

"Hello", I said.

Clay and David walked behind me.

"Hey Russell", said Clay.

"My man", said Russell.

"How are you this morning?" asked Clay.

"I am fine bro", said Russell.

"This is David and this young man is Jake", said Clay.

"How are you guys?" asked Russell while shaking mine and David's hand.

"I am fine", I replied.

"Good man", said David.

"Ok, back the truck up", said Clay.

Russell backed the truck into the barn. There was this huge cylinder shaped storage for holding the milk. Clay hooked a hose to the truck. He turned the knob to the right.

"Alright", said Clay.

"You have got some good company here. Where are the other guys?" asked Russell.

"I gave them a day off. They have been asking for it from a month or so", said Clay.

"So, who is this young man?" asked Russell.

"He is Ron's grandson. By the way, Ron passed away yesterday", said Clay.

"What, Ron....you mean Ron?" asked Russell.

"Yes, Ron passed away yesterday. I was in the barn, I did not even know", said Clay.

"Wo, holy smokes man. He looked perfectly alright to me", said Russell.

"Yes, I also thought the same way. We had the lunch together yesterday", said Clay.

"Man, when is the funeral?" asked Russell.

"We don't know, his body is in the hospital", I said.

"Hospital", said Russell.

"Yes", I said.

"Well, give me a call on my cell phone whenever his funeral is", said Russell to Clay.

"Yes, absolutely", said Clay.

Clay turned off the huge faucet. He then removed the hose and placed it back.

"Alright, you are good to go" said Clay while he wrote something on a copy.

Russell signed the copy and said, "Nice meeting you both."

I and David smiled.

Russell left with his van. Clay moved towards the outside and started moving cows inside. Apparently, it got cloudy outside. David opened the inside gate and slowly and slowly moved all the cows inside. Cows pretty much moved to their respective spots.

"David, do you mind getting that hose for me", said Clay.

"Ok", said David while looking around.

"There", I said while pointing towards a hose which was attached to a faucet on the outside wall of Clay's room.

David picked up the hose, un-tangled it and moved it towards Clay.

"There", he said. Clay placed the hose inside a very long trough.

"Ok, turn it on", he said. I went close to the faucet and turned it on.

"I am not going to pay you", said Clay. All three of us laughed. I moved towards Clay and David.

"You see, you need to take good care of them", said Clay.

A calf moved close to the water trough.

"Can I touch him?" I asked. Clay picked me up and leaned me forward.

"There", he said. I touched the calf above his nose area. The calf got scared.

He moved back.

"See, I told you. I takes time to earn their confidence", said Clay.

"Watch", he waived his hand at the calf. "Come on, come on, it's ok", he said.

Calf moved forward, slowly and slowly. He started drinking water from the trough. Clay gently moved his hand over calf's head.

"Yes, you need to do it gently", he said as he picked me up again and leaned me forward. This time I did touch the calf.

"It is so soft", I said.

"Yes", said Clay.

David sat on the floor.

"What happened?" asked Clay while placing me down.

"I get this, sometimes", he said.

"What happen David?" I asked.

"I get a little nauseated sometime", said David.

"David, we should take you to the hospital", I said.

"No, no, don't worry", said David.

"Are you Ok man?" asked Clay while placing his arm around David's right shoulder.

"Yes, I am fine man, thanks", said David.

"You should take rest", said Clay.

"No, I am fine, I can work", said David.

"Work, of course you can work but only when you are feeling fine", said Clay.

"Alright then, I will take a nap", said David.

I and Clay took David to the room. David removed his shoes and laid on the bed. Clay placed a blanket on top of him.

"Alright, take rest buddy", said Clay.

Clay and I moved out of the room and closed the door.

"He needs help", I said.

"Yes, sure he does", said Clay.

"I will be back", I said.

"Where now?" asked Clay.

"I need to see my mom", I said. I left the barn and reached home.

My mom was on phone.

"Ma", I said.

"Wait sweetie", she said.

I went close to my mom. She smiled as she talked on the phone. After about 2-3 minutes she hung the phone.

"What is it Jake?" she asked.

"Nothing ma, if I tell you something, you won't be angry, right?" I asked.

"What is it Jake?" asked my mom.

"Well, who was on the phone?" I asked.

"It was from the hospital. They have not completed the investigation, although they have removed your grandpa's vital organs for donation", my mom said.

"So, he will be brought here tomorrow?" I asked.

"Yes", she said.

"Ok", I said.

"So, you were going to tell me something", my mom said.

"Yes, ma, I was saying that...ahmmmm", I said.

"What is it Jake?" my mom asked.

"Promise, you won't say me anything?" I asked.

"Jake, you need to speak now", my mom said.

"You know the guy for whom I took pizza", I said.

"Yes, what about him?" my mom asked.

"He has AIDS", I said.

"AIDS, did he tell you?" my mom asked.

"Yes, the poor guy did", I said.

"He is homeless, right, is he not getting treatment?" my mom asked.

"No ma, he can't afford. They threw him out the hospital, since he could not pay the bills", I said.

"Poor guy, he has no family?" my mom asked.

"His wife left him", I said.

"Because of his disease?" my mom asked.

"Yes, he did get a job because people knew he had AIDS", I said.

"But, AIDS does not just spread like that", my mom said.

"Yes, that is what Clay said to David", I said.

"What, Clay, when did Clay meet David?" my mom asked.

"Oops, sorry ma", I said.

"Ok, everything out of your mouth right now", my mom said.

"You know ma, it snowed yesterday, I knew David was going to be sleeping on the bench, I thought why not bring him here. So, I and Clay brought him here to the barn. He took shower and slept. He helped Clay in the morning. He wasn't feeling well so he is sleeping now", I said.

"What? Jake, that guy is here in our barn?" my mom asked while her eyes became huge.

"Sorry ma, I am really sorry. I could not stop myself", I said.

"Clay helped you?" asked my mom.

"Yes, but he is not to be blamed for this, it is all my fault. I lied to him that you allowed me to bring David here. You know ma, he got robbed just before we brought him here. They took his jacket, shoes", I said.

"What is the government doing? What are the charities doing?" my mom asked.

"They do nothing ma, I mean even if they do, it is not addressing the real problem", I said.

"What is the real problem?" my mom asked.

"The real problem is something else. Everyone thinks that giving a few cents, or a burger or something like that to these guys will fix the problem. Some think that maybe providing them shelter will fix the problem. No. These are not the solutions. We need to give them love, which they need most. I mean, we are such a rich nation but still our own citizens are living like street-dogs", I said.

"Don't say that", my mom said.

"Seriously ma, are they any less than street-dogs, tell me", I said.

"It is an offensive word Jake", my mom said.

"But isn't that the right word to describe as to how they live? They take food out of the trash, they sleep on the sidewalk, they don't have any health insurance, and people despise them. They pretend that they don't even see them. I saw from that room, when people reached close to these guys, they took out their cell phones and pretended as if they never saw them. The police demands money from them, so that they could live on the street. They cite them for littering, I mean where else would they put their stuff, if not on the streets?" I asked.

"I have been sending donations to charities in Africa", my mom said.

"What? Africa, we have a worse scenario than Africa in our own backyard. I mean, come on mom, aren't we a society of hypocrites?"

"Hypocrites", my mom said.

"Yes, ma hypocrites. Our own backyard is on fire and we have the audacity to go out there and extinguish fire in others backyards. People would send $10 donation through their cell phone to Red Cross society, which goes and helps people in other countries. I am not saying it is wrong. But, only when we have taken care of every one in need, in our own backyard", I said.

"Hmm", my mom said.

"I mean look at all the bull-shit they show on TV. Donate $1 to support a child for 1 whole month of drinking water in Africa. Bull-shit. Someone in your backyard is drinking water from a bottle left by someone in the trash can", I said.

"Jake, you need to watch your language", my mom said.

"You know why people do that, because they are hypocrites. They smoke day and night and then tell someone not to smoke. On TV they would show oh, I care so much for pets, you can also help these pets by donating $10 a month. I bet, pets have a better lifestyle than some humans in this country", I said.

"Jake, you are speaking way too much. You need to shut-up now", my mom said.

"What? Are you disappointed to know all this ma?" I asked.

"Well, Jake", my mom said.

"Come on ma, truth is not always sweet to hear", I said.

"I am thinking that how could they leave a man with AIDS on the streets", my mom said.

"See, ma, we all are so naïve", I said.

"Is he resting? How long has he had the disease?" my mom asked.

"Around six months", I replied.

"So, he has not received any treatment?" my mom asked.

"They asked him to sit on a wheel-chair and then politely dropped him outside on a bench. He kept looking at their faces. They told him they don't have the resources to treat him. These ass-holes have the resources to send huge piles of money to foreign countries and then say, 'see we are so fucking generous". You know what ma, people like these will realize when they end up on a bench and no one will give a shit about them", I said.

"Jake, shut up. Where did you learn all these words?" my mom asked.

"From home ma, when you and dad used to fight. All I heard was 'fuck-you' and 'fuck-you", I said.

My mom went and sat on a couch, she started to cry.

"No, need to cry ma. We all have to learn. Don't tell me not to smoke, if you smoke ten cigarettes a day", I said.

"Yes, I guess, you are right. We all need to change", my mom said while wiping her tears.

"How much money have you been sending abroad?" I asked.

"Well, about hundred dollars a month to charities", my mom said.

"What? Hundred dollars", I said while shaking my head.

"Jake, we should switch the topic now", my mom said.

"Why? If you don't like me or my topic give me to a charity too. You should leave me, just like you left dad. You see ma, you have to look inside your own self. Maybe, you did not give what dad need and that is why he started looking for another woman", I said.

"Jake, I will slap you now", my mom said.

"Go ahead, that will not change the truth", I said.

"Truth, do you know all the truth?" my mom asked.

"What is the truth ma? The bottom-line, you both did not get along. So many kids in my class have parents who are divorced", I said.

"Jake, your dad was not faithful to me", my mom said.

"But why? Did he not love you from the very beginning?" I asked.

"Jake, it is a long story", my mom said.

"Long-story, yes I know. There is always a long-story", I said.

There was knock on the door. I opened the door. It was Clay.

"Hey Jake, David wanted to see you", said Clay.

"Ok, I will be right there", I said.

"Wait, I am coming too", my mom said.

All three of us walked towards the barn. We reached Clay's room where David was lying on the bed.

"Hey, O, hello ma'am", said David.

"Hi", my mom said.

"I am sorry to bother you all. I was just wondering if you could take me back to the city", said David.

"City, but why?" I asked.

"I guess, I am sick, so I won't be able to work", said David.

"You see this ma. This is happening in our own backyards and we fools are going to help others when our own need our help the most", I said.

My mom stayed quiet.

"Let me see what I can do", my mom said as she left the barn.

"Jake, stop bothering everyone", said David.

"Don't worry David", I said while holding his hand. Clay was sitting quiet on a chair next to the table.

"I guess, I am going to die", said David.

"Don't say that, you will be fine", I said.

"Come on man, don't worry", said Clay as he got up from the chair and came close to the bed.

My mom came back to the room with a laptop in her hand.

"Ok, we can put him on a health insurance", my mom said.

She asked David's information about his age etc. She then typed something on the laptop which she placed on the table in Clay's room.

"What?" she said.

"What happened ma?" I said.

"None of the health insurance will cover him because of his pre-existing condition", my mom said.

"Isn't that awesome, ma", I said.

"I don't believe this", my mom said.

"So what should we do now?" I asked.

"If you get him treated here in this country, we will be bankrupt soon", my mom said.

"Bankrupt", I said.

"Yes, the medicine costs a lot and then the daily expenses would be just out of our scope to afford", my mom said.

"Let us take him to some other country like India or Mexico", I said.

"Let me check", my mom said.

After checking something on the laptop she said, "There is a charitable society in India which treats AIDS patients for free", my mom said.

"Awesome, let us take him over there", I said.

"I need to contact them, but in the meantime we need to take David to the hospital. We can bear few days of treatment's cost", my mom said.

She called the hospital. Within about 15 minutes an ambulance came. They were about to take David in the ambulance when David said, "Bunch of hypocrites".

"What?" asked one of the member of paramedics.

"You are taking me in, just to throw me out later on", said David.

"It's Okay David, we are going to take you to India", I said.

"India, yes for sure. I am sick of this country anyways", said David as they placed him in the ambulance.

A woman from paramedics injected something into David. David mumbled for a while and then he slept. The ambulance left the barn.

"Poor soul", my mom said.

"Finally, you are seeing the truth. You were of the impression that all homeless people are just drug addicts and criminals, weren't you?" I asked.

"I never thought that way", my mom said.

"Appreciate your mom for what she did for David just now", said Clay.

"I am sorry, I guess I am taking out everyone's anger on you", I said.

"Good boy", said Clay.

"I should go and prepare the lunch. I also have to get in touch with this society in India", my mom said.

"Absolutely ma, thanks", I said.

My mom went out of the barn.

"You should take rest too", said Clay.

"Na, I am fine. I was wondering, if I could go out with you on the tractor?" I asked.

"Are you sure? You don't want to rest?" asked Clay.

"Na, I am good", I said.

We started walking towards the tractor, which was parked outside the back door. It was a covered tractor so no worry of cold air coming in.

"Ok", said Clay while picking me up and leaning me forward so that I can go inside. He followed me and sat on the middle seat, I was sitting on a smaller seat on the side.

"It is nice inside", I said.

"You like it?" asked Clay.

"I love it", I said.

"What is that far away?" I asked as David started driving the tractor through field full of snow.

"Be patient, you will find out soon", said Clay.

He kept driving the tractor through the huge open field towards this building which was hardly visible from a distance. The inside of the tractor was getting warm now. We were getting closer to the building.

"Wow, one could hardly see this building from over there. What is in this building?" I asked.

"Patience my friend", said Clay.

He parked the truck outside the building and then held me down. He then moved close to the building and took out a key from his pocket to open a huge lock, in front of the building. We entered in.

"So many vegetables", I said.

"Yes", said Clay.

"But, why do you grow all these in the building?" I asked.

"We have to, the snow will destroy all the vegetables", said Clay.

"Ok", I said as we walked across the building.

"Wow, look at those red tomatoes", I said.

"Yes, we have pretty much everything here", said Clay.

"Everything?" I asked.

"Yes, under all this soil, there are potatoes and onions", said Clay.

"Wow, look at that", I said.

"This is Cilantro", said Clay.

"Neat", I said.

"So, you have never been here before? I mean why not?" asked Clay.

"I told you Clay, we just stayed in the house. My grandpa would come to this place and I would just be playing at the house. My stay at hospital has made me curious about everything. I want to see new things, explore them", I said.

"That is very good", said Clay.

He picked up few pots of tomatoes and moved them to a new place. He then picked up a watering can and started watering the plants. He then moved from one area to other watering plants. He then went to the back of the building, re-filled the can and started watering the plants again. I kept on watching him. I heard sound of a vehicle coming towards the building.

"They must be here", said Clay.

"Who?" I asked.

"The workers who take care of this farm", said Clay.

"Hola", said one guy as he entered the building.

"Hola", said Clay.

"This is Ron's grandson", said Clay.

"Hola", said one guy.

"I am sorry", I said.

"They are saying hello to you Jake", said Clay.

"Oh, hello, I mean hola", I said.

"They don't speak English", said Clay.

"Where are they from?" I asked.

"They are from Mexico", said Clay.

"Awesome", I said.

"They are very hard working people", said Clay.

They both started working. One of them started removing tomatoes from the plants and other guy moved soil with a shovel.

"Don't they speak English, at all?" I asked.

"No, they speak Spanish, although they understand English. I mean American English", said Clay.

"I would learn Spanish too", I said.

"Sure, you will", said Clay while talking to these two guys in Spanish.

"Gracias", said one guy.

"Gracias", replied Clay.

"You are gracias too", I said while waving my hand at them. Clay laughed.

"Gracias means thank you", said Clay.

"Oops, my bad, gracias to you as well", I said. Both men looked at me and laughed, one of them said, "Gracias senor."

"Senor means Mr." said Clay.

"Oh, you too, I mean gracias senor", I said.

Clay gave them some further instructions. One of the guys handed Clay a bucket of tomatoes.

"Those look good", I said.

"These are all organic, no pesticides or insecticides", said Clay.

"What is organic in regard to these?" I asked.

"Organic would be, let me see, well, when things grow with all natural material. I mean there is no synthetic stuff used in growing all these", said Clay.

"Those must be really good tomatoes", I said.

"Wanna eat?" asked Clay.

"Sure", I said. Clay gave me a tomato from a bucket.

"Hmmm, real good", I said while eating the tomato.

"I know, these two guys bring some of the produce to the house and rest is taken to the farmer's market", said Clay.

"Was this washed?" I asked.

"Absolutely, they wash produce before bringing to the house", said Clay.

"Good, because my mom says that we should wash fruits and vegetables before eating", I said.

"Yes, you should, even if the produce is organic, you never know if there is still soil on the produce", said Clay.

"Yes", I said as I and Clay walked towards the tractor.

We got on to the tractor and drove back towards the barn. I saw my mom standing near the back door of the barn. We reached the barn.

"Jake, you need to tell me before you go anywhere", my mom said.

"Sorry ma, I just, a", I said.

"Ok, I talked to Dr. Bharti and she knows someone in India, who could take David to this charitable facility near Bangalore", my mom said.

"What a shame for our nation to be the richest in the world and not be able to provide health facilities to the one in need. They have enough space for poor to live there. In our country, only rich survive. I mean you can't even get your teeth fixed in this country", said Clay.

"I guess, I have never been able to see the world through others eyes. I have been made to believe what is shown to us on TV", my mom said.

"Yes, the reality is not what the media shows us", said Clay.

"Yes, I guess", my mom said.

"Even I am scared now. I mean, what if I or Jake gets some serious disease like AIDS, we would also run out of money, sooner or later", my mom said.

"Exactly ma, I mean, how come a less rich nation like India, be able to provide free healthcare to AIDS patients and we being the super-power can't treat those in need", I said.

"We could, if we stop spending billions of dollars in bombing other nations for petty reasons and not minding our own business", said Clay.

"Yes, it is a huge shame on part of us", my mom said.

"A single fighter jet costs millions to make and then the government says we don't have the money to pay for healthcare of every citizen. You would, if you stop sticking your nose in other's business", said Clay as he looked extremely agitated.

"Yes, I guess. Anyways, Jake, I have prepared the lunch, Clay you should join us", my mom said.

"We usually cook here in the barn; I hardly got time to cook today. I give lunch to those folks as well", said Clay while giving bucket of tomatoes to my mom.

"Folks?" my mom asked.

"Yes, two workers, who work in the green-house", said Clay.

"That was a green-house?" I asked.

"Yes, it was", said Clay.

"I have heard about it in the school", I said.

"Good, today you saw one", my mom said.

"Ok, let us get the lunch here in the barn and we all could eat together", my mom said.

"Very kind of you ma'am", said Clay.

"Don't be", my mom said.

"We could use that table inside my room", said Clay.

"Sure, that would work", my mom said.

We all walked towards the house and brought food in the barn. It took two rounds to bring the food. I was allowed to carry only water bottle both times. Clay took out his cell phone and called the two folks. He talked in Spanish.

"You speak Spanish?" my mom asked.

"Yes, a little bit", said Clay.

"Are they coming?" asked my mom.

"Yes, they are", said Clay.

After about 5 minutes both workers entered the room.

"Hola Senorita", said one worker.

"Hola", said second worker.

"Hola Senor" my mom said

"Ma, you know Spanish?" I asked.

"Just a little bit", my mom said.

"Where?" I asked.

"Dad had workers from Mexico before, so I learned a little bit myself", my mom said.

"Great", I said.

My mom served food to everyone. The two workers took their plates outside. Clay followed them.

"Ma, so sweet of you", I said.

"I wish I had come to the barn quite often in the past", I said.

"You never wanted to, remember. You were just absorbed in the games", my mom said.

"True, but for past one year or so, I have been converted into an extrovert", I said.

"Extrovert, for sure" my mom said.

"You don't believe me, anyways", I said.

We finished the lunch.

"It was very delicious food", I said.

"Thanks", my mom said.

Clay and the two workers entered the room.

"I am sorry, this is Enrique and this is Rodriguez", said Clay.

"Nice to meet you both senor", my mom said.

"Si", said one. They gave their plates to Clay. He took our plates to the back of the kitchen too.

"I can wash them Clay", my mom said.

"No worries ma'am, I have a powerful dishwasher here", said Clay.

"Gracias Senorita", said Enrique.

"Gracias", said Rodriguez.

"De nada Senor", my mom said. The two workers left the room.

"What did you say to them?" I asked.

"O, de nada means it is nothing in Spanish", my mom said.

"You are good", I said.

"Na", my mom said with a smile.

"You can leave everything here, I will clean these", said Clay.

"Thank you so much", my mom said.

"Tired or sad?" I asked.

"I guess, mix of both", my mom said.

"Don't be sad, grandpa was getting very old, right?" I asked.

"Yes, he was on multiple medications. I guess he is not in pain anymore", my mom said.

I saw tears in my mom's eyes.

"Come on ma, you ask me to be strong all the time. Lead by an example, be strong", I said.

"Yes, I am strong", said my mom while wiping her tears. I went close to her and hugged her.

"Jake, you need to take medicines now", my mom said.

"Clay I need to go, I guess, I will see you in the evening", I said.

"Yes sure, take rest", said Clay.

I and my mom left the barn. We reached the house. I was feeling tired and so was my mom. We both slept for about 2 hours, till the evening. I heard a knock on the door. My mom went to the front door; I also got up from the mattress and followed her.

"Ma'am", said Clay.

"Clay", I said.

"How are you feeling?" asked Clay.

"Good", I said.

"How about you?" I asked.

"Good", replied Clay.

"I was wondering if you would like to come with me. I have to buy some homeopathic medicines for the cows", said Clay.

"Homeopathic?" I asked.

"Homeopathy was a common form of medicine in the United States before the modern medicine came. Well, we are certified organic by the United States Department of Agriculture and we have to follow their guidelines", said Clay.

"Sure, can I go ma?" I asked my mom.

"Yes, enjoy. I will cook dinner in the meantime", my mom said.

I went inside; my mom helped me in wearing the jacket. Clay was waiting on the door.

"Let's go", I said to Clay.

"Alright", said Clay.

"Bye ma", I said while leaving with Clay.

Chapter 5

The Birds with no Nest

We reached Clay's truck. He buckled me up. The sun was going down behind the trees far away. The green-house was hardly visible from the barn. Clay moved the truck out to the paved road which led to the city. Within 15 minutes, we reached the city. I kept looking out through the window. I had never seen this part of the city.

"They are here too", I said.

"Who?" asked Clay.

"The homeless", I said.

"Yes, I know, it is like a chronic disease now", said Clay.

"No wonder", I said.

Within about 5 minutes we reached the pharmacy from where Clay had to take medicines for cows. He asked me, if I wanted to stay in the truck, I said it was fine with me. Clay went inside the pharmacy and was back in 5 minutes or so.

"Ok, we are all set", said Clay.

"Hey Clay, can't we go to a shelter for home-less and see if they have any openings?" I asked.

"Openings", said Clay.

"Yes, for these people, you know the one with no home", I said.

"I would not say no because I have been through all this, so yes we will certainly go there, but I don't have much expectations", said Clay.

"Let us go anyways", I said.

Clay drove through the city. I saw many homeless folks, having all their belongings in a shopping cart. I never saw this world before. Soon we reached a homeless shelter. There was a huge line in the front. Clay parked the truck and un-buckled my seat belt. We both got in the line.

"I have been here many times", said Clay.

"Really", I said.

"Yes, I have been turned away many times", said Clay.

"But why?" I asked.

"They can't accommodate everyone", said Clay.

"Hmmm", I said.

"You know what this is all foolish on my part. Let's go", said Clay.

"Wait", I said.

"Jake, you are not well, if your mom found out about this, she is going to be mad. Not only you, I will have to do some answering", said Clay.

"It's Ok, we have a house. It does not really matter. I just want to see, how people are treated in this country when they have no money", I said.

"How people are treated, not only in this country but in any country, people are worse than animals if they have no money", said Clay.

"Yes, but we are better than all. This is the land of opportunity, no?" I asked.

"Not really sure about that anymore", said Clay as we moved ahead in the line. More people came behind us. There was a strange smell in the whole area. Some people had shopping carts next to them and some had plastic bags in their hands.

"How are you doing?" asked a man behind us.

"Fine", said Clay.

"You guys look fine to me, why are you here?" the man asked.

"Oh no, it is not what it looks", I said.

"Wait, we recently got homeless", said Clay.

"Oh, ok, is this your son?" asked the man.

"No, he is my grandson", said Clay.

"What happened to his dad?" asked the man behind.

"He lives with his girlfriend", I said.

"Son of a bitch", said the man.

"What? Watch your mouth, he is my father", I said.

"Easy there bro", said Clay to the man behind.

"Hey screw you, screw this country and screw this world. Fucking god has thrown us into the richest nation on the earth and here we are standing like...fucks", he yelled out loud.

I and Clay kept quiet.

"Okay, don't look back at him", said Clay quietly in my ear.

"Hey, you got a dollar?" the man behind us asked.

"Will a dollar solve your problem?" I asked.

"Yes, it will", he said.

"Clay, could you please give him a dollar", I said. Clay took out a dollar from his pocket and gave it to the man.

"There", said Clay.

"Yeah, bless you man", said the man.

"You should say God Bless you", I said.

"What?" he asked.

"Who are we to bless anyone? You said bless you. I think it is more appropriate to say god bless you", I said.

"Alright, God bless you, happy", he said.

I and Clay kept quiet as we moved ahead in the line. Soon we entered into the building. There was a sign saying, 'no more vacancies'.

"See didn't I tell you", said Clay.

"Ya, can't we talk to anyone?" I asked.

"Do you see anyone to talk to?" asked Clay. I saw a woman wearing a badge passing by.

"Excuse me ma'am", I said.

"What?" she asked in a rude fashion.

"I and and my grandpa have no place to sleep", I said.

"See that sign, we have no more vacancy", she said as she tried to move out of the building.

"Have you got kids?" I asked.

"Yes, I do", she said.

"Would you like your kids to be treated this way by someone if any one of them was standing here for help?" I asked.

She paused for a minute and then left without saying anything.

"These bitches are bad", said the man behind us.

"Watch your mouth man, we have a kid here", said Clay.

"Why don't you both get the fuck out of here, didn't you hear that bitch saying that there is no vacancy", said the man behind us. Clay held the man by his jacket.

"Clay, leave him", I said.

"You be careful buddy", said Clay.

"He is frustrated by all this. He is not to be blamed", I said.

"Sir, how did you become homeless?" I asked.

"None of your business boy", he said.

"We will give you another dollar if you share your story with us", I said.

"Five dollars", he said.

"Alright, five dollars", I said while looking towards Clay.

"There, but no more, ok", said Clay to the man.

"Ok, so what is your name?" I asked.

"My name is Tom Cruise", the man said.

"Tom Cruise, really", I said.

"Ha ha ha", he laughed.

"See, we are wasting our time", said Clay.

"Ok, my name is Jesus", he said.

"Jesus like Jesus Christ?" I asked.

"Yes, Jesus like Jesus Christ", the man said.

"Come on Sir, seriously, how did you become homeless?" I asked again.

"Come with me", the man said.

He moved out of the building, I and Clay followed him. He took us to the end of the street.

"Ok, we can't go no further Jake, we need to be careful", said Clay in my ear.

"You have the gun, right?" I asked.

"Yes, I have a gun. I got a concealed handgun license 2 months back; well Ron helped me in getting it. You know, we need guns on the farm", said Clay slowly to me.

"Ok, then we don't need to worry, right?" I asked.

"Jake, I think we should be heading back to our truck", said Clay.

"Don't worry", I said.

"Jake, you are my responsibility. We can't go no further", I said.

"Please, please", I said.

"No", said Clay.

"What if you were that guy?" I asked.

"Well, alright", said Clay.

The man turned right and moved towards a very old building.

"Was this building on fire?" I asked Clay.

"Maybe", replied Clay as we followed the man. It was dark by now. The street had only one or two lights. There was no traffic on this street.

"Come on guys, don't be scared", said the man.

We entered this building. There were probably 10-15 people in that building.

"This is my room", said the man.

He had a torn mattress, few clothes on the floor, few cans of soda and beans on the floor. He also had a torn couch next to the mattress. There was some light in his room coming from candles that people were using in other rooms.

"Have a seat", he said.

"We are fine", said Clay.

"What, you think that is too dirty for you to sit", said the man.

"Na, I prefer to stand", said Clay.

"So, how the fuck did I end up here?" said the man.

"Yes, we would like to know", I said.

"You see, this world is full of parasites and hypocrites", the man said.

"Ok", said Clay.

"Well, I had a business. One day my store got robbed. I had a gun and I shot the man who was leaving the store after robbery. I was arrested and served 10 years in jail", the man said.

"For what?" I asked.

"For shooting that motherfucker", the man said.

"But didn't he rob you?" asked Clay.

"Yes, he placed a gun in the middle of my fucking eyes", said the man.

"You know law in this country sucks. It turned out that since that man was running away, I was expected to call 911 rather than to shoot him", the man said.

"Yes, you could have called 911, instead", said Clay.

"Yes, I think that now. But, at that moment I just wanted to kill the asshole. That man placed a gun between my eyes and I just wanted to take down the bastard", said that man.

"The adrenaline rush, man", said Clay.

"The worst part started when I was released from the jail. There is this background check bullshit in this country.

Once you go to jail, it stays like a bad sore up your ass", said the man.

"Man, please this is a kid here", said Clay.

"Never mind, I have not heard anything new here. I have heard all these words used by my dad or mom, or someone in the school", I said.

"No, no, I am sorry kid. Anyways, so my business closed long back, then no one gave me a job. I cursed god, nothing happened. I moved from one homeless shelter to next. Government did give me un-employment check for a while though. I mean, one could hardly get an apartment for rent with that check. So, here I am now", the man said.

"You don't have any kids?" asked Clay.

"I had a son who died in a car accident, my wife left with some other guy once I went to jail", said the man.

"Sorry about all that", I said.

"Don't be kid, this is all Karma of being born in this f...sorry", said the man.

"Can't you do some job?" asked Clay.

"Hell yeah, I can do any job man. People are just scared that I am going to stick a bullet in their ass", said the man.

"You don't have any disease, do you?" asked Clay.

"I have gum disease, see", said the man while opening his mouth and showing his teeth.

"Ok, other than gum disease like AIDS, Cancer or some other major disease?" asked Clay.

"No bro, I am fine otherwise, I mean once in a while I get upset stomach, eating all this shit from the trash-can", said the man.

"Ok, would you be willing to take care of cows on a regular basis?" I asked.

"Jake", Clay looked at me with twisted face.

"Bro, I will do any job", said the man.

"Ok, what's your name?" asked Clay.

"My name is Robert Deniro, na, I am just kidding, ok, I am Josh", he said.

"Josh like Joshua?" asked Clay.

"Ya, people call me Josh", the man said.

"Ok, Josh you can come with us", I said.

"What? Josh, we should be going now", said Clay.

"No, he could come with us and take care of cows", I said.

"No, we will come some other time. Your mom must be waiting, we are late", said Clay.

"Oh, you are scared of me, aren't you?" asked Josh from Clay.

"Na, not at all", said Clay.

"This kid has bigger balls than you", said Josh.

"Ok, we need to go and you need to watch your mouth", said Clay.

"I am going to fuck you pussy fart", said Josh.

Clay reached for his gun.

"Wo, I was just kidding man", said the man as he saw Clay moving his hand inside the jacket.

"Take it easy", said Clay.

"I was just kidding man", said Josh.

"If I wanted to harm you, I could have done it by now", he said as he took out a folding knife from his pocket.

"Josh, please place this knife down, we are not your enemies. We were just trying to help", I said.

"This big ass boy is scared of me", said Josh.

"I am scared for this kid, not myself. I have lived on the streets for 5 years, seen numerous assholes like you", said Clay in a loud voice.

"Alright, take it easy guys", I said.

Josh threw is knife to a side.

"Good", I said.

"That is better", said Clay.

"You both should go now", said Josh.

"I see everybody as my enemy", said Josh while holding both his hand to his face and crying out loud.

"Bro, you gotta let someone help you. If you show a knife to those who are trying to help, you will get nothing", said Clay.

"I know", said josh while wiping his tears.

"Ok, two of my men bring vegetable from our farm to sell it in the farmer's market. I can get you a job of advertisement. All you have to do is circulate pamphlets around the city, I mean wherever you possibly could. Is that something you are willing to do? We need to spread the message of our organic produce. Ron and I did that before but we hired a man through an advertisement in newspaper. I guess, you need a job and we need a man for the job, then why not you", said Clay.

"Awesome man, I will do that job", said Josh.

"Ok, I will come tomorrow with the pamphlets. I will give you seventy dollars, if that is fine with you?" asked Clay.

"Seventy dollars, are you kidding me? I have not seen more than ten dollars in years now", said Josh.

"Okie doks, I will see you tomorrow", said Clay.

"Thank you man, what time do you expect to be here? I will be here" said Josh.

"Hmmm somewhere around 2 pm", said Clay.

"Sounds good man, I guess I will see you tomorrow then" said Josh.

"Bye", I said.

"Bye kid, thank you once again man", said Josh.

I and Clay started to move outside the building.

"Who has got a dollar?" asked a man sitting in the hallway.

"Hey, don't bother them", said Josh who was following us.

"Have a safe trip", said Josh as we left the building.

"Thanks", I said as Clay waived his hand. We reached the end of the street and turned left. It was dark in the street.

"Your mom is going to be very angry", said Clay.

"You should call from your cell phone", I said. I gave Clay my mom's cell phone number. He called her number and said, "Yes, this is Clay ma'am."

"What is she saying?" I asked.

"Ok, yes, I will give it to Jake", said Clay while handing me over his cell phone.

"Ma, we are fine. We should be home soon", I said. My mom asked me to come soon as the dinner was ready. She hung up the phone. We reached the truck.

"What the hell?" said Clay.

"Oh no", I said as I looked at the truck. All the tires of the truck were gone as the truck stood on bricks.

"Yes, this happens when you come to this area", said Clay.

"What are we going to do?" I asked.

"I am going to call the police", said Clay.

"No", I said.

"Why?" asked Clay.

"I mean, do you expect to find your tires?" I asked.

"No, but we need to report this", said Clay.

"I bet the tires are here in this area", I said.

"How do you know?" asked Clay.

"I have seen it in movies. Let us go back to Josh, he may know about tires", I said.

"Don't be a fool. Maybe this truck would be gone when we return", said Clay.

"Come on, he lives here, we can call the police anytime", I said.

We walked back towards the building where Josh lived. We reached the building. Josh was sitting outside with someone, smoking a cigarette.

"Hey guys, what happened? You did not leave yet?" asked Josh.

"How are we supposed to leave on a truck with no tires", said Clay.

"What the hell? Someone stole your tires?" asked Josh.

"Yes, all four", said Clay.

"Then you are fucked, ha ha ha", laughed Josh.

"You know anything about who may have stolen the tires?" I asked.

"Who do you think I am? Quicken loans? Ha ha ha", laughed Josh.

"Let's go Jake. He is high right now", said Clay.

"I am just kidding man, I am a funny guy. You should have known by now", said Josh.

"Ok, funny guy, if you could help us, help us know or we are calling the police", said Clay.

"Police, they won't find shit", said Josh.

"Ok, then", said Clay.

"You see that building in the front" said Josh.

"Are the tires there?" I asked.

"No, there is a guy named Radar, give him 5 bucks and he will tell you about the tires", said Josh.

We went inside the building, it was pretty dark inside. There was a man sleeping on a bed made from boxes.

"Hey there", said Clay.

"Yes", he said as he opened his eyes.

"We are looking for our stolen tires? Do you know anything about it?" asked Clay.

"I charge a fee", said Radar.

"There", said Clay while giving him five dollars.

"Ok, you go outside. Talk to a man named Josh, he knows everything", said Radar.

"He sent us here", said Clay.

"Go back to him and he will tell you about you tires. I charge a fee for this information", said the man.

"What, son of a bitch", said Clay while he went outside the building towards Josh.

"Who the hell do you think you are?" asked Clay.

"Just a funny man, told ya", said Josh while laughing.

"Go check your truck", said Josh.

"What? asked Clay.

"Go", said Josh.

"Ok, I am calling 911", said Clay.

"Sure, they are gonna take you in for fake complaint", said Josh.

"Fake complaint, what?" said Clay as he started to walk towards the truck. I followed Clay.

"What?" said Clay.

"What is that all about?" I said as I looked at the truck. We could not believe our eyes. All the tires of the truck were back.

"What did just happen?" asked Clay.

"I have no idea", said Clay.

"You saw that there was no tire on the truck, right?" asked Clay.

"Oh, maybe he asked the guy who stole it to put it back. I guess that he why he sent us to that man. He just wanted to buy some time. What do you think?" I asked.

Clay walked back towards where Josh was.

"Hey this ain't funny", said Clay. Josh looked at us and said, "Don't forget to bring the pamphlets tomorrow."

"Son of a...sorry Jake", said Clay as we walked back to the truck.

"How could they put all the tires back that fast?" I asked.

"They are pro at this", said Clay.

"Pro?" I asked.

"Yes, professional thieves. They practice this day and night, I guess", said Clay.

"Sure. I mean they are really good at it", I said.

"I bet they are", said Clay as he moved around the truck checking each tire. He then bent down and hit the tires with his fist, one by one.

"Not bad, you can't even tell these were removed", said Clay.

"Yes", I said.

"Alright, hop in", said Clay opening the passenger side door. He buckled my seat belt.

He then came to the driver side and said, "Let us get the hell out of this place."

"He is not a bad man", I said.

"Who?" asked Clay while driving the truck.

"Josh", I said.

"Yes, he is such a kind guy. He gave us a set of tires, our own tires, right" said Clay in an angry mood.

"Yes, but he may have not given it back", I said.

"You can take his side Jake, but he is a thief and he is not getting a job tomorrow", said Clay.

"I know you are angry now, but hopefully by tomorrow you will change your mind", I said as Clay drove through the city. We were back at home. Clay entered from the backside.

Chapter 6

The Barn of Hope

"Let us go in front of the house", I said.

"Why?" asked Clay.

"Dinner, aren't you hungry?" I asked.

"Well, I guess I will become like a spoiled child if I keep on eating cooked food. I cook my own food. You guys would be gone soon, so I should really drop you there and come to the barn to make my own meal", said Clay.

"Ok, then you should cook for me and my mom also", I said.

"You mean now?" asked Clay.

"So what would happen to the food that your mom cooked?" asked Clay.

"Exactly", I said.

"Exactly what?" asked Clay.

"What would happen to the food that my mom cooked if you would cook your own?" I asked.

"Alright boss, let's go", said Clay as he parked the truck in front of the house. I knocked on the door.

"There you are, finally", my mom said.

"Sorry about that ma'am", said Clay.

"Wash your hands first", said my mom as I reached for a plate. I and Clay both washed our hands.

"Wow, you made pizza", I said.

"Yes, pizza with a sauce made up of fresh tomatoes", my mom said.

She served pizza to Clay and me.

"Incredible", I said as I took a bite.

"Really good ma'am" said Clay while taking a bite. Clay did not sit and started to walk outside.

"Why don't you sit on the table?" I asked.

"My place is in the barn Jake, not here", said Clay.

"No, you can sit and eat here", my mom said.

"Well, I appreciate that ma'am, but Ron was my brother and boss. You are his daughter. Although, I am just a little less than Ron's age, I still consider you as a boss", said Clay.

"No, don't use this boss word again and again", I said.

"I prefer to maintain my limits, I work here. I get accommodation, food and some money in return. I guess, I want to stay a humble servant", said Clay.

"No, no, we consider our employees as our brothers and sisters", my mom said.

"I appreciate ma'am but we can't deny the truth. I mean there is nothing bad in earning a living of honor, maintaining a limit, right?" asked Clay.

"Yes, absolutely, my dad treated all their employees as brothers and sisters. But, I guess you are right in some way. I always keep a safe distance between me and my boss, even though my boss is a woman", my mom said.

Clay stood there chatting and eating pizza.

"You are done. Come, have some more", my mom said. Clay took two more slices. I also had one more slice.

"I am surprised that you made the pizza", I said.

"Yes, I wanted to use those tomatoes for something", my mom said.

"Can't we expand the dairy and farm?" asked Clay.

"Yes, we can think about it", my mom said.

"Since, Ron is not here anymore, you are not planning to sell this ma'am, although it is none of my business?" asked Clay.

"Well, I am not sure about anything at this point", my mom said.

"No, I completely agree", said Clay.

"We should keep this ma, where will Clay and others go", I said.

"Well, of course Jake, we will take everything in account before taking any decision", my mom said.

We all were finished with the pizza. My mom took the plates from me and Clay.

"Ok Jake, I will see you tomorrow morning", said Clay.

"See you tomorrow Clay", I said.

"Thank you for the dinner ma'am", said Clay.

"You are most welcome", my mom said. Clay opened the front door. I went towards the front door.

"Don't forget to printout the pamphlets for Josh", I said.

"No Jake, no way. He is a thug", said Clay while lowering his voice.

"Thug, he gave the tires back", I said.

"Ok, we will talk about this tomorrow", said Clay.

"Hopefully you will change your mind by tomorrow", I said.

"Good night now", said Clay.

"Clay, who takes care of the cows when you are not here?" I asked.

"Calves, ha ha", Clay laughed.

"Very funny", I said as Clay walked towards the barn.

"Clay, tell me?" I asked again.

"God ha ha", he laughed again.

"Come on Clay", I said.

"Those two guys whom I gave a day off today", said Clay.

"So that means cows were on their own?" I asked.

"What do you mean? I had enough food and water for them", said Clay.

"Ok, I...never mind. Good night", I said.

"Good night", said Clay as he walked inside the barn and closed the front door.

I went inside and slept. Next morning.

"Jake", I heard my mom calling me.

"Sweetie, you need to get up. Grandpa's body will be released today. I have to do a lot of things today", said my mom as she moved her hand through my face gently.

"Grandpa is coming today at what time?" I asked.

"They should be here in 2-3 hours", my mom said.

"So, all the relatives would be coming?" I asked.

"Yes. Ok, I am going to get you ready", said my mom as she cleaned my body with a wet towel. I was unable to take a bath because of plaster. It was a good thing that my jacket covered the plaster, which was going to avoid a lot of my relatives from panicking.

I ate my breakfast.

"Ma, I am going to see Clay", I said.

"Ok", my mom said. I moved out of the house and a car pulled in front of the house.

"Hey young man", said the driver of the car as he moved the window glass down.

"Hello", I said.

"Remember me", he said.

"Oh, yes, Uncle Paras", I said. Uncle Paras was mom's cousin. He was a very well-known doctor and extremely rich too.

"How have you been? What is that?" he asked while pointing towards my arm.

"Oh, I got injured in the swings", I said.

"Really, when?" he asked.

"Few days back", I said.

"Sorry about that", he said as his wife came out from the other side of the car.

"Hello Jake", said Sarah, Paras's wife.

"Hello Sarah", I said.

"Where?" she said while looking at me.

"He got injured in a swing", said Paras.

"Injured, where is your arm?" she asked as she looked very concerned.

"Inside the jacket", I said.

"Is it very bad?" she asked.

"Na, I am getting better now", I said.

"Paras, Sarah", said my mom as she came out of the house.

"Sheela, sorry to hear about your loss", said Paras.

"Yes, very sorry dear", said Sarah. They both hugged my mom one by one.

"Come on in", said my mom as she started to take them inside.

"Ma, see you in a while", I said.

"Sure", my mom said.

I walked towards the barn. The front door was opened. It was a bright sunny day. The snow was still covering most of the field. I entered the barn and the milk van was inside. Clay and Russell were chatting.

"Hey there buddy", said Russell.

"Hello Russell", I said.

"Hey Jake", said Clay.

"Hello Clay", I said. Clay gave a notepad to Russell to sign.

"Alright, you both have a good day now", said Russell.

Russell left the barn.

"So, Jake, how is it going?" asked Clay.

"Good, how about yourself?" I asked.

"I am fine, but that cow right there is pretty sick, since last night", said Clay.

"Really, what happened?" I asked.

"Seems like some type of infection", said Clay.

"So, are you going to call an animal doctor?" I asked.

"Ya, I know a vet, he will be coming in an hour or so", said Clay.

"Poor cow", I said.

"Yep, we have to remove her from the batch. Once we administer antibiotics, we have to remove it from the herd and sell their milk as conventional not organic", said Clay.

"Ok, I am learning something", I said.

"How is your arm?" asked Clay.

"Getting better each day", I said.

"Grandpa will be brought back today", I said.

"Ron...a", said Clay.

"Yes", I said.

"Has your mom made necessary arrangements?" asked Clay.

"I hope so, the relatives are coming in", I said.

"Good, has she made arrangements for, you know", said Clay.

"Arrangements for what?" I asked.

"Never mind, I need to talk to your mom", said Clay.

"Sure", I said. We both walked out of the barn and started to walk towards the house. There were 5-10 cars parked outside the house by now.

"I guess, people are pouring in", said Clay.

"Yes, it looks that way", I said.

We reached close to the house. I climbed the little stairs and opened the door, which was unlocked. I saw many people inside. I recognized some, but not all. I saw my mom sitting on the couch chatting with two ladies.

"Ma", I said.

"Jake", my mom said.

"Clay needs to see you", I said. My mom asked the two ladies to excuse her for a moment. We both went outside where clay was waiting.

"Clay", my mom said.

"Good morning ma'am", said Clay.

"Good morning Clay, how are you this morning", my mom asked.

"Good, how about yourself", asked Clay.

"Well, I have a lot to do today", my mom said.

"Have you arranged for the funeral, like coffin, priest etc? Also, have you decided a resting place for Ron?" asked Clay.

"Yes, I have hired a company and they will take care of everything for us", my mom said.

"Ok, where would be the resting place?" asked Clay again.

"It is a very nice cemetery", my mom said.

"Ron told me once that he wished that he was buried in his own land. He wanted to be a part of these fields forever", said Clay.

"What do you think Jake?" asked Clay.

"Well, ya, whatever grandpa wanted, I guess", I said.

"Hmmmm....." my mom said.

"What are you thinking?" I asked.

"I don't know", my mom said as she started to cry.

"Why are you crying?" I asked while getting close to her and giving a hug.

"Nothing Jake", my mom said.

"Be strong ma", I said.

"Yes, I am", she said while wiping her tears.

"Ok, we will do what dad wanted", my mom said.

"Thank you ma'am", said Clay.

"Ok, I will go and call the company again, they will have to make all the arrangements here", said my mom as she started to walk back into the house.

"What now?" I asked Clay.

"Clay, I am sorry, could you please find an appropriate resting site for dad", my mom said.

"Yes ma'am, I will take Jake with me and let us see an appropriate site", said Clay.

"Thank you", my mom said.

"Alright buddy lets go", said Clay.

"Ok", I said. We both started to walk towards the barn. I heard a car driving towards us. The car came and stopped next to us.

"Doc", said Clay.

"Clay, how are you doing", said the doctor.

"Fine, how about yourself?" asked Clay.

"Can't be better", said the man.

"Who is this young guy?" he asked.

"This is Jake, Ron's grandson, by the way Ron passed away a day before yesterday", said Clay.

"Ron passed away, how?" he asked.

"I don't know, he died a natural death", said Clay.

"Man, he looked perfectly alright to me", said the doctor. He took the car in front of the barn and parked it there.

"My name is Doctor Alvarado young man", he said as he shook my hand.

"Nice to meet you doctor", I said.

"Same here doctor", I said.

"Ok, let us have a look", said Doctor Alvarado as we entered the barn. Clay showed him the cow. After close monitoring Doctor Alvarado asked, "How long she has been acting like this?"

"Since last night", said Clay.

"Hmmm....", said doctor.

"Ok, I am going to write these medicines. In the meantime, I am giving her this injection. Hopefully, she feels better soon", said doctor.

"Sure", said Clay.

"Ok then, you both have a good day now", said doctor as he shook Clay's hand and left the barn.

"Poor cow", I said.

"Yep", said Clay.

"I need to get these medicines from the city", said Clay.

"Ok, let me go and tell my mom", I said.

"You wanna come again?" asked Clay.

"Yes, I want to come. What am I going to do among all the mature people", I said.

"Ok, you can call from my cell phone", said Clay.

Clay dialed the phone in the house.

"Hello, aaa, yes I need to talk to Sheela", said Clay.

"Someone else answered?" I asked.

"Yes, ma'am, Jake wants to talk to you", said Clay.

Clay handed me the phone and I said, "Ma, we have to get medicine for a cow, I am going with Clay. I will be back soon", I said.

My mom gave me the permission to go. "Alright, love you ma, bye", I said.

"Ok, all set?" asked Clay.

"Yes", I said.

"Let's go", said Clay.

"Where are the pamphlets?" I asked.

"Pamphlets", said Clay.

"Yes, pamphlets for Josh, remember", I said.

"No, no. We are not dealing with that guy again", said Clay.

"We gave him our word, right?" I asked.

"But, no, no, I am not going there again", said Clay.

"Clay, put yourself in his shoe and now tell me whether we should give him a shot at earning a bread of honor or not?" I asked.

Clay kept quiet for a while and then started to walk towards his room. I followed him. He had a computer on side of the room with attached printer. He pulled out an advertisement brochure on the screen and hit the print command. He then added a big bundle of papers to the printer. Soon, the printing started and there were like 200-300 papers with printed advertisement.

"What do you think?" asked Clay while showing me one printout.

"Looks great", I said.

"Ok", said Clay while collecting all the printouts and placing them in a bag.

"Time to go", I said.

"Yes boss", said Clay.

"Boss, no. I am your friend", I said.

"Ok, let's go buddy", said Clay while smiling. We reached outside of the barn. I saw some more vehicles parked outside the house.

"Oh shoot", said Clay.

"What happened?" I asked.

"We forgot to find a good site for Ron's resting place", said Clay.

"So?" I asked.

"Let's go fast" said Clay as he started to walk towards the back of the barn from inside. I followed Clay. He placed the bag in the barn. We reached the tractor and both sat inside. Clay drove the tractor through the open land.

"Suggest a good spot", said Clay while driving the tractor.

"How about that tree", I said. There was a tree on the left side of the barn, not towards the green-house. It was like in the midway but on a side to the left.

"Ya", said Clay as he drove the tractor close to the tree.

"What do you think?" I asked.

"Yes, this may be a good spot. They can dig close to the tree", said Clay.

"Ok", said Clay. We drove back towards the barn. We reached the barn and there were two men inside.

"Hey there", one of them said.

"Hello", said Clay.

"Are you Clay?" he asked.

"Yes, I am", said Clay.

"Ok, Sheela has send us to you to find a good resting spot for the diseased", said the man.

"Yes, we have a spot", I said.

"Ok, can you show us?" the man asked.

"Absolutely", said Clay. We got into the tractor. The two got their truck from the front of the house and followed us. Their truck was a little bigger than Clay's and they were able to drive it in the fields covered with snow. We reached the spot. I and Clay came out of the tractor. The two men also reached near the tree and they came out of their truck respectively.

"Ok, near the tree", said one man.

"Yes, right here", said Clay while pointing out towards the exact site.

"Ok, we will get started. Thank you", said one man.

"You are very welcome", said Clay. We both got on to the tractor and drove back towards the barn. Once we reached the barn, Clay picked up the bag of pamphlets and we went to the front. We got into Clay's truck and drove through the path from the back. Within 15-20 minutes we reached the city. Clay parked the truck in front of the parking lot. I stayed in the truck as Clay went to get the medicines. He returned in about 10 minutes.

"Ok, let's go", said Clay.

He drove the truck through the heavy traffic. We soon reached the area where we found Josh, near the homeless shelter. There were people standing outside the shelter. Some were just sleeping outside on the cardboards. We both came out of the truck and started to walk towards the building where Josh lived. We turned right on the street. There were 4 men chatting outside the building while standing. We both approached them.

"Hi there", said Clay.

They all looked at us and none of them spoke.

"Hello", I said.

"What do you want?" asked one of them.

"We are looking for Josh", said Clay.

"Josh", said one man.

"Yes, Josh....Joshua", said Clay.

"Joshua", said one man.

"Yes, him", said Clay.

"You don't know", said another man.

"Know what?" asked Clay.

"He died early morning man. They took him away", said one man.

I and Clay stayed quiet for few moments while looking at each other.

"What, how?" I asked.

"Don't know, someone found him fallen near the shelter", said one man.

"Are you sure it was Joshua....also called Josh?" asked Clay.

"Yes, man. We knew him, good man", said one man.

"Oh no", I said.

"That is un-believable", said Clay.

"Yes man, who gives a damn about us, death is the only escape from this hell", said one man.

"Sorry about that guys, who could know better than me", said Clay.

"You were on the streets bro?" asked one man.

"Yes, man. Hey any one of you wanna do a job?" asked Clay.

"Yeah man", I can do a job said one man.

"I can too", said another.

Three among four men showed willingness to work.

"You don't wanna work?" asked Clay to the man who did not show willingness to work.

"Piss off", he said.

"Ok, I will piss off. Ok, those who want to work follow me", said Clay.

Three men started following Clay.

"Ok, you have to distribute these pamphlets" said Clay.

"Alright, man", said one man. Clay distributed the pamphlets to the men and gave them 30 dollars each. Soon, few more homeless folk from the shelter started to walk towards us.

"What is happening here?" asked one man.

"Nothing", said Clay.

"Wo, they are getting money. Give money to us also", the man said.

"I have no more jobs for today but if I have something in the future, I will give you a chance", said Clay.

The three men whom Clay gave the pamphlets and money started to walk in the street. They went quite far and we saw them handing over the pamphlets to people.

"They are working", I said.

"Seems like they are desperate to work but our bullshit system, well", said Clay as he looked very disappointed.

"Don't worry Clay", I said.

Clay took out a stack of dollars from his pocket and gave ten dollars each to the men who showed willingness to work.

"Bless you man", said one man.

"No, god blesses you all", I said.

"Yes, you all need more blessings than we do", said Clay.

"Thanks", said one man. They all looked very happy. They went back towards the shelter.

"Man", said Clay.

We looked at those three men for a little while as they kept distributing pamphlets to people in the street. We both sat in the truck. Clay placed his head back on the seat and took deep breaths.

"Are you okay?" I asked.

"Ya, I am fine", said Clay.

"At least we got to help someone", I said.

"Ya, when the wind blows to the other side", said Clay.

"What?" I asked.

"Never mind", said Clay as he started to drive the truck through the street. The men whom Clay gave ten dollars each waived at us. We both waived back.

We were back at the barn in about 20 minutes.

"That is what I love about this place", said Clay.

"What?" I asked.

"So close to the city but far away from all the commotion", said Clay.

"Yes, for sure", I said.

Clay parked the car outside the barn. There were 20-30 cars in the area that were parked all the way close to the barn.

"Wow, so many cars", I said.

"Yes, seems like all the family members and friends are coming in", said Clay.

There was this big tent that was installed next to the tree where grandpa was going to be rested.

"Where are you going?" asked Clay.

"Inside the barn", I said.

"What for?" asked Clay.

"I don't know, I will watch you do whatever you do", I said.

"No, you should go and see your mother now", said Clay.

"She would be occupied with all the fine actors", I said.

"Fine actors", said Clay.

"Yes, they would be pretending as if they are so sad for grandpa's passing away. I know how much they really care", I said.

"Don't say that. They might be genuinely sad", said Clay.

"Really, they are here to have their attendance", I said.

"Attendance", said Clay.

"Ya attendance, like the way we have in school", I said.

"Ok, stop cursing them. You don't have to go there if you don't want to, but we should let your mother know", said Clay.

I saw my mom coming out of the door with a lady. They started to chat. My mom had her back towards the barn. I waived but the other lady did not see.

"Clay could you please open the truck's driver side door", I said.

"What for?" asked Clay.

"Please open it, I need to do something.

Clay opened the door; I tried to reach the car horn.

"Why don't you just go over there", said Clay.

"Aaa...it's very high", I said.

"Ok", said Clay and pressed the car horn.

My mom and lady looked towards us. I waived. My mom waived back. I pointed towards the barn with my right hand. She understood that I would be at the barn. I and Clay walked inside the barn. He took the bag of medicines to the back. He then took out a syringe and injected a medicine into cow' shoulder area.

The cow looked very weak.

"I guess, this cow had some karmic relationship with Ron. He is gone, she is sick", said Clay.

"Did he take care of all these cows?" I asked.

"Yes, like his babies", said Clay.

"Sweet", I said.

"Yep, hopefully she feels better", said Clay as he came out of the fence inside which cows lived.

"Hungry?" asked Clay.

"A little bit", I said.

"Ok, come on in, I will fix some sandwiches", said Clay.

We both walked inside Clay's room. Clay went to the kitchen. I sat on the chair next to the table.

Clay brought sandwiches in about 5 minutes.

"There you go bud, here is a veggie sandwich", said Clay.

"Hmm..looks good", I said.

"Dig in", said Clay.

"I will", I said. I started eating sandwich in no time. I was able to use right hand much more efficiently by now.

"Jake", I heard as I saw my mom entering Clay's room.

"What are you enjoying?" asked my mom.

"A veggie sandwich", I said.

"Looks good", my mom said.

"Wait, let me fix one for you", said Clay.

"No, no, I am fine", my mom said.

"Are you sure?" I asked.

"Ok, they are going to have food and everything ready near the tent for the visitors. It is good you had a sandwich. Thank you Clay", my mom said.

"Always", said Clay.

"Ok, I just came to see if you needed anything to eat, I guess you are fine now. Sorry, here are your pills", my mom said as she gave me the pills which she was holding in her hand. I took the pills and swallowed it with a glass of water.

"Good, I should be heading back now", my mom said.

"Let me know if you need my help", I said.

"No, I guess those guys will take care of everything", my mom said.

"Ok, that is great. So, when are they going to bring Ron, I need to see him", said Clay.

"I am not sure if that would be possible. Ron had enrolled himself for organ donation. I guess they must have removed all the vital organs including eyes", my mom said.

"What? We can't see him last time?" asked Clay.

"I need to talk to them, there must be a way of seeing his face", my mom said.

"Yes, please", said Clay.

"Ok, let me find that out, I guess Jake will stay here with you", my mom said as she was leaving the room.

"No problem, he is here with me", said Clay.

"Don't worry ma", I am good.

"Ok, I will see you in a while", said my mom and left the room.

"So what do we do now?" I asked after finishing the sandwich.

"Let us go to the resting place and see if everything is taken care of", said Clay.

"Ok", I said.

We started to walk towards the back gate. Clay went inside the fence and touched the sick cow again. The cow did not move much.

"I guess the medicine has kicked in, she is sleepy", said Clay.

"Ya", I said.

"Ok", said Clay as he came out of the fence.

We took the tractor and reached the area near the tree. There were approximately hundred chairs under a big tent. There was plenty of food on huge tables. There were some individual bringing more food to the tables. A small podium was installed with a huge table next to it.

"What is this table for?" I asked.

"It must be where Ron would be kept for people to see him the last time", said Clay.

"Everything alright", asked Clay to one of the men who were working there.

"Yes Sir, we are good", said the man.

Outside the tent, on the back side there was a big pile of mud.

"Ok", said Clay after looking at the pile. We moved a little further and there was the grave.

"Wow, is this the place where we all end?" I asked.

"Probably", said Clay.

"What do you mean?" I asked.

"Well, unless one is cremated", said Clay.

"Cremated", I said.

"Yes, where the body of a dead person is burned and only the ashes are left", said Clay.

"Seriously", I said.

"Ok, let us go back to the barn", said Clay.

"Let's go", I said. We took the tractor and arrived back at the barn. After entering the barn Clay said, "I will be back; I just need to use the restroom."

"Ok, I will be here near the cows", I said.

"Don't go too close" said Clay.

"Ok", I said. I stood close to the fence. Two calves looked at me curiously. One of them started to walk towards me. I moved back a little bit. The calf came very close to the fence and moved his head through the space in the fence. I moved towards the calf slowly. As I moved close to the calf he started to move back. I stopped and moved back again. The calf moved forward again.

"Playing games with me", I said.

"Who is playing games?" asked Clay as he came back.

"This calf, right here", I said.

"Yes, I know they want to play too, just like you guys", said Clay.

I moved towards the calf again but it went back towards his mother.

"Clay", my mom said as she entered the barn.

"Yes ma'am", said Clay.

"They have brought dad in the coffin; they have applied some cosmetics to his face to look natural. I want you to look at dad and see if everything is alright for the funeral services to begin", my mom said.

Clay and I walked with my mom towards the house. We entered the house where grandpa laid in the coffin on a stand. His face looked as if he was not dead. Clay looked at the grandpa and started crying. My mom started to cry too.

There were some people in the room and they comforted Clay and my mom. Clay approached grandpa again and touched his hands.

"Thank you for everything buddy, you are in a very good place, I know for sure", said Clay. Some more people entered the room and started having a look at the grandpa. One by one they came and then hugged mom. My mom asked me to get close to the grandpa. She picked me up. I touched grandpa's hands which felt very stiff. My mom then placed me down.

"I think we should close it now", said a lady standing behind my mom.

"Yes", my mom said.

My mom went towards the kitchen and talked to someone from the company who were handling the whole funeral proceedings.

A man came to the front. He picked up the wooden cover and was about to place it on top when Clay said, "Wait". Everyone looked at Clay.

Clay removed his wrist watch and placed it around grandpa's wrist.

"Is there something special about that watch?" asked my mom.

"Yes, I have given him my watch so that he could keep track of time until I meet him again in heaven", said Clay as his voice choked.

Everyone stayed quiet. The coffin was finally closed. People started to move outside. Grandpa's coffin was picked and placed in a car parked outside. The path leading from barn to the tree was cleared of snow by the company men. People got into their cars and started driving towards the tree where the funeral proceedings were going to take place.

I, mom and Clay walked alongside the car in which grandpa was taken. It took us about 20 minutes to get near the tree. Cars were parked randomly. Grandpa's coffin was taken and placed on the big table next to the podium. People took out flowers from their cars and started placing those on grandpa's coffin one by one. Some were eating food.

Many relatives and friends gave short speeches on the podium. Everyone praised him for being such a great man throughout his entire life. I heard a car coming towards the proceedings. I looked around and it was my dad with his girlfriend. They had brought flowers too.

My dad placed the flowers on grandpa's coffin and went close to mom and talked to her. He then came and sat on a chair next to me. His girlfriend took a seat next to him.

"Jake", he said in a low voice.

"Dad", I said.

"How are you?" my dad asked.

"Ok", I said.

"What is that look?" asked my dad.

"You should really talk to your gf dad", I said.

"What gf?" my dad asked. I stood up from the seat and went and stood next to grandpa's coffin.

It was time for grandpa to be put to rest. They picked up his coffin and placed it inside the grave. The priest chanted some prayers. My mom picked up a little dirt and threw in on the coffin while crying. Clay also did the same thing and so did many others. Clay looked extremely sad.

I went close to him and said, "Clay, everything will be alright."

"Thanks bud", said Clay.

I then went close to my mom and hugged her. She still had tears in her eyes.

"Everything will be fine", I said.

"For what happens to the children of man and what happens to the beasts is the same; as one dies, so dies the other. They all have the same breath, and man has no advantage over the beasts, for all is vanity. All go to one place. All are from the dust, and to dust all return" but the difference is that "God will judge the righteous and the wicked, for there is a time for every matter and for every work", read priest from a book as people took turns in throwing dirt on grandpa's coffin.

"In God's care you rest above, in our hearts you rest with love", said priest as he read this final line.

People started to walk back towards their cars. I walked alongside mom. I looked back and saw the company men bring a dirt mover to the site. They covered the grave with dirt to the top. Two men brought a big stone and placed it on top of the grave. They then started bringing some bricks and covered the whole grave with bricks.

"So what are we going to do now ma?" I asked my mom.

"We will see", my mom said.

Clay was walking like ten feet away. I reached Clay and asked, "What are we going to do now?"

"I need to see the cows and see how they are doing", said Clay.

"Ok, I will come with you", I said.

"As you wish", said Clay. I went back to my mom and said, "Ma, I will be with Jake for a little while, you can take care of close relatives, who will be staying overnight in the house."

"Sure", my mom said as she got closer to a lady and started to chat with her. I went close to Clay and we started walking back towards the barn. People who came on cars left the funeral area.

There were few who were walking along us, they left their cars parked outside the house. It was evening. The sun was setting behind the trees. I and Clay reached the barn. Clay started placing hay in front of the cows and removed some cow dung.

"How is that cow doing?" I asked.

"She still looks weak to me", said Clay.

"What do we do now?" I asked.

"We can't do anything as of yet. She will get better with time", said Clay.

"Ok", I said and stood there to watch Clay work. He added more water to the trough. There was a basket of tomatoes, jalapenos, cucumbers, cilantro placed on a side.

"Seems like more fresh produce", I said.

"Yes, indeed", said Clay.

"I am going to make a pasta", said Clay.

"Pasta", I said.

"Pasta, with fresh veggies, sounds good?" asked Clay.

"Yes, but there must be plenty of food left from the ceremony", I said.

"Yes, that would be for relatives and guests", said Clay as he picked up the bucket and started to walk back towards his room. I followed him as usual. He took the bucket inside the kitchen. I sat on the chair outside.

"Where did you learn to cook?" I asked.

"I used to cook at homeless shelters sometimes when I was not under severe depression", said Clay.

"Depression", I said.

"Yes, depression, don't worry about it. I am fine now", said Clay.

"I hope it stays that way", I said.

"If I stay here till I die, then yes for sure", said Clay.

Clay started cooking. He came back to the room in the meantime.

"Pasta is boiling", said Clay.

"How much time?" I asked.

"About 10 minutes", said Clay.

"Ok", I said.

"So, how are your studies at school?" asked Clay.

"School sucks", I said.

"Don't use that word", said Clay.

"What?" I asked.

"That S word", said Clay.

"Ok, sorry", I said.

"That's better, no seriously, how's the school?" asked Clay.

"It is ok, I am not too excited to go there every day", I said.

"Why not?" asked Clay.

"I don't know, it is all very boring", I said.

"Boring", said Clay.

"Yes, boring", I said.

"But why?" asked Clay.

"It is same schedule every day to carry the heavy bag around all day", I said.

"Heavy bag?" asked Clay.

"Yes, the school bag", I said.

"Oh the school bag, is it very heavy?" asked Clay.

"You bet", I said.

"Hmmm", said Clay.

"Did you have heavy school bags in your time?" I asked.

"Not so much", said Clay.

"See, they are literally torturing kids with so much heavy load and so much pressure", I said.

"Ya, I know the competition is so stiff", said Clay.

"Why can't parents have just one kid?" I asked.

"One kid", said Clay.

"Yes, like the one kid policy they have in China", I said.

"Ya, maybe that policy would come to United States too if we keep on expanding at a fast rate", said Clay.

"Everyone is fighting for the little resources", I said.

"You seem to have pretty good general knowledge", said Clay.

"Yes, I mean top schools take only few kids. What is with this world anyways? Top school, top grades or you will starve to death", I said.

"You have a long way to go", said Clay.

"I know, it scares me", I said.

"Don't worry, you will be fine", said Clay.

"How is your pasta cooking?" I asked.

"Oh yes, pasta", said Clay as he walked back into the room. Clay started to work in the kitchen again. I went outside his room and moved towards the back of the barn where cows were.

"Clay", I heard my mom saying as she entered the barn.

"Ma", I said.

"Jake, you and Clay should come for the dinner", my mom said.

"Clay is cooking pasta ma", I said as she got closer to me.

"Pasta", my mom said.

"Ok, so you would be eating pasta with Clay then", my mom said.

"No, I mean if you want me to join you over there for dinner, I am fine with that too. I just don't want Clay to be eating alone. I guess grandpa used to eat with him all the time", I said.

"Yes, absolutely, you should give him company", my mom said.

"When is David going to India?" I asked.

"Oh, it just skipped totally from my mind. Let us see, a day after tomorrow, maybe. We will have to see if his health is stabilized", my mom said.

"Great, thanks ma, you are very kind", I said.

"Less than you", my mom said.

"Na", I said.

"Jake", said Clay as he came towards the back of the barn.

"Pasta is almost ready, ma'am you should join us too", said Clay.

"Oh no, I have to take care of the relatives and friends, but thanks though", my mom said.

"Ok, you both have a good time", my mom said.

"Thanks ma", I said. She left the barn

"Let's go", said Clay.

"Yes, I am feeling hungry again", I said.

We went inside and started eating the wonderful pasta that Clay had cooked.

"Wow, this is really good", I said while eating.

"Thanks", said Clay.

"No, I am serious, it is so fresh", I said.

"Yes, no frozen stuff here. All natural, organic and fresh, can't beat that", said Clay.

"I bet", I said.

"Have some more", said Clay while trying to hold my plate.

"Yes, why not", I said while letting Clay take my plate to the kitchen.

"There", said Clay as he returned with more pasta in the plate.

"Wo, that much", I said.

"Come on, you are a young man", said Clay.

"Ok, I can try", I said. The pasta was so good that I finished the whole plate again.

"Now we are talking", said Clay once I finished the pasta.

"Ah, I am really full", I said.

"Me too", said Clay.

"So what now?" I asked.

"Well, I guess back to have a look at the cows", said Clay.

"You never rest", I said.

"I had rested for 5 years, the worst rest ever. Street benches, sidewalks, homeless shelter, all I was doing was resting", said Clay.

"Sorry about that", I said.

"Don't be, must be my bad karma", said Clay.

"Na, maybe the broken system of this country", I said.

"I can't agree more", said Clay.

"Why don't people stand up to get all this. I mean, if a person has committed crime, whatever the reason might be, don't they deserve a second chance", I said.

"Yes, they do, but who cares what is below", said Clay.

"Below", I said.

"Yes, below, do you ever care that insects die under your shoes every time you walk on the street or somewhere else?" asked Clay.

"Of course I do, I always watch my feet", I said.

"Well, you are an exception Jake, most people have no time to look out of their cell phone screens while walking", said Clay.

"Yes, I agree with that", I said.

"No one cares, trust me. Politics, charities, sending donations to other countries when our own people suffer is the height of hypocrisy that our nation is under right now", said Clay.

"Well, then why don't you do something about it?" I asked.

"What can we do?" asked Clay.

"Protest", I said.

"Protest for what? Our protests fall on dumb ears", said Clay.

"Hunger strike", I said.

"Hunger strike, who gives a damn Jake", said Clay.

"Join politics", I said.

"It is not easy and those who are fair initially become biased when they reach that place", said Clay.

"Martin Luther King protested, Mahatma Gandhi protested, Nelson Mandela protested", I said.

"Yes, you are right, those were solid warriors, I would say", said Clay.

"I mean what the heck? How could we be the richest nation and a superpower and still let our people sleep on the streets with no food, healthcare, house, I mean come on. I think each citizen of this country matters", I said.

"Not really", said Clay.

"You know what, I think it is a shame on part of the leaders of our nation if even a single man or woman has to sleep on the street", I said.

"So what are you suggesting? Should the five star hotels be opened for them?" asked Clay.

"Five star hotels, why not?" I said.

"What?" asked Clay.

"Yes, why not five star hotels", I said.

"Ok, stop this argument Jake, it is not going to lead anywhere", said Clay.

"Do you know how many people in New York City sleep in homeless shelters each night?" I asked.

"No idea", said Clay.

"Me neither", I said.

"Wait what, are you kidding me now? You asked the question as if you knew the answer", said Clay.

"Let us check on your computer", I said.

"Computer", said Clay.

"You have internet on that one, right?" I asked.

"Of course", said Clay. We went and sat next to Clay's computer. He entered the query in the search engine.

"Wow", said Clay.

"Sixty two thousand", I said.

"Oh man", said Clay.

"That many people in the best city of the world", I said.

"That is true but a lot of people are to be blamed for their own plight", said Clay.

"Maybe, but you were not be blamed for your own plight, the system was, right?" I asked.

"Well, yes, but there are lot of people who are addicted to drugs and some who are lazy and don't want to work, you know", said Clay.

"Sure there must be many, but there must be a lot of genuine cases too, right?" I asked.

"Yes, of course", said Clay.

"They are basically homeless because the system screwed them up, somehow", I said.

"I would say that system screwed all but certainly some like me", I said.

"What about David?" I asked.

"Ya, David, well we can't change the way people think", said Clay.

"Have you seen the movie Philadelphia?" I asked.

"Yes, Hanks had AIDS and Denzel was his lawyer. But, that was a movie", said Clay.

"A lot of technology shown in movies few years back has become a reality now", I said.

"You know a lot of stuff, considering your age", said Clay.

"I am learning each day", I said.

"Good", said Clay.

"So, did police officers asked for money from you?" I asked.

"Not all, but there were some who demanded money for letting me sleep on the street", said Clay.

"That is sick", I said.

"I know, but what could we do?" asked Clay.

"A lot", I said.

"Lot, like what?" asked Clay.

"I don't know, file a complaint to some higher officer", I said.

"Once you are on the street, all you care about is food and a place to sleep, you don't have the energy to pick fight against the powerful", said Clay.

"I can't believe all this, we are shown entirely different side of the coin", I said.

"Yes, you see the other side only when you are on the other side", said Clay.

"That is very sad", I said.

"I am not saying that everyone is bad. There are honest cops out there. There are people who help, they are god fearing people", said Clay.

"Why God fearing and not God loving?" I asked.

"No, there are certainly God lovers out there too", said Clay.

"But still issues persist despite all the work done by these charities", I said.

"Of course, most of the facilities are not even safe to sleep", said Clay.

"Not safe. What happens there?" I asked.

"People get robbed all the time?" I asked.

"Who would rob a homeless man?" I asked.

"Extremely sick people, you know like scavengers who feed on the dead", said Clay.

"Maybe David never had a chance to meet good people", I said.

"Well, someone may have tried to help him but, you never know. Some people at homeless shelter are good and some just treat you as trash. It all depends, not everyone is good and not everyone is bad out there. It is balanced. The good and the evil", said Clay.

"Ok, there should be some good people trying to help the one in need, no?" I asked.

"One expects so, it is nice to say and hear, although the real life is entirely different", said Clay.

"It is all about person to person then", I said.

"Of course it is. Sometimes all you need is words of love, not a few cents", said Clay.

"I guess so", I said.

"Ok, you want some ice cream?" asked Clay.

"You have ice cream", I said.

"Yes, ice cream made from milk of our own cows with fresh strawberries from the farm", said Clay.

"I would love to have some", I said. Clay went inside and brought ice cream for me in a cup.

"There you go", said Clay.

"Where is yours?" I asked.

"Na, I have it all the time, you go ahead", said Clay.

"This is good", I said.

"Thanks", said Clay. I finished the ice cream and Clay took my cup back to the kitchen. Clay returned back to the room.

"So, have you ever tried to meet your daughter?" I asked.

"No", said Clay.

"She would be thinking that I am dead by now. Also, she was too busy with her own kids that she had hardly any time to think about anything else", said Clay.

"You can call her and tell her that you are doing fine now, no?" I asked.

Chapter 7

The True Knowledge

"No, I am not interested. I have seen a lot in life, I guess in the end it is only our own selves and God that truly matters", said Clay.

"You still believe in God after what you have undergone?" I asked.

"Yes, I believe more in God than ever before", said Clay.

"How did that happen?" I asked.

"When I was alone, sleeping outside sometimes on a cardboard, sometimes on a bench, all I was doing was praying. My prayer was finally heard when God sent Ron", said Clay.

"So you think that God had send grandpa", I said.

"Absolutely", said Clay.

"But why didn't he send someone sooner?" I asked.

"Gold is purified only after heating. I had to go through this pain and agony in order to be able to stand in front of God", said Clay.

"So everyone who is homeless is basically getting purified then, right?" I asked.

"No, not necessarily, it may get even worse for some", said Clay.

"Why worse for some and good for some?" I asked.

"You are a question machine, aren't you", said Clay as he laughed.

"I mean, why would God let some to sleep in five star hotels and some to sleep outside in cold with no food?" I asked.

"Only he could answer that question", said Clay.

"He", I said.

"Yes, God", said Clay.

"But where do we find him?" I asked.

"In your heart", said Clay.

"In my heart", I said.

"Yes", said Clay.

"You are saying that God, the creator of this whole universe resides in my heart", I said.

"He resides in everyone's heart", said Clay.

"How is that possible?" I asked.

"Everything is possible for God", said Clay.

"Then why doesn't he give a house for everyone to live in", I said.

"Frankly, I don't know the answer to that", said Clay.

"How many Gods are there?" I asked.

"What do you mean how many Gods, there is only one God", said Clay.

"If there is only one God then why are there so many religions?" I asked.

"Well, people have their own beliefs", said Clay.

"But if there is only God then why do people have so many beliefs?" I asked.

"Well, everyone has come up with their own way of worshipping and praising God", said Clay.

"Do cows give white milk everywhere?" I asked.

"Of course", said Clay.

"All cows eat grass or Hay, right?" I asked.

"Yes", replied Clay.

"Then why do we have separate religions when we know that a cow's milk is white whether it is in US or Brazil, it does not matter", I said.

"Yes, what has cow milk to do with God?" asked Clay.

"It is just a metaphor. If there is one earth, one sun then the way leading to the God must be the same also, no?" I asked.

"Yes, it should be the same but who will teach people", said Clay.

"We are Christians, right?" I asked.

"Of course", replied Clay.

"I have gone to church where they say that way to God is through Jesus only", I said.

"Yes, that is right", said Clay.

"But, don't you think that it was possible only till the time Jesus was in a human form on this earth", I said.

"No, I think it is still possible. Jesus is the way", said Clay.

"If Jesus is the way then the Buddhists who believe in Buddha would never see God, right?" I asked.

"Well, they may through Buddha", said Clay.

"Ok, so now you are saying that some will find God through Jesus and some will find God through Buddha and others.

Think for a second, it is the same sun which gives light to Buddhists and Christians. One sun, not two, not three, I mean Christians don't have their own sun. If in this physical world we are given light and energy by one sun. How can we think that the path leading to God may be different", I said.

"I am not sure Jake, but I did not understand that example fully", said Clay.

"If God created this huge universe, how could we think that the path leading back to him will be different? It makes no sense. I understand that we all need a teacher in our lives at every stage", I said.

"Teacher" said Clay.

"Yes, teacher, when we are born our parents become our teachers. They teach us to how to speak, walk, eat etc. Then we have teachers in the school. I guess, on spiritual path many teachers came at different time points but essentially said the same thing", I said.

"What same thing?" asked Clay.

"That there is only one God", I said.

"How do you know so much stuff?" asked Clay.

"We were in New Orleans once. There were two men who were saying that we should fear god on a loud speaker close to Mississippi river. One of them asked me if I believed that Jesus died for our sins. I said, I guess he died for sins of those who were alive at that time. You know, he cured the sick, made a blind-man see again. The man asked me, so you don't think he died for our sins kid? I said, no. He said why not? I said if he had died for our sins too, then why the hell would we be here? Wouldn't we be in heaven with him? The man did not say anything as he had no answer", I said.

"You said all this?" asked Clay.

"Yes, I did", I said.

"But, I mean how do you know all this stuff? You are so young for all this", said Clay.

"When I go to church every Sunday, I listen with my ears opened", I said.

"So you think that Jesus did not die for our sins?" asked Clay.

"Think about it Clay. If he died for yours and mine sins, you would not have lived on a street for 5 years and I would not have been sitting here with a broken arm. All of our sins would have been paid off by Jesus and we would be have been chatting like this in Heaven, not in this barn", I said.

"Hmmm", said Clay.

"I think every mystic has come to this earth for a specific amount of time and they took some marked sheep to the other side", I said.

"Marked sheep", said Clay.

"Yes, just like a shepherd has certain sheeps that he takes care of", I said.

"So, that would mean that all the great saints that came, took care of certain souls only?" asked Clay.

"Exactly, how could they have taken care of our souls because we were not even born at that time", I said.

"So, that means our going to church means nothing", said Clay.

"Yes, it means nothing", I said.

"No, no, I am not willing to accept that. I have placed my faith in Jesus and he is my savior", said Clay.

"We have cows in the barn, right?" I asked.

"Yes, of course", said Clay.

"Grandpa, you and two other men took care of these cows", I said.

"That is correct", said Clay.

"Since Grandpa has died, he cannot take care of these cows? Can he?" I asked.

"No he can't", said Clay.

"You will take care of these cows along with two other men", I said.

"That is correct", said Clay.

"Let us say Grandpa was Jesus. Do you think grandpa could take care of these cows?" I asked.

"What? I got confused there. So, you are saying if Ron was Jesus", said Clay.

"Yes, my point is that Grandpa is not able to take care of cows now", I said.

"Yes, but Jesus heals us spiritually", said Clay.

"Have you seen Jesus?" I asked.

"No", said Clay.

"If Jesus came and stood in front of you, would you recognize him?" I asked.

"Yes, I would", said Clay.

"How?" I asked.

"What do mean, how? I would know it is Jesus", I said.

"If you have not seen him ever, how would you know it is Jesus and not some other powerful entity?" I asked.

"I would know because my heart will tell me so", said Clay.

"But your heart could be wrong too", I said.

"No, I will know and my heart will know that it is Jesus", said Clay.

"But, you will see him with your eyes, not heart. Your heart will only attest to what you see with your eyes. I mean you could believe or nor believe, but the decision would be yours. What if Jesus appears in front of you and he was not even close to what we have pictured him in the church. What if he was a black man or Chinese?" I asked.

"He was a middle eastern man, much like us", said Clay.

"But how do you know? You only know what others have told you? In some pictures they have made Jesus completely white skinned. How is that possible? He was in Middle East, the sun is heavy in that region and so people have tanned skin. We are trying to picture him based on our convenience and what we like", I said.

"Then what, it is all about faith", said Clay.

"But faith develops only when you see something with your own eyes", I said.

"Not necessarily", I said.

"Ok, do you know that people thought that sun revolved around earth initially", I said.

"Never heard of it", said Clay.

"Everyone thought that sun revolved around earth", I said.

"How is that linked to Jesus?" asked Clay.

"It is. Those who thought that sun revolved around earth stick to their believes and those who thought earth revolved around sun stick to their. What is the fact? We know now with proof that it is earth which revolves around sun", I said.

"Ok, what has that do with faith", said Clay.

"The question here is that who do you have faith on? What we are taught in church or what we see with our own eyes", I said.

"You don't see with your own eyes that earth revolves around sun. You can't even tell. You have faith on scientists? Don't you?" asked Clay.

"Yes, we do. But, scientists have seen this by themselves. They have used telescopes and satellites and run numerous equations to figure out that earth revolves around sun. But in a church we don't know, whether the person who draws Jesus's image has actually seen him or not", I said.

"I am not sure where you are taking this debate but I believe in Jesus and I have faith that he is my savior", said Clay.

"Ok, no harm in believing even if it is right or wrong", I said.

"I know it is not wrong", said Clay.

"You think it is not wrong not that you know", I said.

"Whatever", said Clay.

"Ok, I believe that cows have wings and they fly", I said.

"You are making fun of me. You are a little devil, aren't you", said Clay

"No harm in believing something. I believe in what I see", I said.

"You don't have to cut open your heart to know that you have a beating heart inside", said Clay.

"Yes, but you need to cut open someone to know that, right?" I asked.

"You have to, but we trust others who have seen a heart, like doctors, don't we?" asked Clay.

"Yes, we do have to believe", I said.

"Yes, you do believe them, even though you have not seen the heart yourself", said Clay.

"So you are saying that priests have seen Jesus?" I asked.

"Not priests, but someone has seen him. That knowledge is transferred down", said Clay.

"Your heart example does not apply here because we can still see heart inside a person if we go to a hospital. But, we can't see Jesus, physically, can we?" I asked.

"Not physically, but spiritually", said Clay.

"Ok, now that brings me back to the initial question. If you have not seen the physical form of Jesus, how will you recognize the spiritual? Those people during the time of Jesus, who have seen him in his physical form, will recognize him in his spiritual form, no?" I asked.

Clay kept quiet.

"If an entity stands in front of you, that entity maybe Buddha, Krishna or Jesus but you won't know", I said.

"You would, Buddha would look like Buddha and Jesus would look like Jesus", said Clay.

"You mean that Buddha, as we see in sculptures or images. Come on Clay; if you have not seen him then how would you know it is Buddha? You can't just compare his spiritual form to a painting, can you?" I asked.

"Ok, so what is the solution then? We need to believe in something", said Clay.

"Believe in what you see, not in what others tell you", I said.

"See what?" asked Clay.

"See the spiritual form of Jesus", I said.

"But how would I know if it is Jesus if I have not seen him in physical?" asked Clay.

"You just answered your own question", I said.

"Did I? Yes, you are right. We can't recognize the spiritual form unless we have seen the physical. So, you are saying that we can't find God then", said Clay.

"I never said that. We can, of course, but we need a teacher, who is at the level of the father and at our level at the same time", I said.

"You are scaring me with your knowledge. How come you know...I mean", said Clay.

"I don't know, I guess curiosity", I said.

"So, tell me how I could find God?" asked Clay.

"You need to find a teacher who is at the level of God and at our level", I said.

"Why is that important?" asked Clay.

"John the Baptist was at the level of the father and at our level. When he died Jesus said that John has gone back to the level of the father, now he can't deliver you bread from the heaven. I will deliver you the bread from heaven. I will show you the way or simply I am the way", I said.

"Wow, you are just incredible. You are no kid", said Clay.

"Now, in my opinion Jesus has also gone back to the level of the father, just like John. Jesus can't deliver us bread from the heaven just like John was not able to do so when he went back to the level of the father", I said.

"What are you?" asked Clay.

"Come on listen", I said.

"I am listening", said Clay.

"So you need someone who could deliver you bread from the heaven now", I said.

"Where do I find such an individual?" asked Clay.

"When your time will come, God will automatically bring you in touch with such an individual", I said.

"You are very clever, you have answered my questions by not even answering it", said Clay.

"Ultimate answer is known only by God", I said.

"Very true, every few years one crazy individual predicts that this world is going to end, but nothing happens", said Clay.

"Yes, I have heard such stories. Those are on news sometimes", I said.

"Some people sold their houses, cars, even quit their jobs. When nothing happened they had nowhere to go", said Clay.

"Yes, that must be really funny", I said.

"They literally had to get the help from their friends and relatives when the world does not end", said Clay.

"People like those deserve to be homeless, not you, ha ha ha", I laughed.

"No, seriously, I wish no one was homeless", said Clay.

"Yes, I am just kidding", I said.

"I am just angry at people who start all the crap at first place", said Clay.

"They should be put inside jails", I said.

"Ya, they should but they are not breaking any law. It all comes down to laws in this country", said Clay.

"At least people could boycott them", I said.

"Sure", said Clay.

"I think we should all understand that only God knows everything", I said.

"Yep, no doubt about it", said Clay.

"We should listen to the priests but use our own brains too", I said.

"We should always use our brains. Let's go outside and see the cows again", said Clay. We went outside and walked towards the back of the barn.

"Every animal has soul", I said.

"Sure", said Clay.

"We should not eat them", I said.

"Ok, but the food chain continues", said Clay.

"Yes, but we are not animals so we shouldn't be part of the food chain", I said.

"Who says we are not animals?" asked Clay.

"We are biologically, but not socially", I said.

"What do you mean?" asked Clay.

"We don't live in jungle", I said.

"Neither do these cows", said Clay.

"Yes, but what I am trying to say is", I said as Clay paused me.

"Look here", he said while entering the fence.

"What happened?" I asked.

"Look at her", said Clay.

"She looks better now", I said.

"Yep, that's what it seems like", said Clay while gently touching the cow on the head area. "They are very sensitive", he said.

"Clay, give her some more medicine", I said.

"More medicine won't help her, she will get better with time", said Clay.

"I should go and see my mom now", I said.

"Yes, of course. If I don't come back then it is a good night from me", I said.

"Yes, sure, have a good night", said Clay as he came out of the fence and placed his hand on my right shoulder.

"I guess, I will see you tomorrow then", I said.

"Hey, when are you returning to school?" asked Clay.

"I don't know and I am not excited to return back to the same boring schedule", I said.

"You can come here once in a while, I mean over the weekends and when your school is off", said Clay.

"I would love to", I said.

"Alright then, I guess if you are leaving tomorrow then you will see me before going", said Clay.

"Absolutely, bye", I said.

"Bye Jake", said Clay. I left the barn and went to the house. My mom was talking to a lady.

"Jake", my mom said as I went inside the house.

"Ma, I am here", I said.

"Good", my mom said.

"Are we going back tomorrow?" I asked.

"Yes, sweetie, we have to leave early in the morning. We will go home first and I will drop you to the school, you don't have to take the bus tomorrow", my mom said.

"Ok, can we meet Clay before leaving?" I asked.

"Yes, I have to meet with Clay before leaving. I guess, I will have to take charge of the barn and everything else over here", my mom said.

"Are you going to quit your job?" I asked.

"No, no. I just have to take care of the finances and Clay will keep me updated", my mom said.

"Ok, you are the new boss now", I said as I went close to my mom. She gave me a hug and said, "I am just taking care of things which dad built with so much hard work. I guess I was the only child so the whole responsibility rests on my shoulders now"

"Can we come here every weekend?" I asked.

"Yes, we can think about that. I am not sure if it would be possible every weekend, but in a month or so, certainly", my mom said.

"No ma, I want to come here on every weekend", I said.

"Ok, we will come here every weekend", my mom said.

"Thanks ma", I said and walked towards our room. My mom also came to the room. She changed my clothes.

"So, the guests have gone to sleep?" I asked.

"Yes, everyone has to leave early in the morning", my mom said.

"Ok, I am very tired now and should sleep too", I said.

"Yes, I will be back soon. I have to make sure that everyone is comfortable", my mom said and left the room. I laid down on my mattress and I don't remember when I fell asleep.

In the morning.

"Jake", my mom said.

"Hmm..." I said while rubbing my eyes.

"Jake, sweetie its morning wake up, we need to go", my mom said.

"Aa, ma I want to sleep more", I said.

"Come on baby, we need to go. You have to go to school. Remember how many days you have missed", my mom said.

"Ok", I said. I went to the restroom. My mom gave me a bath since I could not do it myself because of the plaster on my left arm. I had to keep my left arm up while bathing. She then got me dressed up.

"Ok, the breakfast is ready, come soon", she said as she left the room. I went outside in about 5 minutes or so. There were 10-15 relatives around the kitchen area. They were all busy in eating breakfast.

"Jake", my mom called while giving me a plate.

"Mom, did you call Clay?" I asked.

"Yes, I already called him and he took his breakfast to the barn", my mom said.

"That is incredible", I said.

"Yes, you should finish soon. We need to see him before leaving", my mom said.

I sat on a chair next to the kitchen shelf and started eating the breakfast.

"Hey, what happened to your arm?" one of my relatives asked.

"I fell off of a swing", I said.

"Oh no, when?" she asked.

"Few days back", I said.

"I am Savannah, your mother's cousin", she said.

"Hello Savannah, nice to meet you", I said.

"Same here", she said as she walked towards my mom and started chatting with her while looking towards me.

"Ma", I said.

"Yes", my mom said while coming close to me.

"I am done. We can go and see Clay now", I said.

"Sure, give me a minute", my mom said. My mom went to talk to two ladies who were sitting in the dining area. She talked to her and then returned back where I was sitting.

"Ok, let's go", my mom said. I got off the chair and we both walked outside the house. It had snowed again. The whole area was surrounded by snow. Cars were covered with snow too. We both walked towards the barn and saw Clay walking towards his truck.

"Clay, where are you going?" I yelled from a distance. Clay stopped and looked at us.

"Nowhere, I was just going to move the truck to a side for the milk van to enter the barn" said Clay. We kept walking towards Clay.

"How are you Jake?" he asked.

"I am good, I have to go to school today", I said.

"That is good", said Clay.

"Well, I hope you will be able to manage the whole barn", my mom said.

"I hope so, I certainly can't fit in Ron's shoes", said Clay.

"No, you will be fine", my mom said.

"Thanks ma'am, I will keep you updated with email. Also, we may have to hire 1-2 more men", said Clay.

"Hire, one of those homeless guys", I said.

"Jake", my mom said with a twisted face.

"What? Why can't they do this job?" I asked.

"We will see whom we have to hire, ok", my mom said.

"Ok, you are the boss now", I said.

"Come on now", my mom said.

"Ok, Jake if I find a suitable homeless guy for this job then I will certainly hire, ok", said Clay.

"Thanks Clay, they need an opportunity more than anyone else", I said.

"Who could know better than me", said Clay.

"You could take me with you and we can interview some. What do you say?" I asked.

"You have to focus on your school from now on", my mom said.

"I will ma, I could do this on the weekend or in holidays", I said.

"Ok great Mahatma, whatever you say", my mom said.

"Why did you call me Mahatma?" I asked.

"It is a Sanskrit word. You know about Sanskrit, the ancient language of India. It is still spoken in parts of India. In fact, English is derived from Latin and Latin is derived from Sanskrit. Maha means great and atma means soul, so Mahatma means a great soul, aren't you one? Always, worrying about others, I think you need to focus a little on yourself too", my mom said.

"Oh that's why they called Gandhi as Mahatma Gandhi", I said.

"Yes, his full name was Mohandas Karamchand Gandhi, but people called him Mahatma Gandhi because of his great deeds", my mom said.

"Wow, ma, you know a lot of stuff. I am impressed. You have made me interested to go back to school and read a book or two about Mahatma Gandhi", I said.

"That would be great. You can also read about Nelson Mandela, Martin Luther King", my mom said.

"Sure", I said.

"Ok Jake, I will see you over the weekend", I said while moving my hand for a handshake.

"Come here", said Clay as he brought me close for a hug.

"I enjoyed my time here", I said.

"Me too, you were a great support. I am going to miss Ron a lot now", said Clay.

"Get you an assistant", my mom said.

"An assistant....na, I will get used to it with time", said Clay.

"Ok then, we should be going now", my mom said.

"Yes, absolutely ma'am", said Clay.

"Jake, I don't know, I feel like going to dad's resting place before we leave", my mom said.

"Yes, sure, we can go there. We will have to take the tractor since the snow was heavy last night", said Clay. We all went to the back of the barn from inside and got into the tractor. Clay drove the tractor to the grandpa's resting place. There was a gravestone with grandpa's name and the year of his birth and death engraved on it. The area was not covered with much snow because of the branches of the huge tree taking the pile of the snow on its leaves. My mom sat near the grave. She closed her eyes for two minutes. Clay looked sad too.

"Ok, let us go", my mom said. Clay drove us back to the barn. We went to the front of the barn and walked towards the house. Clay accompanied us. There were only 2-3 cars parked outside. Most of the relatives had left the house. There were few who were preparing to leave. In few minutes they came out. My mom thanked all for coming. Everyone left and it was only our car parked outside.

"So, I guess, I should just lock the house then", my mom said.

"Yes ma'am lock the house and please take the keys with you", said Clay.

"Are you sure you won't need to use the house for anything?" my mom asked.

"No ma'am, I am self-sufficient at barn", said Clay.

"Very well", my mom said. She went inside the house and brought the two pieces of luggage outside.

"Let me help you with those", said Clay as he went close to my mom and picked both bags. He then placed the bags in the back side of our car.

"Ok Jake", said Clay while coming close to me and hugging me.

"Bye Clay, I will see you soon", I said.

"You sure will", said Clay as he picked me up and took me towards the passenger side. He then buckled me up to the seat.

"Thank you Clay", my mom said.

"Oh no, thank you both", said Clay.

"Bye", I said from inside the car.

"Bye, have fun", said Clay as he waived back at me. My mom drove the car from the front path. I kept looking back. Then she turned left and slowed the car one more time. I waived at Clay who was now on the left side. He was still standing there and waived back at me. My mom also waived at him and drove the car towards the city.

Chapter 8

Back to the Concrete Jungle

The traffic was heavy early morning. We reached house in about 45 minutes. I reached for my bag when my mom said, "No don't pick that up." I stopped and asked, "Why not?"

"Your arm", my mom said.

"Yes, but I can use right arm", I said.

"You never like carrying that bag and today when I am telling you not to carry it, you want to carry it", my mom said as she looked irritated.

"Ok, but what about books?" I asked.

"Give that bag to me. I will carry it and take you to the class", my mom said.

"Are you sure? Wouldn't you be late for your job?" I asked.

"No time for all this. Oh no, your medicines" my mom said as she went into a complete panic mode.

"Calm down ma", I said. She reached for her bag and took out the pills and gave it to me with a glass of water. I swallowed the pills.

"Good boy", she said while holding hers and mine bag. She locked the house and drove me to school. She then carried my bag all the way to the class. A teacher was already in the class. We were a little late.

"Hi", my mom said to the teacher.

"Hello, how are you Jake? I heard about your accident", the teacher said.

"I am fine now", I said.

"Come on in, you can give me his bag" my teacher said to my mom.

"Thank you, so nice of you", my mom said.

"You are very welcome", said my teacher as she took my bag in her right hand and held my right hand with her left and took me to my seat. Everyone in the class was happy to see me. Jatin and Justin stood up and came close to my seat. Teacher walked back towards my mom. They both left the room.

"How are you?" asked Jatin.

"Great", I said.

"Hey bud, how is your arm?" asked Justin.

"Much better", I said.

"Nice to see you Jake", said Sarah while sitting on her seat.

"Thank you Sarah", I said.

"Let me help you", said Justin as he took a book out of my bag.

"Thanks Justin", I said.

"Hey, that's what friends are for", said Justin.

Teacher returned back to the class.

"Are you comfortable Jake?" she asked while approaching me.

"Yes, ma'am thank you, I have very helpful friends here", I said.

"Good, I am very glad to hear that. If you need anything, just let me know", said my teacher.

I saw our principal entering the room. He came straight towards me.

"How are you doing Jake?" asked principal.

"I am fine Sir", I replied.

"Listen, Alwyn is back. I don't want any issues between you and him, ok", said principal.

"Yes Sir there won't be any problem. I am hurt so I won't be doing anything stupid anyways", I said.

"I am glad you recognize your previous action as stupid. Whatever, I expect you to behave like a good boy and if someone bothers you in any way, come straight to me. Don't go around beating kids", he said.

Everyone in the class laughed.

"Alright, quiet now. Clara, you can continue", said Principal Jacob as he left the class.

Teacher taught us about milk production and distribution. I was laughing inside. I had seen all this live, in real life. Sessions changed, teachers came and went. Every teacher inquired about my health. I felt special. It was time for lunch.

"Jake", said Justin.

"Yes", I said.

"Let's go for lunch", said Justin.

"Let's go", I said. We arrived in the cafeteria.

"You sit here, I will get your lunch", said Justin.

"Thank you so much", I said. I sat on a table and Justin, Jatin and Sarah got into the line. I saw Justin talking to the lady in the cafeteria and pointing towards me. She gave Justin another plate. Justin brought two plates in his hand. He placed my food plate in front of me.

"There, enjoy", said Justin.

"Thanks", I said. Jatin opened the juice can and removed the foil from the burger.

"Enjoy", said Jatin.

"I am so lucky to have friends like you", I said.

"Come on now, enjoy the burger", said Jatin.

"Does it hurt?" asked Sarah.

"Sometimes, but it's not much", I said. We saw Alwyn walk inside the cafeteria with two boys. His walk was still pompous. He came towards our table.

He looked at me and said, "Oh here is the handicap boy." He did a high five with a boy who was with him after saying these words to him.

"Go away Alwyn", said Sarah.

"Or else?" asked Alwyn.

"Have you forgotten the punch?" asked Jatin.

"Oh, so are a tough boy now", said Alwyn.

"Hey listen Alwyn, I am handicap, are you happy now? You can punch me if you want. There, hit me on my arm", I said while moving my arm with plaster towards Alwyn.

"Come on hit, if that makes you happy", I said. Alwyn looked at us. He made faces and went in the line to get his food.

"Wow that was intense", said Justin.

"He is a jerk", said Jatin.

"Yes, for sure", said Sarah.

"So, what did you do all this time?" asked Sarah.

"I saw the real world", I said.

"Real world?" asked Justin.

"Yes, the real world. The truth, the reality of our great nation", I said.

"What do you mean?" asked Sarah.

"There are people out there who have no homes, no money for food or healthcare", I said.

"What? How is that possible? There are government run programs and so many charities out there", said Sarah.

"Sarah, if there are hundred holes in a water tank, you fill ninety nine but leave one, water is still going to leak, through that one hole", I said.

"Ok, then", said Sarah.

"I know there are homeless shelters out there but you have no idea how those facilities are managed. There are more than sixty thousand people sleeping in homeless shelters tonight in New York City alone", I said.

"Sixty thousand", said Jatin with eyes wide open.

"Yes, sixty thousand and that is the official number. But, there may be thousands who sleep on public benches, outside churches and some just sleep on the floor, wherever they find space", I said.

"How do you know all this stuff?" asked Justin.

"It's a long story", I said.

"But, I have never seen anyone sleeping outside", said Justin.

"How many times have you been out in the night?" I asked.

"Sometimes, to see a movie", said Justin.

"See a movie, right. The homeless people don't go to movie theaters. They don't have ten dollars to spend on entertainment. For them even few cents matter", I said. All three of them were quiet and listening to me.

"Some are extremely sick and can't afford medications", I said.

"What?" asked Sarah with extreme surprise.

"Yes, there are people out there with AIDS, one of the most dangerous diseases. They can't afford medication", I said.

"But isn't government supposed to help them out?" asked Jatin.

"Yes, government is supposed to take care of needs of every citizen. But, remember that one hole analogy, there is always a hole through which the water flows out, although slowly. I am surprised to see people sending money to other nations for help, when our own citizens are living on the street like street dogs", I said.

"Yes, that is certainly something that needs to be addressed", said Sarah.

"Hey, maybe we can write a letter to the President", said Justin.

"Letter to the President, days of presidents like Abraham Lincoln are gone. Our presidents just fly over the affected areas now. Remember, how president Bush flew over New Orleans during Katrina. It is a shame. If I was the President, I would have got down there on a boat to see things by myself. I would not have left the place, till everyone who needed help received it", I said.

"President Obama is better, no?" asked Sarah.

"Only in speech, I don't think he has done anything remarkable. He is just reaping the fruit of Martin Luther King", I said.

"Are you saying he is a bad president?" asked Jatin.

"No, I am saying that he has not brought the 'CHANGE' that he wanted to bring. His campaign said 'Yes We Can", yes we can what, travel in air force one", I said. Everyone laughed.

"Yes, he is certainly travelling in air force one", said Justin.

"The complete slogan should have been, yes we can travel in air force one from now on, ha ha", laughed Sarah.

"Ha ha, yes that would fit the best", I said.

"But, I like him", said Jatin.

"Of course you do, my Indian friend. Why wouldn't you, he represents minorities", I said.

"Come on, don't be a racist now", said Sarah.

"Racist and me, hell no, I helped a black guy with AIDS, his name is David", I said.

"You helped someone with AIDS?" asked Sarah.

"How?" asked Jatin.

"It's a long story. He is now going to India for treatment", I said.

"Coming back to the original topic, why did you say that Jatin would like President Obama for sure?" asked Justin.

"Well, because he is from a minority and if Obama can become president then everyone in minority has a shot at it. I think, people want to become president for the sake of becoming president. Not for changing this country. They spend thousands of dollars on white house dinner parties when people out there are taking food out of the trash cans", I said.

"What, food out of the trash?" asked Sarah.

"Yes, food out of the trash can, while these politicians sip French made five thousand dollars' worth of bottles of wine", I said.

"Really, they drink that expensive wine?" asked Justin.

"Oh, even more. They hire chefs who charge thousands of dollars making one time meal when our own people eat from leftovers", I said.

"What can we do?" asked Sarah.

"You know, I read somewhere, If you want the change, then be the change", I said.

"So how do we become the change?" asked Jatin.

"A law has to be passed that if any citizen sleeps on the street or eats from the dumpster then the president of the country will have to sleep on the street too", I said.

"What? That's not going to happen", said Jatin.

"Yes, I agree with Jatin, that is a stupid idea. How could we make the president of a country to sleep on the street? What about his security?" asked Justin.

"Let us say, I have 5 kids and I have 5 beds in my house. Would I ask one of my kids to sleep on the floor or I myself would sleep on the floor? Would I share my food with everyone in the family or I will just fill up my stomach and let my kids go hungry?" I asked.

"I guess, Jake has a point there", said Jatin.

"So you are saying that president should sleep on the street if any citizen has to sleep on the street?" asked Sarah.

"Yes, this should be a freaking law. Any person who accepts the position of the president of the United States would be deemed as the father of the nation. No father would drink expensive wine while letting his kids take food out of the trash", I said.

"Is that really possible?" asked Jatin.

"Everything is possible, we just need to try", I said.

"But again, if a president has to sleep on the street then what about his security?" asked Sarah.

"The president should make sure that no person sleeps on the street. He should make sufficient arrangement for everyone or he will have to face the consequences. He would have to dress like a homeless guy and go out there. No one gives a damn about those folks anyways. Most people don't even look at them. I saw people took out their cell phones when they approached a homeless guy pretending they were too busy to see them", I said.

"Would you accept such a challenge?" asked Justin.

"Without a flinch", I said.

"I guess the big question still remains unanswered. How do we make this mandatory?" asked Sarah.

"Yes, you are right. We won't be able to do anything. We are just kids", said Jatin.

"We could, we just have to put the first step forward", I said.

"What would be that first step?" asked Jatin.

"I don't know yet but I will try to find out soon", I said.

"Let us go guys, the lunch time is over", said Justin.

We all went back to the class. There were two more sessions after lunch. I attended both and my mom came to the class just 5 minutes before the session was about to end. She took my bag and drove me home in the car. I ate a sandwich, took my medicines and went to sleep. I woke up late in the evening. Watched TV for a while, ate dinner, had my pills and went to sleep again. My mom took me to the school again, the following day. The sessions in the school started as usual.

It was time for lunch again and I was worried to face my three friends. I had no clue what I was going to tell them from the previous day's discussion.

"So Jake, ready for lunch?" asked Jatin.

"Yep", I said. We walked to the cafeteria.

"Alright, Mr. Jake, you go and have a seat, we will take care of your food", said Justin. He, Jatin and Sarah got in the line. I sat on the table thinking what I was going to say. I felt like running away from the school.

"So, Mr. Jake", said Jatin as he placed my food plate in front of me.

"Hey, I really appreciate all this. You are my awesome friends", I said.

"Ok, eat the food now, let me help you", said Sarah as she removed the foil from the taco.

"Nice, taco", I said.

"Yep, hopefully no more burgers", said Justin.

"Man, I would love if they serve East Indian food once in a while", I said.

"Jatin must be eating it every day", said Justin.

"You all can come to my house or let me think, I can ask my mom to cook food for all of you. I can bring it tomorrow if she manages to cook it today", said Jatin.

"No, don't bother your mom. My mom cooks Indian food sometimes. She is getting better every day", I said.

"I love Mexican food and pizza", said Jatin.

"Seems like everyone loves others food, ha ha", I laughed.

"Ha ha, right. Mexicans want American food, Italians want French, British want Italian", said Justin.

"But, I have seen that people of all ethnicities somehow love Indian food. I don't know why?" I asked.

"It's the spices bud. Many of those spices have therapeutic benefits, so our bodies just love them", said Jatin.

"Yes, I guess Jatin has a point", said Justin.

"I agree, so Jake did you think as to how one could make the President live with the people on the street?" asked Justin.

I swallowed the taco down my throat and said, "Yes, absolutely."

"Ok, what is it?" asked Sarah.

"What?" I asked.

"Come on Jake, how could this be achieved?" asked Jatin.

"We have to start the process", I said.

"Start the process, which process?" asked Jatin.

"We, I mean, I have to sleep where the homeless people live", I said.

"Wo, what?" asked Justin.

"What will that achieve? You are not a Hollywood star that everyone will follow you. You will be another homeless among thousands, just one extra number", said Sarah.

"Yes, you are right, but, if all four us sleep outside, our parents, their friends, their relatives, you know", I said.

"So, you are suggesting that rather than providing home to those in need we should leave our houses and become homeless too?" asked Jatin.

"Yes, that is a great point. We will add to the problem and not solve it", said Sarah.

"I think you should stick to the original plan. If people are homeless and government fails to provide housing then the president should sleep on the street, like a good father would do", said Justin.

"I agree, we can't sleep on the streets, we are too small. Someone may kidnap or kill us", said Sarah. We all laughed at what Sarah said innocently.

"Yes, we could be kidnapped", I said.

"Yes, not a good idea buddy", said Justin.

"But coming back to the original problem, how do we make the president to sleep outside on the street?" asked Sarah.

"We should write to president", said Justin.

"What, write to the president that he should sleep on the streets because we request him to do so", I said. Everyone laughed.

"No, well, ya, I guess that's not going to work", said Justin.

"We can bring homeless to our house", said Jatin.

"Na, some of them have their head messed up", I said.

"What?" asked Sarah.

"They develop criminals like behavior. They start to hate the whole society and treat everyone as their enemy", I said.

"Wow, you seem to know a lot about them", said Jatin.

"Yes, just recently", I said.

"So, what should we do?" asked Justin.

"Fire president", I said.

"He will be fired after few years automatically", said Sarah.

"That is little disrespectful, don't you think guys", said Justin.

"Disrespectful, ask the person eating food from the trash, he will tell you what disrespectful means", I said. All three of them got quiet and started looking down.

"Yes, that is disrespectful. We are all immigrants. We came to America to make it a better land but people who need the healthcare most are out there living like street dogs and those with common cold are getting impressive healthcare", I said.

"Are you talking about the homeless people or sick people?" asked Justin.

"I am talking about the screwed up system of this country. A person who commits crime can't find a job. If that person can't work, what do we expect him to do, hmmm? How is that person supposed to pay for rent, food and health care? Aren't we creating more criminals this way? I mean if I commit a crime and I can't get a job and no means to support myself. What am I going to do? Someday, I am going to go out there and stick a gun up someone's ass, right?" I asked.

"Wo, calm down Jake", said Justin.

"Calm down, my ass, I am sick of all the bullshit in this country", I said.

"You shouldn't use bad words", said Sarah.

"Sorry Sarah", I said.

"Don't worry. I think you are just thinking too much about all this", said Jatin.

"Yes, you are right, I need to work on my anger", I said.

"Let us talk about something else", said Jatin.

"Yes, let us talk about Hollywood stars, what they wear, which cars they ride, what kind of dog they have", I said.

"Come on Jake, stop the sarcasm dude", said Jatin.

"Isn't that true, look at all these kids, what do you think they talk about? Oh, dude this new game came today, I am going to get it. My dad called my mom a bitch. My mom called my dad an asshole. We bought a new house. We bought a new car. I am going to blah blah school next year. I got A plus grade in all subjects. They have no idea in which system they live. They are trying to build their lives on dynamite. Sooner or later it will explode", I said.

"Jake, you need help, no seriously", said Jatin.

"You all including them need help. You need to remove the curtain of hypocrisy. Our country is in super debt but we can't stop borrowing money from China. Really, have we lost all moral values? Are we not the America that our ancestors built with a dream?" I asked.

"You need to look at the positive side as well Jake", said Sarah.

"Yes, there is a positive side and we are on that side right now. What if we are on the negative side? Have you ever imagined?" I asked.

"You need to be optimistic, not pessimistic", said Justin.

"Forget it guys, what are you all doing on Saturday?" I asked. All three said nothing much.

"Let us go to downtown", I said.

"Manhattan?" asked Jatin.

"Somewhere around there", I said.

"Would our parents let us go alone?" asked Sarah.

"Tell them, it's a school trip", I said.

"Ok, I guess we all can ask our parents but chances are very slim", said Sarah.

"I have an idea", I said.

"I can call Clay and he could take us around", I said.

"Who is Clay?" asked Jatin.

"Oh he is the most awesome person you would ever meet. Ok, I will talk to my mom and then she could talk to your parents for approval. I don't think it would be a problem", I said.

"But your mom could take us around like the way she took us to hospital", said Jatin.

"No, we need Clay. He knows places that I want to show you all. You have only seen one side of the coin, I will show you the other side", I said.

"Ok, sounds good to me", said Justin.

"Yep", said Jatin.

"Let's go guys, it is time for next session", said Jatin. We all walked back to the class.

The school sessions ended as usual. My mom came to pick me up. This is from the lunch time on the following day.

"Ok, so let's continue the interesting talk", said Justin.

"You mean the president on the street talk", I said.

"Yes, of course", said Jatin.

"Ya, guys I have come up with no idea", I said.

"You are boring Jake", said Justin.

"So now I am boring. How about you become more interesting to compensate my boring effect", I said.

"Easy guys, we are not going to fight among ourselves", said Sarah.

"Hey, how about we form a new charity", said Jatin.

"A new charity, as if we already had less", I said.

"No, I think that would be a good idea, we might be the youngest to start a new charity like such", said Justin.

"Charity is not the solution guys", I said.

"Then what is the solution?" asked Sarah.

"Fix the damn system", I said.

"What about the system?" asked Sarah.

"I told you, we all need less monitoring from government. They have all of our information in their systems. Anyone can view our criminal record. Just imagine how it would be if I don't get a job ever for punching Alwyn?" I asked.

"You mean never?" asked Justin.

"Yes, if I was an adult, the information would have been added to my background history and I would have been screwed for life", I said.

"That is why too much system is bad. I mean it looks good until you, yourself are trapped in it", said Jatin.

"Exactly bud", I said.

"So what should we do to change this system?" asked Sarah.

"Protest", said Justin.

"Where?" asked Jatin.

"Social media", said Justin.

"Na, it would be a protest and will stay a protest", I said.

"But at least we will do something", said Sarah.

"Sarah, no one is going to change this system just because we want it to be changed", I said.

"What should we do, hmmm", said Sarah.

"We have to be a part of the system", I said.

"We are already part of the system, aren't we?" asked Jatin.

"Of course we are part of the system, what I meant was that we need to be a part of policy making", I said.

"Part of the policy making", said Sarah as she looked a little confused.

"We need to send one of our guys at the top level so that this could be implemented", I said.

"How?" asked Jatin.

"I don't know how, all I know is that this would be the only solution", I said.

"But we are doing all this for homeless people, aren't there already sufficient people taking care of this problem?" asked Justin.

"I know, they are taking care of the tail of the problem", I said.

"Tail, what do you mean?" asked Sarah.

"No one is taking care of the reason which gives birth to homelessness or leading sick people to live on the streets. Everyone is trying to fix the wound, not trying to fix the reason for wound", I said.

"Little complex for my small brain", said Justin.

"Why do you wear seatbelt?" I asked.

"To protect us during accident", said Sarah.

"Yes. We need a seatbelt for people socially", I said.

"We need a social seat belt?" asked Jatin.

"Aa ha", I said.

"We need to protect people from becoming homeless at first place. We need to fix the system which leads people with severe diseases out on the street", I said.

"That is not an easy thing to achieve", said Justin.

"I know", I said.

"Should we take food from our house to these people?" asked Sarah.

"I don't know, some people may be out there because they are lazy and don't want to work", said Justin.

"Even a lazy person would want to work if he has to take food out of a trash can. No one likes to be in that situation", I said.

"Some of them may be out there, just waiting to die then", said Jatin.

"Yes, many of them go for alcohol or drugs to numb their senses", I said.

"So you are saying that we need to help people from becoming homeless rather than help them after they become homeless", said Jatin.

"Exactly, it is like vaccination", I said.

"Vaccination, you mean that injection thing?" asked Justin.

"Yes, injection thing", I said.

"So you are going to develop a vaccination like thing to avoid sick people or broke people from living on the streets?" asked Jatin.

"We are going to do it together, not I alone", I said.

"Well, we are honored Sir, ha ha", joked Justin.

"Guys, isn't background check a good thing?" asked Jatin.

"No", I said.

"Why not?" asked Jatin.

"I don't think it serves any good", I said.

"Don't people know beforehand, if someone is a criminal or not?" asked Sarah.

"If a person has served prison time, paid his debt, there is no reason to stamp him as a criminal for rest of that person's life", I said.

"Would you like a criminal in your house, fixing your dishwasher?" asked Justin.

"I would have absolutely no problem at all", I said.

"Then you are different, not everyone thinks that way", said Jatin.

"Yes, I know", I said.

"So, basically you have no solution whatsoever", said Sarah.

"Right now, no", I said. It was Friday.

"Are you taking us tomorrow to show the other side of the city, I mean wherever you wanted to take us?" asked Jatin.

"Yes, I talked to Clay and he will be at my house tomorrow. You should all get ready early in the morning", I said.

"Sounds good", said Jatin.

My mom picked me up after the school. The same schedule followed for rest of the day. I slept at night. My mom woke me up early in the morning. I was waiting for Clay. Doorbell rang, I went to the door and it was Clay.

"Clay, nice to see you", I said while moving my hand forward for a handshake.

"Jake, how are you?" asked Clay while shaking my hand.

"I am awesome, how about yourself?" I asked.

"After Ron, it's very depressing out there", said Clay.

"No wonder, come on in", I said.

"Na, I guess we should be going", said Clay.

"Hello Clay", said my mom as she came close to the front door.

"Hello ma'am", said Clay.

"How is everything on your front?" asked my mom.

"Slowly and slowly things are getting back to normal", said Clay.

"That is good to know", my mom said.

"Should I go now, ma?" I asked.

"Yes, here are the directions to all of your friends' houses", said my mom while handing me over few pages with maps and directions on it.

"Thank you ma", I said.

"You have a good day ma'am", said Clay.

"Yes, you all have a good time too", my mom said. I and Clay walked towards the truck. My mom also came out of the house. We were all set to go. I waived my hand and said bye to my mom. She responded back in the same way.

Chapter 9

Flying in the Flock

"Ok, so we are going to Jatin's house first", I said.

"Let me see that", said Clay while taking the page in his hand.

"Ah, ok", he said while handing me the page back.

We reached Jatin's house and he was waiting outside. We picked him up and moved on.

"Hey Jatin, this is Clay", I said to Jatin as he sat on the window side of the front seat. I moved to the middle. The front seat of Clay's truck was old style seat where three people could sit comfortably.

"Hello Sir", said Jatin.

"Just Clay", said Clay while moving his hand forward for a handshake. Jatin shook Clay's hand. We moved from house to house picking up Sarah and Justin. They both sat in the back seat. I introduced both of them to Clay.

"Aren't you guys tight in the front?" asked Justin.

"Na, I am fine, are you guys ok too?" I asked.

"Ya, I am good", said Clay.

"Absolutely, there is still plenty of room here", said Jatin.

"So, where are we going?" asked Clay.

"Homeless shelter", I said. Clay nearly stopped the car. People started to honk from the back.

"What?" he asked.

"Yes, Clay. Is that a problem?" I asked.

"Did you ask your mom about this?" asked Clay.

"Of course I did", I said.

"Ok, let me pull over to a side and call her", said Clay.

"No", I said.

"Why not?" asked Clay.

"Because I want to show them other side of the coin", I said.

"What other side of the coin?" asked Clay.

"They have only seen nice affluent part of the town. I want to show them where poor people live. I mean the place where people live on streets like dogs", I said.

"That's a little rude", said Clay.

"But isn't that a fact. It's time we start to face the reality", I said.

"Do you guys really want to go to that area?" asked Clay. Everyone said yes.

"You know if something happens out there, your parents are coming after me", said Clay.

"Nothing is going to happen Clay", I said.

"How could you be so sure?" asked Clay.

"Ok, we will just drive through that area. We we won't even get out of the car. Is that ok?" I asked.

"Yes, I guess", said Clay. He drove the truck to the part of the city where majority of homeless population lived. Soon we reached the street where the homeless shelter was.

"Slow down", I said.

"What are all these people doing here?" asked Sarah from the back seat while looking out the window from the right side. Jatin and Justin were also looking towards the people.

"They don't have a home. They are out here in a hope to get a bed to sleep and food to eat", I said.

"I can't believe this is happening in world's greatest city. I mean, at least that is what we call it", said Sarah.

"My god, look at these fellows, they are sleeping on the sidewalk", said Justin.

"Yep, I told you", I said.

Sarah started to cry.

"Sarah", I said. She did not respond but kept on crying.

"Ok, let's get out of this place", said Clay.

"No", she said while wiping her tears. We reached end of the street. Clay turned right towards that old building where Josh lived. There were two persons sleeping on the sidewalk with a shopping cart placed on the side.

We all looked on the left side.

"Damn", said Justin while looking out of the window on the left side.

"What is this place?" asked Sarah.

"This is the place where people screwed by our system end", I said.

"Yes, absolutely, I used to live like that", said Clay.

"You?" asked Sarah.

"Yes, little angel, I was homeless for five years", said Clay.

"Five years!" said Jatin as he looked extremely surprised.

"Yes, you know some of them suffer from severe diseases", I said.

"You told us about that", said Jatin.

"So friends, you see, this is the other side of the coin or picture, whichever way you may want to see it", I said as we drove through the street where many more people were sleeping in the sidewalk.

Jatin looked sad. I looked back; Sarah and Justin were looking out of the windows.

"So, where are we going for lunch?" I asked. None of them relied.

"Guys", I said.

"You see, that's why I said it was a bad idea to come here", said Clay.

"Come on guys, cheer up", I said. No one responded. I placed my right hand on Jatin's shoulder and said, "Come on Jatin, cheer up bud." Jatin did not say anything.

"Clay, let us go to the pizza place", I said.

"I am not hungry", said Sarah from the back.

"Me neither", said Jatin.

"Come on guys, we have to eat something. We can go to Times Square and have fun there", I said.

"I am not interested Jake", said Justin.

"Come on now, due to all this", I said.

"I would like to go home", said Sarah.

"This is life. Some enjoy, some don't. Some are sick some are healthy", I said.

"I feel cheated", said Sarah.

"Cheated, but why?" I asked.

"None of these things are told to us in the school", said Sarah.

"I know, I was surprised too, I never thought this happening in our own city", I said.

"So these people always sleep on the street?" asked Sarah.

"No, sometimes they do get into shelters. Government is doing the best it can. There are a lot of people helping the homeless but demand exceed the supply. I know they need to work on their system further. It's a mix of good and bad people out there. The system is put to test only in time of extreme need", said Clay.

"But everyone should be taken care of", said Sarah.

"Yes, that should be the most ideal situation", I said.

"Where does all the money for making atom bombs come from?" asked Justin.

"From the pockets of these people", I said.

"Ha ha", laughed Clay.

"We don't know that. The disparity between the rich and the poor in this country is greater than any other country. Also, the homelessness is present in the developed countries only", I said.

"Why so?" asked Sarah.

"In developing nations, I mean we call them developing but I think they are more developed than us, people live in slums, no one is homeless", I said.

"So you are saying that slums is a good thing", said Jatin.

"No, slums are not a good thing, but it is still better than being homeless. We now have tent cities close to major cities in many metropolitan area of United States. Tent cities are nothing but slums of the developing nations. In tent cities people don't have real house, just tents. Guess what, tents protect one from rain, snow etc. I read on the computer that a lot of homeless people are now resorting to live in these tent cities", I said.

"To avoid living on the street, right? But wait, then why don't these people also go and live in the tent cities?" asked Justin.

"Well, they are too broke to afford to buy a tent and pay the rent in a tent city", said Clay.

"You have to pay rent in a tent city too?" asked Jatin.

"Yes, you do. When you live on someone's property, you got to give the rent", said Clay.

"But, if people start living in tent cities everywhere, wouldn't we be like the developing nations?" asked Sarah.

"Western countries are worse than poor countries. For example, you can't afford to get a damn teeth fixed in this country. Citizens of our country go to other nations to get their teeth fixed. Well, I should actually call them rich nations because even a poor can afford to get the teeth fixed in those nations", said Clay.

"Yes, that is true. Many people from our country travel to Mexico to get medical care", I said.

"That's a shame and we call ourselves the richest nation on the planet", said Justin.

"It is the richest nation but only for the rich, poor people have no place in this country. Poor people are either put behind jails or shot by the police because they break some kind of a law out of millions of laws in this country", said Clay.

"So we need to fix the healthcare", said Jatin.

"President Obama promised that he was going to fix the healthcare. Did he fix it, hell no, you still need insurance. Everything is still the same", I said.

"We need Universal healthcare, where every citizen receives healthcare not because they can afford it, because they are the citizens and have right to get it. It should be like police services, which are free to everyone. Guess what would have happen if police services become paid. A police officer would come to a man stabbed in the stomach with knife still inside and ask, sir can I please see your police insurance card", said Clay and everyone laughed.

"Ha ha ha, that is possible too. The way we are finding ways to charge citizens for something, we may be charged for police services in the future too", I said.

"Where do we go now?" asked Clay as he kept driving on the street.

"In front of the mayor's office", said Sarah.

"What, mayor's office?" I asked.

"Yes, let us go and question him as to what he doing to stop the rise of this problem", said Sarah.

"Na, that won't help at all", said Clay.

"Why not?" she asked.

"Sweetie, we can't just go out there and talk to Mayor", said Clay.

"Then how do people talk to him?" asked Justin.

"Well, there are special occasions where people, you know, high level politicians meet etc." said Clay.

"What is that? Mayor for president board", said Jatin.

"Where?" I asked. Jatin pointed to the right side, where a small park was.

"Stop Clay", I said. Clay pulled the car to the right lane and stopped it.

"What, the mayor is running for president", I said while looking at an advertisement board in the park.

"What, why is it so weird?" asked Clay.

"Jake punched mayor's son", said Jatin.

"Jatin, come on", I said.

"What, you punched mayor's son, what other feats have you accomplished?" asked Clay.

"He is a bully", said Sarah.

"Well, then it is not a bad thing to do", said Clay.

"Yes, very true", said Justin.

"So, I know now why you were surprised to see him running for president", said Clay.

"I wonder what would happen if people like these become president", I said.

"He can't fix his own city, how would he fix the nation", said Sarah.

"Exactly Sarah, you are right about that", I said.

"Hey, look there, mayor for president. Look at all the cars. Clay lets go inside", I said.

"What will we do there?" asked Clay.

"Let's go, it will be fun. We have to do something anyways", I said.

"Don't we need tickets to get in?" asked Sarah.

"Ideally one does, I guess", said Justin.

"We can try", I said.

"Ok, let me find a parking, although it is going to be a challenge", said Clay. He drove the truck through the street looking for a parking spot. He turned left and there was a spot but he had to do a parallel parking.

"You are good", I said to Clay as he parked the truck. We got out of the truck.

We walked towards the center where mayor was campaigning. We reached the front and there were three security men outside.

"Yes Sir, how may I help you?" asked one security guy.

"Good, hey can we see this campaign?" asked Clay.

"Sure, you have an ID on you?" asked one security guy.

Clay took out his ID and showed it to him.

"Are these young guys with you?" asked another security guy.

"Yes, they are", said Clay.

"Ok, be careful that you don't make any kind of nuisance inside", said the security guy.

"Oh no, they are all very well behaved", said Clay.

The security guy removed the security barrier. We walked in though this hallway till we reached a door. Clay opened the door. We entered inside, found seats and sat. There was a huge crowd inside.

There was someone giving a speech. Soon this man introduced mayor as a candidate for the President of the United States of America. Mayor Ronald Deed came up to the podium and started giving speech. He promised to change America and a lots of blah blah blah! He gave a 45 minute speech. I almost slept during his speech. Others were bored too. The mayor offered to answer some questions from the crowd. A guy got up and asked, "So, how do you plan to address the issue in Afghanistan?"

"Well, we will send some ground troops to stabilize the situation over there", said mayor.

"Clay", I said.

"Aa ha", said Clay.

"Ask him, what he meant by stabilize", I said.

"What? You want me to stand up in front of hundreds of people and ask this question, no way", said Clay.

"Please, please", I said.

"No, sit quiet now", said Clay.

"Clay, please just one question", I said. Clay did not respond. Mayor was answering someone's question, "Yes, we will add thousands of more jobs by expanding the crude oil production", said the mayor.

"Clay", I said a little loud.

"Yes, you have any question", asked mayor while pointing towards us.

"Oh no", said Clay.

"Yes, we do", I said.

"Oh you", said mayor while looking at me.

"Clay ask him the question", I said.

"Ok, yes Sir we do have a question", said Clay as he stood up from the seat. A guy brought a microphone and handed it to Clay.

"Go ahead, shoot", said mayor.

"So, what are you doing for the homeless population?" asked Clay. I looked at Clay with surprise.

"Well, the best we could do. We are providing homeless shelters, free meals and other facilities to the homeless folks", said mayor.

"Do you know that just two blocks from here, around 20-30 people were sleeping on the sidewalk because there was no more space in the shelters", said Clay.

"Yes, we are aware that we are unable to cope up with growing homeless population", said mayor.

"Ok, so you are aware. Is there something that you are doing to take care of that issue right now?" asked Clay.

"You see, we have regular meetings about this issue and we are asking for more funding to provide resources to the homeless", said mayor.

"I was homeless for five years and I did not see a single thing improve in that time frame. I guess, this was the same time frame in which you have been a mayor of New York City, no?" asked Clay.

"Oh no, you are wrong about that. In past five years we have opened two more homeless shelters", said mayor.

"Just two", said Clay.

"So what do you want us to do, convert the whole city into a homeless shelter?" asked mayor. There was a huge commotion in the crowd.

"I am sorry, what I was trying to say is this, considering the number of homeless folks, it is just not possible to accommodate them all", said mayor.

"As a mayor you need to make sure that no one sleeps on the sidewalks, right?" asked Clay.

"Ok, next question", said mayor.

"I am not finished yet", said Clay. All the media cameras were pointed towards Clay.

"Next question", said mayor. No one stood up. Everyone in the crowd was looking at Clay.

"I guess no more questions", said mayor.

"What kind of car do you drive?" asked Clay. Mayor did not respond. We saw a man walk towards Clay. He took the microphone from Clay and said, "Please answer the questions, if you want our vote."

Mayor looked very irritated. He shook his head.

"Ok, what has that question to do with all this?" asked mayor.

"Just answer the question", said the man who was still holding the microphone.

"A Ford 150", said mayor.

"What?" asked the man.

"Yes, I drive a Ford 150 and a Lincoln SUV", said the mayor.

"I thought you drove a BMW and a Mercedes. I have seen you coming out of a BMW this morning. I also saw a picture of you in newspaper with you standing next to a Mercedes", said the man.

Mayor was quiet for few seconds.

"Yes, I now drive these cars but initially I had those two. But, I don't understand what this has to do with my being a president", said the mayor. Clay took microphone back from the man.

"I believe these two cars are highly expensive. Also, these are not American cars", said Clay.

"Oh come on, American cars sell in Germany and other parts of the world", said mayor.

"Do you have kids?" asked Clay.

"Yes, I do", said mayor.

"Do they sleep in a nice comfortable bed of your luxury home or do they sleep on the streets with no food?" asked Clay.

"What? What are you trying to say? My kids should sleep on the street just because there are people out there who are lazy to work", said mayor.

"Lazy, is that how you describe people whose last hope is you?" asked Clay.

"I did not mean that. I am saying that most of those people are either criminals, drug addicts or just too lazy to work", said mayor.

"How do you know all that? Maybe you could tell to which category I fell when I was a homeless?" asked Clay.

"I don't know", said mayor.

"Ok, let me tell you. I had a criminal record on my background history for a crime that I did not commit. I was not a criminal, a drug addict or lazy to work. I could not get a job because of criminal record on my history. How would you explain that?" asked Clay.

"Well, that is the way our system is designed", said mayor.

"So, what are you proposing to fix this system?" asked Clay.

"We need to make sure that the background check system works effectively. We don't want to hire child predators as teachers of the schools, do we?" asked mayor.

"But what if that child predator has already spent 10-12 years in jail for the crime? Should we give that person a second chance or just let him go and stand in front of the homeless shelters?" asked Clay.

"We do give second chances. We have several programs", said mayor.

"Where were these programs when I was homeless?" asked Clay.

"You may not have availed them", said mayor.

"Where should I have gone to avail them, Paris?" asked Clay. The whole hall was filled with a huge laughter.

"No, to the facilities where these programs are run", said mayor.

"I went to the homeless shelters and no one told me about such programs. Let us talk about the universal healthcare. Obamacare is penalizing people for not having insurance, really. That is not what we asked for. We need universal health care in this country. If you become the president of this country, would you bring universal healthcare in this country like in Canada and India?" asked Clay.

"That would not be in my hands alone", said mayor.

"Nothing is in your hands. There are so many people out there with no food, water, healthcare and home. How could we expect you to fix this country when you can't fix this city?" asked Clay. The whole crowd immersed in a huge laughter again. Everyone was enjoying this conversation.

"No single person could fix everything", said mayor.

"At least you could drive regular cars and use the rest of the money for the city. I bet, if every politician in this city stops driving expensive cars, we would have so much money that there won't be a short supply of funds", said Clay.

"Oh maybe next thing you will say is that we should all wear under wears only and that will save money for the City too, no?" asked mayor.

"If I was the mayor of this city, I would not sleep in my mansion when many folks are sleeping on the city streets. I will go to bed when every citizen has a bed to sleep on. If I can't find a shelter, I will pay and let them sleep in a motel. Would you sleep in your house if one of your own kids is out there sleeping on the street like a street dog? I bet not", said Clay. The whole hall filled with loud cheers and claps when Clay said this.

"It is very easy to make big claims and very difficult to execute them", said mayor.

"You are not even making those claims. All we need to know is whether you would sleep on the street if you can't make arrangements for all, yes or no?" asked Clay.

"Yes, I would sleep on the street", said mayor.

"Alright, then you should get to work ASAP as there are probably more than a thousand who would be sleeping out in the cold tonight", said Clay.

"What? A thousand?" asked mayor with surprise.

"See, you don't know the statistics of your own city, how would you know the statistics of the whole country?" asked Clay. The crowd clapped and cheered again.

"I will look into this today and you will see the difference by tomorrow", said mayor.

"No, no, we don't need a difference. A good father would not eat or sleep until one of his kids is hungry or has no place to sleep. You have to promise that you would not eat or sleep until every other citizen of this city has. If you fail to accomplish this, then you will have to sleep on the street, tonight", said Clay.

"Ok, you are crossing the line now. Security", mayor yelled. Three security guys started to walk towards Clay. They took his microphone and held him from his arm. They started to push him towards the exit. We all followed Clay. Few persons from the media followed us all the way to the exit. They had their cameras pointed at Clay. There were like 10-15 individuals who surrounded Clay with microphone in their hands.

"How do you feel Sir?" asked a lady.

"Extremely bad", said Clay.

"What do you expect to do now, since you were literally thrown out?" asked a man.

"Common citizens have to face this on daily basis", said Clay.

"What do you mean?" asked another lady.

"Go to a homeless shelter and you will know what I am talking about", said Clay.

"How long have you been not a homeless?" asked a man.

"Around 3 months", said Clay.

"What did you do before you were a homeless?" asked a lady.

"I was an engineer and designed bridges", said Clay.

"So you are an engineer", said a man.

"Yes, I am. So, when the mayor said that every homeless person is a piece of crap, he was wrong", said Clay.

"Are these your kids?" asked a lady.

"No, they are kids of someone I know very well", said Clay.

"How did you feel coming here? What's wrong with your arm?" asked a lady from me.

"I was injured on a swing", I said.

"On a swing?" asked a man.

"Yes, on a swing", said Clay.

"That means our city parks needs care too", said a lady.

"Absolutely, everything in this city needs to be fixed", said Clay.

"We should be going now", said Clay.

"Sir, Sir", all of them said while walking along with us. Clay did not respond. We all got in the truck. They kept their cameras pointed towards our truck. All of them were asking questions of some kind. Clay started driving the truck. They got to a side.

"Oh boy, they are a nuisance", said Clay.

"Yes, they were like bees around honey", said Sarah from the back seat. We all laughed.

"I am hungry now", I said.

"Me too", said Justin.

"Ok, I know a place where we can all eat a good pizza", said Clay.

"Yeah", I cheered.

"That would be fun", said Justin. Clay drove us towards a pizzeria. We went inside the restaurant. We sat on a table and a waitress approached us.

"Hello, welcome to Zuzzini Pizza", she said.

"Thanks", said Clay.

"Oh, you are that guy from the TV", said the waitress.

"What?" said Clay.

"Yes, you were on TV, there you are again", she said as she pointed towards a huge TV.

"Ah, Ok", said Clay. I looked at the TV and all of us were in the TV.

"Hey, me too", I said.

"Yes, look at Justin", said Sarah while laughing.

"What are you doing to your hair?" I asked Justin.

"Don't know", said Justin.

"He is camera conscious", said Jatin while laughing.

"Can I have your autograph?" asked waitress while handing over a pen and a notepad to Clay.

"Well, alright", said Clay as he signed on her notepad.

"Thank you, ok what can I get you in drinks?" she asked.

"I will have water", said Clay as he looked towards us.

"Lemonade", said Jatin.

"Water", said Sarah.

"Ice tea", said Justin.

"Ok, I will get back with your drinks. In the meantime you can have a look at the menu", said the waitress.

"Ok, thanks", said Clay.

"So, you are a celebrity now, hmmmm", I said to Clay.

"We all are celebrities now, ha ha", laughed Clay. We looked towards TV and they were showing scenes from inside the hall when Clay was asking the mayor some tough questions. The bottom of the screen said, 'New York Mayor gets roasted by a homeless man.'

"Ha ha ha, you roasted him", I said.

"No you roasted him you little devil", said Clay. "Listen", I said.

"They are just playing the recording from that hall", said Clay.

"Hey, we are all in that shot", said Jatin.

"Man, I am popular", said Justin.

"Wait till our parents find out about this. I told them that we were going to the Times Square to have fun", said Sarah.

"Na, they would not say us anything", said Jatin.

"Why not?" asked Sarah.

"They may not recognize us", said Jatin.

"Are you kidding me", said Sarah.

"No, she has a point", said Justin.

"We can say that we were asked to come inside and listen to mayor's speech as we were having fun in the area", I said.

"They may not buy it", said Sarah.

"Nothing to worry about guys; just say Jake took us in there. I will deal with them. I will say that I was curious to listen to mayor as his son is a bully in the school, you know something like that", I said.

"Ok, you better come up with a good excuse then", said Sarah.

"Don't worry Sarah enjoy the feeling of being a celebrity ha ha", I joked.

"That was pretty intense", said a man as he came close to Clay.

"Thanks", said Clay.

"Ya, we need intelligent folks at higher positions. I think the mayor of this city is a super dumb guy. He has no knowledge of this city. Good job back there, you knocked him right to the ground", said the man.

"Thank you, actually it was this young man who insisted me to ask a question", said Clay while pointing towards me.

"Really, congrats young man", he said while shaking my right hand. The waitress came with drinks.

"Ok, you guys have fun", said the man as went out of the restaurant.

"There are your drinks", said waitress.

"Thanks", I said.

"No problem, have you decided what you are going to order?" asked the waitress.

"No, but let's decide right now", said Clay.

"I am good with a veggie pizza", said Sarah.

"I can have a margarita pizza", said Jatin.

"Ok, one veggie and one margarita then", said Clay.

"Ok, anything else?" asked waitress.

"Guys", said Clay.

"Can I have a pepperoni pizza?" asked Justin.

"Justin no, I am a vegetarian and strictly against killing animals for the pleasure of our tongue", I said.

"Ok", said Justin.

"You should have a spinach tofu pizza, you will love it, I bet", I said.

"Tofu spinach, I have never heard of it", said Justin.

"Yes, we do have a baked tofu spinach pizza, I love it", said the waitress.

"Ok, let's have that one too", said Clay. The waitress left.

"What's with the vegetarian stuff?" asked Sarah.

"Where do you think all the meat comes from?" I asked.

"My mom gets it from the grocery store", said Sarah. All of us laughed except Sarah.

"That is where you buy it from. It comes by killing animals in slaughter houses", I said.

"Killing animals, you mean like cows and dogs?" she asked.

"No not dogs, but in China people eat cats and dogs too", I said.

"What, dogs and cats, no", said Sarah as she looked very surprised and sad at the same time.

"Yes, sweetie they do", said Clay.

"But why, don't they have fruits and vegetable to eat?" asked Sarah.

"I bet they do. I guess they must have developed a taste of eating them", said Clay.

"That is yukky", said Sarah.

"Yes, it is. Do you know they kill pigs to get bacon", I said.

"What they kill pigs to get bacon?" asked Sarah.

"Sweetie, you don't know anything", said Clay.

"Did both of you know?" asked Sarah.

"Yes", said Justin.

"Aa ha", said Jatin.

"You both know this and you still eat animals", said Sarah.

"Didn't you?" asked Justin.

"No, I did not know that bacon came from pigs", said Sarah.

"Pepperoni pizza is made from cow and pig's meat, I mean of course after killing them", I said.

"My mom never told me this", said Sarah.

"Why would she? We have this notion in the western countries that we get proteins only from animal sources", said Jatin.

"Very true", said Clay.

"How do you guys manage to meet up the protein needs?" asked Justin.

"Beans, cereals, milk, pulses, bread, cheese, yoghurt, nuts, popcorns, I mean it is a huge list", said Jatin.

"Are you a vegetarian too?" asked Sarah.

"Of course, I have never eaten meat and I am perfectly alright", said Jatin.

"My mom used to give me meat but when I found out on you tube, I stopped eating it", I said.

"What did you find?" asked Sarah.

"I saw videos by PETA", I said.

"PETA, what does that mean?" asked Sarah.

"People for ethical treatment of animals", I said.

"What do they do?" asked Sarah.

"They make sure that animals are treated ethically", I said.

"You mean ethically till their necks are cut off", said Justin.

"Ouu that is rude", said Sarah.

"What, that is the truth, isn't it?" asked Justin.

"Is it true?" asked Sarah while looking at me.

"Yes, it is. They just make sure that animals are treated ethically before they are killed for meat", I said.

"But, why do we have to kill animals if we can get proteins from so many other sources?" asked Sarah.

"Addiction of the taste buds", said Clay.

"Yes, that is right. People love to eat meat for its taste, I mean with time they get hooked to it", I said.

"It is very cheap too", said Justin.

"Yes, that is true", I said.

"But isn't the government doing anything about it?" asked Sarah. We all laughed except Sarah.

"It is a multi-billion dollar industry", said Clay.

"Yes, government would not shut it off. So many people would go out of business, many jobs would be lost", I said.

"They can grow vegetables and pulses", said Sarah.

"Yes, they could but they won't", said Clay.

"You mean the animals will keep on dying then?" asked Sarah.

"Yes, they will", I said.

"That is not good", she said.

"We know sweetie, it is a very huge messed up system", said Clay.

"Who started all this?" asked Sarah.

"It's been going on forever. People have been eating meat for centuries", said Clay.

"You mean animals have been killed for our food for that long", said Sarah.

"I really don't know if there is anything wrong in eating meat. Lion eats meat, is it bad, I don't think so", said Justin.

"By the way you are not a lion", I said. Everyone laughed except Justin, who looked a little irritated by the whole conversation. I could understand his anger. He did not get to eat pepperoni pizza today.

The waitress brought pizzas one by one. Everyone enjoyed the pizzas. We were finished with eating our lunch in about an hour. Clay dropped all of my friends to their respective homes. It was time for him to drop me to the house.

"It was fun, wasn't it?" asked Clay.

"Absolutely", I said.

"I should be heading to the pharmacy to get some medicines and then I will go back to the farm", said Clay.

"Hey, can I come with you? I mean tomorrow is Sunday so you could drop me back here, no?" I asked.

"You have to ask your mother about this. I don't think she will agree. By the way did you see your doctor yet?" asked Clay.

"Yes, I went to see the doctor yesterday and he said that everything was fine. They will be removing the plaster next week", I said.

"That is good to know", said Clay as he stopped the truck in front of the house.

"Ok, let me go and ask my mom. I will be right back", I said. I walked towards the front door and rang the bell. My mom came out.

"Jake, hey, I saw you all on the news today", my mom said.

"Sorry ma, it is my entire fault", I said.

"Fault what fault?" she asked.

"Taking them all to hear the mayor's speech", I said.

"That is good. You all learned something about the politics of our country. Didn't you?" she asked.

"Yes absolutely ma. Thanks", I said.

"No worries come on in, ask Clay to come in too", she said.

"Ma, can I go to the barn and stay there with Clay?" I asked.

"What?" she asked.

"Sorry", I said.

"Aaa, we were there few days back. Well, sure why not, I could also go there and see dad", my mom said.

"Awesome ma, that would be fantastic. So, what time do we leave?" I asked.

"In an hour or so", my mom said.

"Ok, so should I tell Clay to leave?" I asked.

"Ya sure", she said. I moved towards Clay's truck. I reached close to the passenger side of the truck. The window was open.

"Clay, mom said she would take me to the farm. She would stay there too. She wants to see grandpa", I said.

"Great. You are a very lucky young man", said Clay.

"Ha ha", I laughed.

"I guess, I will see you in an hour or two then", I said.

"Absolutely, I will be waiting", said Clay.

"Bye", I said. Clay waived back and left.

I went back to the house. My mom stuffed a bag with my clothes and we were all set to go to the barn. She drove to a grocery store close by. We entered the store. There was a huge TV inside the store on which they were showing the same news.

"There you are again", said my mom as she looked at the TV.

"Ya, how many times do they show the same news?" I asked.

"As many times as they possibly could, they show all the masala news", my mom said. I laughed.

"Is that you on TV?" a lady in the store asked.

"No, it is not him", my mom said.

"He looks like him", the lady said.

"No ma'am that is not me", I said as I and my mom started to walk away from her. Soon I saw the lady taking out a camera from her bag and pointing it towards us as she started to follow us.

"Ma'am", she said.

"Please, respect our privacy. I told you, this is my son not the boy in the TV", my mom said as we kept on walking towards the vegetable section. The lady was very stubborn. She kept following us.

"What do you do?" she asked my mom.

"Would you please mind your own business", my mom said.

"How does your son know Clay?" she asked. My mom did not reply.

"He works in our farm", I said.

"Jake", my mom said while looking at me in an angry mood.

"How long has he been working in your farm?" she asked. We did not respond. My mom picked up a bag and started adding some apples to a bag. She placed it in the shopping cart. She picked few more items from the section and placed in the cart. The lady was still pointing her camera towards us. My mom was looking away. I was actually looking straight into the camera.

"Jake, don't look at her", my mom said.

"Sorry", I said as I looked away from camera.

"Hello", the reporter said.

"Ma'am please leave us alone. We don't appreciate what you are doing. If you want to talk to me, let us shop first", I said.

"No, Jake. You are not talking to anyone", my mom said.

"See, I can't, so you are just wasting your time", I said. The lady did not move. She was stubborn as a horse.

"Jake, please help me here. I am a journalist and if I present your interview to the editor of my news channel, my job may be permanent. I have a boy, just like you. We are going through a tough financial time, trust me", she said and took out a card from her bag. She showed the card to my mom.

"Sorry to know that", my mom said while she looked at the card.

"What is that card?" I asked.

"Never mind, Ok, you can talk to him but please keep it plain and simple", my mom said.

"Ok, thank you so much", she said as she turned on her camera.

"So, today I am here at this Buddha grocery store. I have in front of me a young man who was present with the man who roasted New York's mayor during his presidential campaign. So, what is your name?" she asked.

"Jake", I said.

"How do you know Clay?" she asked.

"He works at our farm", I said.

"How long has he been working at your farm?" she asked.

"Three months", I said.

"What did he do before that?" she asked.

"He was homeless", I said.

"A homeless, who gave him a home?" she asked.

"My grandpa", I said.

"Where does your grandpa live?" she asked.

"He died few days back", I said.

"I am so sorry. Was he your paternal or maternal grandfather?" she asked.

"He was my maternal grandfather", I said.

"Sorry for your loss", she said.

"So, your grandpa gave Clay a job also, when Clay was homeless?" she asked.

"Yes, he did", I said.

"Wasn't Clay able to get job somewhere else?" she asked.

"No, he had a criminal record entered on his background check", I said.

"You mean on his criminal record and that was showing up on his background history", she said.

"Yes, something like that", I said.

"Which grade are you in?" she asked.

"I am in seventh grade", I said.

"I am sorry, what happened to your arm? Oh yes, you fell from a swing", she said.

"How do you know?" I asked.

"I saw it on the news. You responded to this question", she said.

"Ah, Ok", I said.

"Where is your grandpa's farm?" she asked.

"I don't know, it is outside the city somewhere", I said.

"Were you invited to that event?" she asked.

"No, I was interested in listening to mayor's speech", I said.

"Are you a fan of mayor?" she asked.

"Fan, no", I said.

"Oh, I am sorry, so why were you interested in his speech?" she asked.

"I met him at the school", I said.

"At the school?" she asked.

"Yes, his son studies in my school", I said.

"So, you must be his son's friend", she said.

"Opposite of friend", I said.

"What do you mean? Is he not friendly to you?" she asked.

"He is not friendly to anyone. He is a bully", I said.

"Mayor's son is a bully? Did he say you something?" she asked.

"Ok, it is getting too much now", my mom said as she approached close to me.

"Please ma'am, it is very important to get this information out. It may be very helpful to a lot of people", the lady reporter said.

"I don't know if it is right for him to give such type of interviews. He is so young for all this", my mom said.

"There are movie stars younger than his age ma'am", the reporter said.

"Oh no, I don't want him to gain that type of attention", my mom said. The lady reporter was turning her camera on and off during my interview. She was turning it on only when I was responding to her questions.

"So, I would be popular then", I said.

"Sure, absolutely", she said.

"Ok, I don't want to be popular then. I don't want to give this interview just for the sake of becoming popular", I said.

"You can help the society with this interview. People would know more about the mayor and this way they will be able to elect the right candidate for the position of president", the reporter said. I looked at my mom. My mom said to me to continue with the interview with her face gesture.

"Ok, so you wish to continue?" she asked.

"Yes", I said.

"Perfect", she said as she turned her camera back on.

"Ok, so you were telling us something about the mayor's son?" the reporter asked.

"Yes, ma'am he is a bully. He scares everyone in the school", I said.

"Did he bully you as well?" the lady asked.

"No, I did not stand to his bullying", I said.

"What did you do?" she asked.

"Nothing", I said.

"Don't be scared", she said.

"I am attending the anger management classes", I said.

"Anger management", she said.

"Yes, the school's principal made it compulsory. The mayor would have filed a police report if I did not agree to it", I said.

"Police report, why?" she asked.

"I punched his son", I said.

"You punched his son?" she asked looking very surprised. She also had a naughty smile on her face.

"It was an impulse. I did not realize when I punched him. Everything happened so fast", I said.

"So, why didn't they took this with police?" she asked.

"Mayor held me by my arm very strongly and I had bruises on my arm. If he pressed charges against me for assault on his son then I could have pressed charges against mayor for assault too. I mean, that is what principal told me", I said.

"Wow, you never told me that the mayor hurt you", my mom said. Reporter turned the camera off.

"Ma, it was not very serious. Principal Jacobs protected me", I said.

"You should have told me about all this", my mom said.

"Sorry ma, I thought you would be worried for no reason", I said. Reporter turned the camera back on.

"Ok, so mayor of New York City held you by the arm?" she asked.

"Yes, he did", I said.

"Your right arm, right?" she asked.

"Yes ma'am, my right arm before the injury", I said.

"Ok, so were you in a hospital?" she asked.

"Yes, for few days, for the injury I sustained in my left arm as fell from the swing", I said.

"Is his son still a bully?" she asked.

"Yes", I said.

"Wow. Has the principal done anything about it?" asked the reporter.

"Mayor threatened to have the principal fired", I said.

"What?" she asked.

"Yes, that is absolutely true", I said.

"Jake, what are you doing here?" asked Officer Trevino as he walked towards us. He had a shopping cart in front of him.

"Officer Trevino, hello sir", I said.

"Hello young man, how are you doing?" he asked.

"Great", I said.

"We nabbed that guy", said Officer Trevino.

"You mean that guy who hit that man?" I asked.

"Yes, that hit and run car case", he said.

"Great, that is awesome news", I said.

"We could not have done without you", he said.

"Thank you", I said.

"Hi there", said reporter to the officer.

"Hello ma'am", said officer.

"Jake helped you in finding a hit and run suspect?" she asked.

"Yes, he did", said officer.

"How exactly?" she asked.

"I was staying in the hospital and saw this guy hit and run over by a car. The car stopped for a while and then fled. I saw that the car was red and this is what I told officers Randall and Trevino. They showed me few pictures of the cars and I picked one with the closest resemblance", I said.

"Yes, he is right. Finding a hit and run suspect is a very tedious job sometimes", said officer. My mom had moved a little further in the aisle to get some more items.

"Ok, I guess, I should be get going now", said Officer Trevino while shaking my hand.

"Yes, Sir, it was nice meeting you", I said while shaking his hand.

"Have a good day ma'am" he said as he started to move away from us.

"You too Sir", said the reporter.

"Ok, that was great on your part", she said.

"Ya, it was Ok. I saw police officers shooting a homeless man too", I said.

"What?" she asked.

"Yes, officers shot a homeless man who had a can in his hand. They claimed he had a gun in his hand. I never saw a gun", I said.

"What? You saw all this while you were in the hospital?" asked the reporter.

"Yes, through a window in my room", I said.

"But, you were injured, weren't you?" she asked.

"Yes, but I used to get bored sleeping on the bed. Once in a while, I would stand next to the window and see the sunrise and sunset, people jogging near the lake", I said.

"So, you are a very curious boy then", she said with a smile.

"A little bit", I said.

"Did you tell anyone that the homeless guy was carrying a can and not a gun?" she asked.

"Yes, I told detectives Garcia and Bush about this. They came to meet me. They have told me that I may have to go to the court to testify this some day", I said.

"Wow, that is very brave of you", she said.

"Yes, David told me that police officers bothered him for no reason. Some even demanded money", I said.

"What? Really?" she asked.

"Yes, that is true", I said.

"Who is David?" she asked.

"Oh David is a wonderful guy. He was homeless. I saw him from the hospital's window. He has AIDS so no one gave him a job. People came to know about it, you know just like the movie, 'Philadelphia', you know", I said.

"Yes, it is a great movie", the reporter said.

"Ya, I love Denzel, I mean Hanks was great too", I said.

"Yes, they both are terrific actors", the reporter said.

"So, David had AIDS and what happened then?" she asked.

"He could not get heath care. He had no job. He came to know six months back that he had AIDS. I and Clay took him to the barn and he got sick there. My mom called ambulance and he was taken to the hospital. I mean, he had no money so my mom paid his bills. She also paid for his air ticket to India. He will be treated in India for free. Their government does so much more for the sick people", I said.

"Really? Are they accepting people from other countries?" she asked.

"Yes, they have this charitable hospital which gets funding from the government and donations. The healthcare cost in India is almost negligible as compared to United States. They have universal healthcare system", I said.

"Wow, yes I knew a little about it. Even Canada has that", said the reporter.

"I am sorry, I did not ask your name", I said.

"That's fine, I am Susan", she said.

"Ok, Susan, I am not saying that India and Canada are perfect nations. They have their own problems but we claim to be a super power and our own citizens have to go to other countries to get their teeth fixed. I know many living on the southern part of the country going to Mexico. They are able to afford it there. I mean if Mexicans can fix theirs and our teeth then why can't we fix just our own", I said.

"Ha ha", Susan laughed.

"You have good points there but many people have already tried to address this issue in documentaries", said Susan.

"Ok, the solution is to fix the cause not fix the effects", I said.

"Cause, what cause?" she asked.

"The cause, you know for people living on streets with no healthcare and food", I said.

"So, you are saying that the cause for all the suffering needs to be fixed rather than the suffering itself. Wouldn't it be like saying well we are going to treat the disease before it ever happens, how is that possible?" asked Susan.

"It is possible. Have you never heard of vaccination?" I asked.

"Of course", said Susan.

"Ok, we vaccinate to prevent disease, right?" I asked.

"Yes", said Susan.

"So why not vaccinate people against homelessness", I said.

"I have no clue to what you just said", said Susan.

"Ok, no problem. We can achieve this by smoothening the job finding for the homeless", I said.

"How?" asked Susan.

"By finding jobs for the homeless", I said.

"But there are people who are too sick to work, no?" asked Susan.

"Yes, there are. There will be provisions made for those people too. If they can't work then they can't work. We are still going to take care of them", I said.

"I guess, most of the things you are suggesting are already in effect", said Susan.

"There are programs out there but they are not one hundred percent effective", I said.

"How do you know?" asked Susan.

"I know because David was out there living like a street dog", I said.

"Street dog that is an insulting word", said Susan.

"There is no other word to compare their plight to. They live on the street, they eat from trash cans, and they have no health care available. They are citizens of this country but merely citizens. Their lifestyle is no different than street dogs", I said.

"Ya, you should not use that word, homeless folks may be sensitive about that", said Susan.

"They call themselves street dogs. I did not give them this name. They gave themselves this name. In movies black people call each other 'nigger' all the time. They would say something like, 'What's up yo nigga'. I mean, really! If a white man calls a black man that word then it becomes racist, seriously?" I said.

"Where did you learn all that? Your parents allow you to watch that kind of programming?" asked Susan.

"This is all there in the movies. Not only movies but programs on local channels too", I said.

"You should not watch all that", said Susan.

"You know our society is so fucked up that I can't even define it. When I go to a mall, I see almost naked women posters in front of the stores selling women underwear. What kind of impression would a young mind like mine would take from there? Also, in summer girls wear extremely small dresses that you can't help staring at them. That is all provocative. I am a teenager, I do what I see, right?" I asked.

"Well", said Susan

"We have to trim our hypocritical ways. People spend; I don't know a huge amount of money for caring for people abroad when our own people live on the streets. We can't lift our weight and we have become donkeys for others. Our own house is on fire and we are trying to extinguish the fire in others houses on fire. First we arm the terrorists and then we save our own ass from them", I said.

"What, what did you say?" asked Susan.

"Give me a break now. Don't tell me that you don't know all this stuff", I said.

"What stuff?" asked Susan.

"We armed Osama to fight against Russia and then he kicked our ass", I said.

"Who armed him?" asked Susan.

"You are a journalist, you are supposed to know this", I said.

"I am surprised that how come you know all this", said Susan.

"It is general knowledge. We did arm him. When he got pissed at us, he kicked our ass, although, we got him in the end", I said.

"Are you supporting Osama's actions?" asked Susan.

"Hell no, I am criticizing the actions of our dumbass leaders", I said.

"You need to show some respect", said Susan.

"Respect my ass. Have you ever thought that all the wars we have been involved in have been against weak nations? I mean nations with very little or no military power. Accept it, our country has been run by bully leaders who target the weak. I mean we never had war with Russia, China, India or other nuclear power nation. Have you wondered why?" I asked.

"Why?" asked Susan.

"Because they can kick our ass back or retaliate with a nuclear bomb. But, with Iraq, Afghanistan and other countries, we feel like yeah, we are fucking strong. We can beat anyone. We have enough nuclear power to roast the whole earth like hundreds of times. Can you imagine how fucked up we are? Sorry for my language but that is the best way to describe it", I said.

"Do you hate our country?" asked Susan.

"I love my country. I hate the politicians who suck. Gone are the days of Lincoln. This is the age of puppets. I mean puppet presidents. We need president with balls. Oops, sorry", I said.

"It's ok, so you are saying that the presidents lately have lacked in spirit?" asked Susan.

"They want to be president for the sake of becoming president. I did not miss a single speech by candidate Obama. Change, yes we can and blah blah. What change? People are out their eating from trash cans and he is sipping on expensive champagne and wine. You know, that is real shame", I said.

"So you are suggesting that we need leaders who could take a stand?" asked Susan.

"We need leaders who look into their own soul. President Obama during campaign criticized President Bush for everything from Iraq war, bad economy and blah blah. We spent billions of dollars and hundreds of lives were lost in going after weapons of mass destruction in Iraq and we did not find shit there. You know why?" I asked.

"Why?" asked Susan.

"Because there were no weapons of mass destruction there at first place", I said.

"So how do we get that type of presidents to run this country?" asked Susan.

"By looking at the facts. We don't need another politician to screw this country. You know, first father screwed the nation and then son", I said.

"You mean family of bush, right?" asked Susan.

"Yes, you are right", I said.

"I won't be that harsh against them. They did quite a bit for this country", said Susan.

"Politicians don't do shit. They just sit in big houses, fly in air force one or other big planes, drive in luxury cars, stay in luxury hotels, eat food in five star hotels. They are not doing anything great for this country, just another burden on the resources", I said.

"Wow, that is extremely rude", said Susan.

"Rude, I am just using my first amendment rights, freedom of speech. I have freedom to my opinion. If I think politicians are parasites, well, I have my opinion and I am free to express that opinion", I said.

"No, I understand. We need all these rights or we would be just like some countries run by dictators", said Susan.

"I had so many expectations from Obama. A lot of black folks had expectations from him. What has he done? Every week or so we see a black man being shot", I said.

"I don't agree. He has done a lot for black community", said Susan.

"Yes, attend functions and praise King", I said.

"No, that is not true. There are racists in this country, we can't change everyone's way of thinking", said Susan.

"Of course, we can't, but we can punish those who break the law", I said.

"They are already punished", said Susan.

"Would you agree that the leader of a nation is like a father of the nation?" I asked.

"Yes", replied Susan.

"Would you sleep in your bed if your son sleeps out on the street hungry with no food and no bed?" I asked.

"Absolutely not", replied Susan.

"Then how could the mayor of this city or president of this great nation let our own people eat food from trash when they eat in five star hotels?" I asked.

"Well", said Susan.

"They took a huge responsibility but did not stand up to it. They just want to be in these positions for the sake of getting in these positions", I said.

"Yes, I guess then", said Susan.

"Only those who are willing to face punishment for not doing their job effectively should apply for these positions. I mean this is not a grocery store job. They should take it if they could stand up to it", I said.

"But those individuals are very few. I mean people who are completely broke", said Susan.

"Where do you live?" I asked.

"In this city", said Susan.

"No, I mean which part?" I asked.

"Why?" she asked.

"I can show you that part of the city where you would feel worse than slums in a third world country. Even slums have some standards. There are no standards where these people live. Sky is their roof, hard sidewalk is their bed, trash is their food, alcohol and drugs are their medicine and death is their hope", I said.

"Ok, where is this part of the town?" asked Susan.

"I don't know the directions but it is where the major homeless shelter is. It is like three blocks away from the center where mayor gave a speech recently. You will find out, just go to the homeless shelter in that area", I said.

"I certainly will. That may be a good story to cover", said Susan.

"Yes, bring the facts in front of the people. They would be surprised how opposite our politicians work in respect to what they say. We need accountability from now on", I said.

I saw my mom approaching us. She had a lot of stuff in her cart.

"So, is the interview over?" my mom asked.

"Yes, ma'am, thank you so much. You have a great boy here. He is certainly different. I have not seen anyone of his age with so much knowledge", said Susan.

"Thank you for the kind words", my mom said.

"Well, thank you Jake. You will see this report maybe by tomorrow on the TV. I will certainly edit some parts so that someone is not offended", said Susan as she placed her camera back in the bag.

"Great, don't forget to go there", I said.

"I won't. Bye. You both have a good night now", said Susan as she walked away from us.

"Thanks for letting me talk to her ma", I said.

"Sure", my mom said.

"So you have got everything you needed?" I asked.

"Yes", said my mom as we walked towards the checkout counter.

She paid for the grocery items and we were back in our car riding towards the farm.

Chapter 10

No Solace in the Barn

We reached the farm in about 20 minutes. My mom drove straight to the resting place of grandpa. She sat there quietly for 5 minutes or so. We then drove towards the barn. Clay was moving some bags of cow food inside.

"So, you want to see him or you want to go to the house?" my mom asked.

"What do you want me to do?" I asked.

"So you are worrying about what I really care?" asked my mom.

"No, I don't want you to feel that I am always spending time with Clay and not with you", I said.

"Ok, go and tell Clay that I will be cooking nice pad thai noodles today", my mom said.

"Really, that is going to be awesome", I said. My mom removed my seat belt and I came out of the car. I went inside the barn, talked to Clay and then I was back in car again. My mom then drove towards the house. We went inside the house. She started preparing the meal in about 10-15 minutes and I turned on the TV.

"What!" I said as I looked at the TV.

"What happened?" asked my mom.

"They shot another homeless man", I said.

"Who shot who Jake?" asked my mom.

"Never mind ma, just looking at the news", I said.

"Ok", my mom said.

I kept watching the news. Once the shooting news was over, another program started. On this program they were asking some experts about their views on what Clay said during the mayor's campaign. I kept watching the program. My mom was done with cooking the meal in about 30 minutes or so. Clay came to the house. My mom served him food. He took the food and went back to the barn.

The next morning, I went to the barn after taking permission from my mom. I saw Clay on a tractor, ploughing some parts of the farm land. Clay saw me. He drove the tractor towards me. He placed me inside the tractor and closed the door.

"Wow, so you are ploughing the land", I said.

"Yes, got to prepare it for the crop", said Clay.

"You are continuously on TV", I said.

"Well, that is what TV folks do. Once they have some news in their hand, they just keep on running it again and again.

"Wait, look at those vehicles", I said while pointing with my right hand. There were 4 vehicles which entered our farm. There was big dish on one of these vehicles.

"You have got to be kidding me", said Clay.

"Are these people from the news channels?" I asked.

"Son of..." said Clay as he looked extremely agitated. We saw those TV reporters with cameras and microphones walking towards us. Clay started driving the tractor further and further away from them. There was water in the fields. Reporters stopped as they could not continue to walk through the mud.

"Yeah, so they thought they could get to us", said Clay.

"Ha ha", I laughed. We saw reporters going back towards their vehicles.

"What are they doing", said Clay.

"Are they going inside the barn?" I asked.

"They are trespassing", said Clay as he took out his cell phone and dialed 911.

"Yes, I have some news reporters on our property. They are trespassing. Ok, yes. Thank you", said Clay on the phone.

"What did they say?" I asked.

"They are sending someone", said Clay as he started to drive towards the barn. Someone saw us driving the tractor towards the barn and started calling others from inside the barn. There were 5-6 cameramen and 10-15 other folks with huge microphones in their hand. They were all looking towards us. Cameramen had their cameras pointed at us. Clay stopped the tractor at a distance.

"Let us wait for the law enforcement to show up", said Clay.

"Ok", I said. Within about 4-5 minutes we saw two police cars pulling around the barn area. Two police officers came out of the cars. They went close to these reporters and started talking to them. The reporters were pointing towards us. A reporter took a paper out of his pocket and showed it to one of the officers. The officer asked us to come closer with his hand gesture. Clay drove close to the barn. Clay moved out of the tractor and then held me and placed me on the ground.

"Hi there", said officer.

"Hello", said Clay.

"You called about people trespassing on your property?" asked officer.

"Yes, I did officer", said Clay.

"These folks are here to interview you. They work for reputed news channels", said officer.

"I don't want them on my property", said Clay.

"Sir, sir", said one reporter as she approached Clay.

"Ma'am, ma'am you need to stay back", said second officer.

"Sir, the democrats are in talks to offer you to run for president. Are you accepting their offer?" asked a lady.

"What offer?" asked Clay as he started walking towards the lady.

"Sir, you haven't heard yet? The head of Democratic Party wants to give you ticket to run for president", said the reporter.

"Wait what?" asked Clay. The reporters started talking to each other. Clay's phone rang.

"Yes, this is me. What? But why? I simply asked a question, nothing more. Ok I need time to think over it", said Clay.

"What?" I asked from Clay.

"I can't believe this. They are offering me to run for president. For president, really", said Clay.

"That would be awesome Clay", I said.

"Sir, Sir are you accepting the offer?" asked a lady.

Clay stayed quiet.

"Sir, please answer the question", asked another reporter.

"No, I don't want to get involved in dirty politics", said Clay.

"What?" I asked.

"Yes, this is not for me. I belong here. I need to take care of these cows, this farm. Ron gave me a new life. I owe him a lot", said Clay.

"No, you should run for President Clay. People need individuals like you. You have been screwed by this system. Now, you have this great opportunity to fix it", I said.

"Yes, but I will be swimming among sharks. What difference of one honest individual make when the whole system is screwed up", said Clay.

"Someone has to take a stand Clay", I said.

"Ok, it is too much for me, please leave us alone now. I need time to think over it. This has come as a great surprise", said Clay.

"Sir", said a reporter.

"Yes", said Clay.

"What would you do for homeless folks if you become the president of this nation?" asked a lady.

"Jake could answer better", said Clay.

"What?" I asked.

"Yes, you are the one who asked me to stand up in that hall and ask the question. You helped David to be sent to India. Now, you want me to run for president so why don't you answer why I should run for President", said Clay.

"Jake", said a reporter.

"So, what would Clay do for the homeless folks?" asked one reporter.

"Nothing", I said.

"Nothing!" said a reporter with surprise.

"Yes", I said.

"But he was very much concerned about them", said a reporter.

"We are not concerned about the homeless, jobless, people with no healthcare. We are concerned with the reasons giving rise to all this", I said.

"What reasons?" asked a reporter.

"We would like to fix the cause, not the effect", I said.

"Cause aa, effect, I am sorry could you please elaborate", said a reporter.

"Yes. Why do you drink filtered water?" I asked.

"So that we may protect ourselves from harmful bacteria and other chemicals that maybe present in the water", said the reporter.

"Right, similarly we would make policies to protect people from becoming homeless at first place rather than helping them after they are on the streets", I said.

"How would that be done?" asked a reporter.

"By giving them job", I said.

"Some of them don't want to work", said a reporter.

"Some but not all. Most of them want to work but could not find job because of prior criminal record sticking around like a bad sore", I said.

"But that is important, right? I mean, I would not hire a child molester as a babysitter", said a reporter.

"Sure, not as a baby sitter but maybe as a truck driver", I said.

"Well, I would hesitate to do so", said another reporter.

"So you are saying that the person should not be given any job. That person may have spent time in prison for his deeds and maybe a changed person altogether", I said.

"How do you know all this stuff kid?" asked a reporter.

"Oh boy, see what comes next", said Clay while smiling.

"You are more stupid than you look", I said to the reporter. Everyone laughed.

"See, I told you", said Clay while laughing.

"Wow, you need to learn some manners kid", said the reporter again.

"You need to learn how to interview people without pissing them off and calling them kid again and again. Maybe I know more than you, so who would be a kid then?" I asked.

It was a huge laughter this time. Even the officers started to laugh. The reporter felt embarrassed, he cursed at me and went back to sit in one of the vehicles.

"Ok, so Jake you were saying that the criminal history should not prevent someone from getting a job", said a lady reporter.

"Exactly, if the person has served time for it, then there is no need to punish that person for rest of his or her life", I said.

"So you are basically against background check", said another reporter.

"Yes, I am against it", I said.

"Won't that make our society unsafe?" asked a reporter.

"People who committed severe crimes are in jail. What bothers you? Once they have served their time for the crime they have committed they should be free to take any job", I said.

"Ya that is not very safe", said one reporter.

"How would you feel if the officer here gives you a criminal trespass ticket and that stays on your record forever?" I asked. The reporter did not respond.

"Yes, how would you feel if that stays on your record forever? You can't get a job anywhere just because people would think that you are a criminal of some sort who trespasses onto others property", said Clay.

"Let me give him a trespassing citation", said Officer.

"No Sir, please", said the reporter.

"What happened now? Why are you scared? If you want the law to be strict then you should let it be applied to you as well", said Clay.

"Yes, let us give citation to all the reporters here", I said. Officer pulled out book from his car. He wrote something on a page and asked for everyone's identification. Reporters started pleading with the officer.

"I need your identification now. I am not going to say again", said one officer.

"Sir, we are reporters. We have to go to places to cover news", said one reporter.

"You need to seek permission before getting onto a private property", said officer. I saw my mom getting close to us. She walked through the barn.

"What is going on here?" asked my mom.

"Ma'am are you the owner?" asked officer.

"Yes, I am", my mom said.

"Alright ma'am, these are the reporters who came here to interview Clay. He has been offered to run for the President by the democrats", said officer.

"You mean run for the President of the United States?" my mom asked.

"Yes, mom", I said.

"Wow, Clay", my mom said.

"Ya", said Clay.

"So all these folks are here to, oh, I got it now", my mom said.

"Ma'am Clay gave us a call that some folks were trespassing on the property", said officer.

"Ok", my mom said.

"Do you want me to cite them?" asked officer.

"Let me talk to Clay and Jake for a moment", my mom said.

"Sure", said officer.

"Ma'am please, we were just doing our job", said a reporter.

My mom, I and Clay walked towards the barn.

"Clay, are they, I mean is the democratic party seriously offering you a shot at presidency?" my mom asked.

"Yes ma, that is true", I said.

"But how is that possible? I mean just because you were on TV for a while. I mean is that enough for them to consider someone?" my mom asked.

"Maybe, they have very low standards", said Clay.

"Don't say that. You are a great person", I said.

"Great person in what way?" asked Clay.

"You did not give up", I said.

"Yes, you must have suffered a lot but you got through all that", my mom said.

"Yes, but that does not mean that people will elect me to that position", said Clay.

"Anyways, what should we do with the reporters?" my mom asked.

"I guess we should let them go with a warning. Giving them a citation would be a little harsh", said Clay.

"Yes, I agree", my mom said.

"Ok, ma'am, I don't want to give any interview. Please ask officers to make them leave and not to come back without our permission", said Clay.

"Ok", my mom said. We walked outside. My mom told the officers not to give a citation to the reporters. She also asked officers to tell reporters to leave and not to return to our property without our permission. Officers did as my mom told. Reporters left.

"Thank you", my mom said to the officers.

"Just doing our job ma'am. You all have a good day now", said one officer as he moved inside the car. Both officers got into the car and left.

"Clay, yeah", I said.

"What?" asked Clay.

"You are popular. You could be the president of this country. President, I mean president", I said.

"Ha ha", laughed Clay.

"Yes, congrats Clay. I did not greet you earlier but that is just incredible. This country may need a common man in the highest post", my mom said.

"Who would vote for me?" Clay laughed.

"People, of course", I said.

"People want to hear fake promises which I can't provide them", said Clay.

"Ok then don't promise them anything. Just do your job. Fix the criminal history thing. Fire corrupt officials, impeach corrupt judges, you know", I said.

"Corrupt judges, where did the judges come into all this?" asked Clay.

"Our country has the highest number of minorities in the jails. Some judges are corrupt from top to bottom. Yes, I am talking about federal judges. The one who are supposed to protect the civil rights law in this country. It is a shame when they don't do what they are paid to do", I said.

"How do you know all this?" asked my mom.

"General knowledge with a little bit of curiosity, right?" asked Clay.

"Ya, a little bit", I said.

"So what about judges?" my mom asked.

"They are the worst criminals of our society. They literally force people to become criminals. If a person does not get justice in courts, what is that person going to do. Let me tell you, self-justice", I said.

"Some people do get justice in the courts", my mom said.

"The rich, privileged ones, sure", I said.

"I don't agree with that", my mom said.

"How many times have you have to go to a court ma?" I asked.

"I can name some judges of the fifth circuit of appellate court in New Orleans, who are more than corrupt. There are few in federal court of Washington DC too", I said.

"What have they done?" asked my mom.

"What have they not done, this should be your question. They have not served justice, the freaking thing for which they were made judges. No wonder they were blood-sucking lawyers at some time", I said.

"Ok, we can't criticize the whole justice system now", my mom said.

"Of course not, there are some judges with maybe 5% honesty level", I said.

"That is 95% corrupt level", said Clay.

"Exactly", I said.

"But judges of federal courts are immune from getting fired easily", said Clay.

"Yes, that's why they have become the dictators of our nation. They throw the racial minorities in jails. You were out there, you know how great our system is", I said.

"Ya, it is horrible", said Clay.

"These judges will learn a lesson when they would be seeking justice and some corrupt judge would screw them", I said.

"Yes, that is the only way they would learn a lesson", said Clay.

"You know legal system is not there to provide you justice. It is whether a lawyer knows the judge personally or not. I know it is hard to believe but our system looks flawless only when we are not the ones seeking justice. I am talking about legal system at this point", I said.

"But officers were here in no time", my mom said.

"We are not minority ma. I am talking about people in minority. You have no idea how they are screwed, first by lawyers and then by judges. It is like dual rape", I said.

"So no one is doing anything about it?" asked my mom.

"Who would do anything about this? The rich don't care because they are able to hire best lawyers who have contacts with the judges. The poor can't find lawyers and are forced to pursue their cases as Pro-Se and guess what happens then; their cases are thrown out of the courts just because they lack legal skills. Seriously, the purpose of the legal system was to serve justice or to test people's legal skills", I said.

"What is Pro-Se?" my mom asked.

"It is when someone fights his or her own case in a court of law", I said.

"So we need to fix healthcare, background check, legal system and the list is getting longer and longer", said Clay.

"Yes, the foremost is the legal system", I said.

"I did not know all that stuff", said Clay.

"You should read cases where judge's bias is evident in their rulings. You can't help but laugh", I said.

"So, are you planning to protest in some way, I hope not", my mom said.

"I can't do anything about it", I said.

"Clay might be your way of bringing this change", my mom said.

"I know, but it is going to be an extremely tough task considering that you are moving solely on truth and not on false facts", I said.

"I agree with you ma'am, it is an extremely difficult task and I am not sure if I will able to handle this", said Clay.

"Why not?" I asked.

"I am getting old", said Clay.

"You are aging like a fine wine, the more it ages, the better it gets", I said and laughed. My mom and Clay laughed too.

We heard vehicles heading towards the barn. We all went outside. There were three cars which parked in front of the barn. The doors of the cars opened.

"Mr. Clay", said a man while approaching us.

"Yes", said Clay.

"My name is Aaron Keen and I am the regional director for democratic party", said the man while shaking Clay's hand.

"Hello there", said Clay.

"Hello ma'am, hi there buddy", said the man.

"Hello", my mom said.

"So, you already know what we offered you. We don't usually do that. You see we need you to run in this campaign", said the man with a fake smile on his face.

"I don't like two faced people", said Clay.

"What?" the man asked.

"Yes, two faced individuals", said Clay. Three more men came out of the car and stood close to Aaron. They looked like security guards to me.

"So, you want to use me to gain more popularity for your party", said Clay.

"Anything wrong with it, we will pay you good amount for it", said the man.

"Pay?" asked my mom.

"We will have him withdraw at the last moment, so need to worry about winning or losing", Aaron said.

"What makes you think that I will agree to it?" asked Clay.

"Money, I guess everyone needs it", Aaron said.

"You know, you should leave now, we are done here", said Clay. Aaron went back to the car and talked to someone sitting in the car. The man from the car came out and shook Clay's hand.

"Sir, my name is Kenneth Red and I am the actual regional director for democrats. Whatever just happened here was just a small test to see if you were really what you said. I mean, we wanted to see if you were after money and power, just like everyone else or you actually wanted to make a difference", he said.

"Sorry Sir", said Aaron.

"I guess you got your answer then", said Clay.

"Yes absolutely. It would be an honor to have a common man run for the president of this country", said Kenneth.

"You guys wanna come in for ice tea, maybe?" my mom asked.

"That would be very kind of you ma'am", said Kenneth.

"What happened to your arm, oh ok, I saw that on TV. It was the swing, right?" asked Aaron from me.

"Yep", I said. We all walked inside. The security guys stayed outside. My mom started making the ice tea and we sat in the living room.

"Nice house", said Kenneth.

"It is my grandpa's", I said.

"Where is he?" asked Kenneth.

"Ron passed away few days back", said Clay.

"Sorry to hear about that", said Kenneth.

"So, Clay, have you given speech in front of people before?" asked Kenneth.

"Nope", Clay said.

"We will need to train you", said Kenneth.

"Train to say lies", said Clay.

"Giving a good speech is essential to become the president", said Kenneth.

"I have not accepted your offer to run for the president yet", said Clay.

"You have not", said Kenneth with a little surprise.

"I thought you have", said Kenneth while looking at Aaron.

"No, you have got some other idea; I am not running for president. I would have to say so many lies, which I can't", said Clay.

"No, you just have to tell people that how you would make this country better, that's all", said Kenneth.

"Ya, I alone won't be able to do anything. What difference did President Obama bring? Nothing at our level, I mean at the level of people who need the help most. He has not done anything different to fix the system but is rather penalizing people for not having health insurance. We did not need another form of health insurance. We wanted universal healthcare. No wonder doctors in this country are millionaires, they overcharge for everything", said Clay.

"See, that is a very good point. But, we can't use things against our own party. President Obama belongs to Democratic Party and we need something to support him, not to go against him", said Kenneth.

"There goes the political crap", said Clay.

"We have to be a little political, after all it is politics", said Kenneth.

"I won't be able to appreciate him for doing nothing different. I feel sad for President Bush, whom candidate Obama blamed for everything", said Clay.

"That is the way it works. You have to prove that you are better than others or you fail", said Kenneth.

"I can only pursue this, if I get a chance to speak truth", said Clay.

"We can't let you speak against the member of our own party, Clay", said Kenneth.

"See, that's the whole point. I have not even agreed to your proposal and you guys have started with the no to do list, already. Is this just a source of income for you guys?" asked Clay.

"Well, not really. We do get one of our best candidates out there", said Kenneth.

"One of your best puppets, not candidates", said Clay.

"Truth is just not possible", said Kenneth.

"Why not?" asked Clay.

"How could you provide a nice house, car, a great job, top healthcare to every individual? That is just not possible", said Kenneth.

"Then don't promise all that", said Clay.

"We need to promise all that or else people would not vote. No one wants to hear the truth that all of this could not be accomplished", said Kenneth.

"We need to tell the truth. If this could not be accomplished then say it. If we don't have the resources then we need to say this", I said.

"Wow, you seem to have a lot of knowledge, aa, Jake, right", said Kenneth.

"More than you could even imagine", said Clay.

"Ok", said Kenneth while smiling.

"I mean, of course there is a limit to everything. We hit a wall after sometime. China has a one child policy because they could not cope up with expanding population. If we can't cope up with our population then let us have a one child policy", I said.

"No, no we can't do it here. We are democratic nation, like India, not communist like China. We can't impose this on people. They have a right to choose", said Kenneth.

"Of course they do but those who give birth to babies at young age with no career or job should not be allowed to take money from the government. They should suffer for their stupid mistakes", I said.

"No, we can't punish for something like that. We need to show that we would help them in every circumstance", said Aaron this time.

"Aaron, do you have kids?" I asked.

"Yes, two lovely kids", said Aaron.

"Why two, why not one, three or five?" I asked.

"I guess, we are pretty happy with two", said Aaron.

"No, because majority of individuals in our society are having two kids. Two kids has become a status symbol", I said.

"Status symbol", said Aaron.

"You know a presidential candidate stands on a stage with his wife and kids during campaign, kisses two kids and kisses the wife to show that he is a family man, right?", I asked.

"Wow, you really are something, ha ha ha", laughed Kenneth.

"Ya, that is the whole purpose of dragging your whole family to the stage. What purpose does it solve, except make one look nice and generous and a family man of course", I said.

"People like to see family men", said Kenneth.

"That's the whole point. Our society has become so copy and paste that our true feelings have just sunk to the bottom somewhere. You do this, as it will look good, we should buy this car and this phone because every other moron is buying it", I said.

They all laughed.

"Where did you learn all this young man?" asked Aaron.

"From the same society which sometimes makes me sick. Well, I am already sick", I said.

"So what should we do? We live in the society and we have to pretty much have to flow with it", said Kenneth.

"Flow with it, why? Why can't you flow in a direction you wish to flow in", I said.

"Well, one could", said Aaron.

"Very few have swim against the current. Gandhi, King, Mandela are few examples", I said.

"You see, world is not how you see it", said Kenneth.

"Yes, I have seen other side of the painting", I said.

"Other side?" asked Aaron.

"Yes, the other not so pretty side", I said.

"Ok, where?" asked Aaron.

"In the city, amongst the richest live the poorest", I said.

"What do you mean?" asked Kenneth.

"I meant exactly what I said", I said.

"Ok, continue", said Kenneth.

"It all sounds so repetitious", I said.

"Ya, I mean, he is talking about the folks who are broke and on the streets", said Clay.

"Yes, then what, we can't fix everything", said Kenneth.

"Why would you? You drive Porsche and Mercedes, you don't give a shit about those guys when you eat in top restaurants", I said.

"No, no, you are wrong about that, we do care about those people. I always help them by giving them, you know few dollars", said Kenneth.

"How would you feel I break your legs and throw you on the street. Then, I approach you and give you few dollars and say, see how kind I am, I just helped this crippled fellow", I said.

Kenneth and Aaron looked extremely angry.

"Jake, come on, I feel sorry on his behalf", said Clay.

"Here's your tea", my mom said as she entered the room.

"I guess we should be leaving now", said Kenneth.

"What happened?" my mom asked.

"Nothing ma'am, we are just getting late", said Kenneth.

Kenneth and Aaron moved out of the house and left.

"What happened?" my mom asked.

"They did not like our honest point of views, they are all snakes", I said.

"Jake, watch that", my mom said.

"Sorry ma, these people, they all speak in the same tone", I said.

"So, what is the verdict here?" my mom asked.

"There is no way I am running for President and swim with these sharks", said Clay.

"Good decision", I said.

"Ok, that was your decision and I guess you chose to do the right thing", my mom said.

"I guess, I should be going back to the barn", said Clay.

"Have the ice tea", my mom said.

"Sure ma'am", said Clay as he drank the whole glass. I also picked up the glass and drank it.

"Ice tea in icy conditions, wow that feels awesome", I said.

"Ha ha", my mom laughed.

"Yes, I bet you can't beat that feeling. Nice tea ma'am", said Clay.

"Thank you", my mom said.

"I will see you in a while", I said to Clay.

"Sure buddy, see you", said Clay as he left the house.

I sat on the couch and turned on the TV. The news of Clay not accepting the Democratic Party's offer was playing.

"Ma, can you believe this?" I asked.

"What Jake?" my mom asked.

"It's on the news so soon. I mean, what are these people. Did they call Kenneth or Aaron or they called the news channel. Whichever way, it was extremely fast", I said.

My mom sat next to me and started listening to the news.

"Wow, I can't believe this, they hardly left this place", my mom said.

"Yep", I said.

"Let me go and tell Clay about this", I said.

"Ok, I will prepare the lunch in the meantime", my mom said. I went outside and walked towards the barn. Clay was outside, fixing something in the truck.

"What happened?" I asked.

"Drive belt is giving issues", said Clay.

"It was on news", I said.

"What?" asked Clay.

"That you have declined democrats offer for running for president", I said.

"You have got to be kidding me", said Clay.

"No this is true, see on your TV", I said. I and Clay went inside Clay's room and they were showing some advertisements. After the advertisements were over they started the same news of Clay again.

"It is a slap on their face", I said.

"No, we shouldn't think like that", said Clay.

"Come on Clay, they are trying to defame you. They are saying that you are not a true patriot since you did not accept to run", I said.

Clay stayed quiet.

"Can't we call them and tell them not to say all these words?" I asked.

"It does not matter to me", said Clay.

"So they would say anything about you and you won't do a thing about it?" I asked.

"What can we do? Sue them for defamation. Do you have any idea how much attorneys cost in this country?" asked Clay.

"I know they charge a lot of money", I said.

"Hiring attorneys is a luxury these days", said Clay.

"Really, are they that expensive?" I asked.

"Yes, in some cases their bills pile up to millions", said Clay.

"Millions, really", I said.

"There is the guy", said Clay.

"Oh, Kenneth, I guess he went straight to the news channel complaining about you", I said. Clay laughed.

"Yep, he is a cry baby. He is trying to label me with all kinds of notorious stuff", said Clay.

"Can't we do anything to stop him from saying all this?" I asked.

"In this country, no", said Clay.

"I guess we should turn off the TV rather than turning off our mood", I said.

"Good idea, let us go to the green-house", said Clay.

"Ok", I said. We went to the greenhouse, spent a little time there. We picked up few baskets of fresh veggies. Clay then drove the tractor towards grandpa's resting place. Clay spent few minutes there and then we came back to the barn. We both went to the house, ate the meal. Clay returned to the barn.

Chapter 11

The Bird with Patience

It was morning and time for us to leave for the city. I met with Clay and told him to see him next week. My mom drove me to the school after going to the home first.

It was lunch time and all of my friends were sitting on the table as usual.

"So, it seems like we are all very popular now", laughed Jatin.

"Sure buddy", I said.

"So, what was that news about Clay being not patriotic?" asked Justin.

"That is all crap, don't worry about such news", I said.

"Is Clay going to do something about it?" asked Sarah.

"What could he do?" I asked.

"I don't know", said Sarah.

"Can't he run for president without anyone's help?" asked Justin.

"You mean independent?" I asked.

"Na, I am not really sure about it. You need a lot of money to campaign", I said.

"But we all are popular now", said Sarah.

"Maybe", I said.

"Why don't we cash in our popularity", said Sarah.

"We have a lot to do in our studies, we don't have time for all this, no?" asked Justin.

"Yep", I said.

We talked about various issues during the lunch hour.

My mom picked me up from school and I was back at home.

"So ma, this plaster is going to be removed tomorrow, right?" I asked.

"Yes, sweetie, we will go there in the evening", my mom said.

The following day, in the evening, I was waiting outside the doctor's room.

"Jake, hello ma'am", said nurse Cindy.

"Cindy, nice to see you", I said as I approached her. She gave me a hug.

"I saw you on TV, you are popular now", said Cindy.

"Ya, a little bit, I guess", I said.

"How have you been ma'am?" asked Cindy.

"Great, how about yourself?" asked my mom.

"Good, thanks for asking", said Cindy.

I was taken into the room where my plaster was removed. It was a little painful process. I was able to move my arm now.

"Wow, that feels good", I said.

"That is great, Doctor John would be here to see you shortly", said Cindy.

I waited in the room. Within about 5 minutes John entered the room.

"Hello young man, seems like your arm is in perfect condition now", said John while moving my left arm up and down, left and right.

"Fold", he said. I folded the arm.

"Perfect, ok Cindy, can you call Sheela in", said John. Cindy left the room and brought my mom in.

"Ma'am, looks like Jake is all set", said John. My mom had tears in her eyes.

"Thanks", my mom said.

"Don't cry ma, I am fine now", I said.

"Ok, young man, I have written some medicines for you. Take these on time and good luck to you", said John as he shook my hand.

"Thank you so much", I said. John left the room.

"You take care now", said Cindy.

"Thank you Cindy", I said.

"Just doing my job, you take care now", she said and left the room.

"Ok, are you ready to have fun?" my mom asked.

"Absolutely", I said.

We left the hospital. My mom took me to an Indian restaurant where we had a fantastic meal. We were back at home and I was all set to go back to the school with both functional hands.

The next morning I took the school bus to get to the school. Everyone in the bus was happy to see my plaster gone and my arm functioning again.

"Hey nice to see you, now you can punch Alwyn with both hands again", said Justin.

"No, from now on Gandhi's no violence policy", I said.

"No violence policy, but why?" asked Justin.

"We can achieve much more without violence than we could achieve with violence", I said.

"What are we trying to achieve?" asked Sarah.

"A grade, ha ha", laughed Justin.

"No you fool", said Jatin.

"Come on guys", I said.

"I am serious; we should follow the no violence policy. If someone says us something, we should not say anything back", I said.

"How is that possible?" asked Justin.

"Ok, a man used to eat tobacco leaves and spit in front of a man's house. The man from the house used to come out every day and clean the area with a cloth and bucket of water. The man kept spitting every day and the other man used to clean it every day, until a day came when this man felt very ashamed to spit in front of his house. The man who used to spit went inside this man's house cried and apologized to this man. From that day onwards, he stopped chewing the tobacco leaves and never spit again in front of that man's house", I said.

"Wow", said Sarah.

"I would have punched him", said Jatin.

"No, you should not say that", I said.

"Yes, but that is a very difficult thing to do", said Justin.

"Absolutely", I said.

"I know some people would just shoot someone on such issue", said Jatin.

"Yes, we watch such news every day. A man shot another man over loud music. Shooting happened among neighbors over, I don't know something", I said.

"Ya that is true", said Sarah.

"But how would that theory fit where people are hard core criminals?" asked Jatin.

"It won't, a very dirty cloth has to be washed. There is no getting around it", I said.

"So, how do we determine, which is a dirty cloth and which not?" asked Sarah.

"With experience, if someone abuses you instead of stabbing you, there is a clear difference there, no?" I asked.

"There is, but law does not work that way", said Justin.

"No it does not", I said.

"There we are", said Sarah as we reached the school.

"Ok, we will continue this topic in the lunch break", said Sarah.

"Sure", I said.

We went inside the classroom. After few sessions it was time for lunch break.

We followed the routine. I also got in the line this time.

"Hey, I can't thank you enough for all of yours help during past few days", I said.

"Hey, that's what, guess what?" asked Jatin.

"Ya, I know, that's what friends are for", I said.

"Yeah", said Jatin while making thumbs up gesture.

We all got our plates and went and sat on the table.

"Hey Justin, where is Alwyn?" asked Sarah.

"Don't know, it is good to not have him around", said Justin.

"His dad is mayor and a very rich man, he does not need to study. He will take care of his dad's business anyways", said Jatin.

"Ya, maybe", I said.

"So we were talking about being patient", said Justin.

"Yes, it is a very hard thing to achieve", I said.

"How hard could it be, more than a walnut, ha ha", laughed Jatin. We all laughed.

"It is actually much harder than a walnut", I said.

"How do you know?" asked Sarah.

"If it was not hard enough then the whole world would have followed it and we would have been a much peaceful world", I said.

"Yes, I guess", said Justin.

"I know, people are fighting over religion", said Sarah.

"Isn't that just non-sense?" I asked.

"Ask those who fight on the name of religion", said Jatin.

"Yes, I know. People have forgotten the real essence. I mean, aren't religious places just places of business", said Justin.

"Yes, most of them are. Some people are taking it as a full time profession", I said.

"But if there is only one God then why do people fight?" asked Sarah.

"Good question Sarah. There is no need to fight if there is one God, but if there is a separate God for Christians, Jews, Muslims, Hindus, then yes, fighting makes sense", I said.

"What religion do you follow?" asked Jatin.

"I follow no religion", I said.

"So, you are not Christian?" asked Sarah.

"I am a human being and that is all I know. If I was born in a Hindu family, would that make me a Hindu automatically, no", I said.

"No, you are right, just because you are born in a particular family does not mean that you have to follow their religion", said Jatin.

"Are you Hindu?" asked Sarah.

"Yes, my parents are Hindu so I guess I am Hindu too. But, I like Jesus", said Jatin.

"See, even if you like Jesus, you will be forced to like Krishna", I said.

"Yes, I know, one time I said to my mom that I wanted to buy this picture of Jesus, she said that we are Hindus, not Christians", said Jatin.

"I think all the religions have to stop pretending as if they own a particular mystic. Christians have to stop pretending that they own Jesus. Jesus belongs to all. Similarly Hindus have to stop pretending that they own Krishna, he belongs to all", I said.

"Good point. George Harrison, the famous singer of the Beatles group believed in Krishna. Despite being born in the west, he could not control his love for Krishna. In fact, he has sung many songs in praise of Lord Krishna", said Sarah.

"Excellent example Sarah, I just gave you an A plus for that", I said and laughed. Everyone else laughed too.

"You know, one day we were in New Orleans and they were saying that Jesus was better than all other Gods because he died for our sins and blah blah. You see, if there is one sun and we all get light from it then how could there be so many gods? A sun does not say, well, this person is of this religion so I won't give light to him or her. The sun gives its light to everyone, irrespective of religion, race, country or color. We have a lot to learn from Sun", I said.

"Good point, the sun never discriminates, it has never asked for anything back. It just gives", said Sarah.

"If Sun has no religion then what religion would a ray coming out of the sun have?" I asked.

"No religion", said Justin.

"Yes, no religion at all. We have divided this earth but we have been unable to divide the sun. Think of it. If we were able to divide the sun then the stronger ones would have robbed weaker ones of light", I said.

"Sure, that is what humans do. We divide and then try to own everything we could", said Sarah.

"People are immersed in illusion. They think that their way of finding God is the best. There are some who don't believe that God exists. I guess those folks are better than those who do believe that God exists but they think that he could be found by only their method. Even Christianity is divided, Catholic, Baptist, Methodist etc. There is no limit to what our evil minds are willing to do" I said.

"I guess, we have come far away from our main topic of 'patience", said Jatin.

"That is true. But, maximum people in this world are killed over religion", I said.

"True, once in a while we encounter riots between Hindus and Muslims in India", said Jatin.

"Yep, we fight over religion too. Don't you hear in news that someone was trying to make a mosque and it was burnt here in US, you know stories like such", I said.

"Yes", said Sarah.

"I mean come on, aren't we kids of one God. If we are, then what is the fight about?" I asked.

"That is true. But, people have their own idols that they like to worship. Also, there are certain things said in the scriptures which make one believe that one religion is better than another", I said

"But why can't people understand this simple thing?" asked Sarah.

"Christians don't own Jesus, Hindus don't own Krishna, Buddhists don't own Buddha. They were individuals who came from the level of God to our level. If there is only one God then the question of who is better than other does not arise. They were at our level and also at the level of God", I said.

"How is that possible? How could they be at our level and also at the level of the God?" asked Sarah.

"In their physical form, they are at our level but from inside they are at the level of God", I said.

"You mean spiritually", said Sarah.

"Yes, spiritually", I said.

"Yes, they must be really powerful. Jesus arose from dead", said Sarah.

"Yes, they are like small seeds. No one can imagine that such a big tree could be present in a small seed. But, if we plant the seed and give it the right conditions then it could become a huge tree", I said.

"So, you are saying that we all have...aaa", said Jatin.

"I am saying that we all have the potential to rise spiritually. All we have to do is provide the right conditions", I said.

"So, what are the right conditions?" asked Sarah.

"To be in the company of someone who is at the level of God and at our level at the same time, just like Buddha or Jesus", I said.

"But many Christians believe that we can get to God only through Jesus", said Sarah.

"That was true till the time Jesus was among us in his physical form. Once he left his physical abode, he could have taken care of only those individuals whom he initiated on the path at that time", I said.

"The truth is, no one knows everything for sure", said Jatin.

"Yep, I agree", I said.

"But different religions claim as if they know the best", said Justin.

"Yes, that is the whole problem", I said.

"If there is one God and we all his kids then that makes us all brothers and sisters spiritually, correct?" asked Jatin.

"That is absolutely true", I said.

"Then why would a brother kill his own brother over the same father?" asked Justin.

"That is the whole point", I said.

"I think we need to go back to the original topic", said Justin.

"What was the original topic? Ha ha", laughed Jatin.

"No clue", I said. Everyone laughed.

"Guys, time to go back to class", said Sarah.

We all went back to class.

This interaction was from the following day during the lunch.

"I hate math", said Sarah.

"Ya, me too", said Justin.

"Hey, I saw your interview on TV yesterday", said Jatin.

"Really, which channel?" I asked.

"On channel 5", said Jatin.

"You were incredible man", said Justin.

"You think so", I said.

"Absolutely, you have a lot of knowledge considering your age", said Jatin.

"I don't think many students watch new channels around here", I said.

"Yep, they are too busy with Bieber and Swift", said Sarah.

"Are you too?" I asked.

"Hell no", said Sarah.

"Ha ha", I laughed.

"So anything new today?" I asked.

"Nope", said Jatin.

"You were telling us about the no-violence strategy yesterday", said Justin.

"Oh yes, that's right. So, the thing is to offer your second cheek if someone slaps on your first", I said.

"But what if someone slaps on your second cheek too?" asked Justin. Everyone laughed.

"Ha ha, good point. I have no idea, hmm, maybe to offer the first cheek again", I said.

"Ha ha you are funny. So, we should keep offering our cheeks till the next person has either killed us after slapping us a million times or that person just gets tired", said Jatin. Everyone laughed.

"Ya, ha ha something like that", I said.

"Not a very good approach", said Sarah.

"Yep, but Jesus asked us to use this approach, I mean offer the second cheek", said Justin.

"Sure, that's what we know. He got us confused, he should have clearly told us as to what do in case one gets slapped on both cheeks", I said.

"I would say slap back", said Jatin.

"Ya, that would be appropriate in that scenario since we offered generosity, we accept something back in return too, no?" I asked.

"I guess so. I think that philosophy does not apply to all case. I mean, if someone kills one of our family member then are we going to offer the second member to be killed too or are we going to stop the person from committing the crime again?" asked Jatin.

"Great question Jatin, I have no idea buddy. I guess after the second slap we have to figure out on our own", I said.

"You punched Alwyn, he hit you once on the shoulder", said Sarah.

"Yes, that was an impulse", I said.

"What would you do now, if he hits you again? Don't you think submission represents weakness?" asked Jatin.

"Yes, sometimes it becomes important to take action", I said.

"Exactly", said Jatin.

"Yep, I mean, if we don't do anything then the other person just thinks that he could keep on doing whatever he feels like doing", said Sarah.

"So, we should change that line to something like this, 'If someone slaps us on our one cheek then we must slap back on his cheek, not punch him", I said. Everyone laughed.

"Ha ha, ya, don't punch. Give equal back, not more not less", said Jatin.

"That is good one Jake. I know some people would just shoot if someone slaps them", said Justin.

"So the punishment should be according to the crime. No punishment could lead to more crime in my opinion", said Sarah.

"Yes, I guess so", I said.

"Perfect way of solving this problem would be to just do whatever one feels correct in that particular situation", said Jatin.

"Look who is here", said Sarah.

"Alwyn, see there", said Justin. Alwyn was looking towards us. He threw a piece of bread at us and laughed with his friends.

"He is not going to change. A punch, a week of suspension and he is still where he was", said Sarah. I picked up the piece of bread and started to walk towards Alwyn's table.

"Jake, no, what are you doing?" said Sarah.

"Wait, I will be back", I said.

"Hey Alwyn, seems like you threw a bread at us", I said.

"Yes, I did, what are you going to do about it?" asked Alwyn.

"Do you know how many people take out these pieces of bread from the trash and eat it every day", I said.

"What?" asked Alwyn.

"Yep, the food that people throw goes into trash cans where many poor homeless people get their food from", I said.

"Tell this story to your friends because I don't give a shit", said Alwyn.

"You need to respect the food and thank God for what you are getting to eat. Some people don't even get this much to eat in whole day and you are just throwing it away", I said.

"People throw food all the time. At home my mom and dad throw stuff they don't like. They would eat a little bit chicken and throw the rest. In restaurants people eat just a little bit and throw the rest. What's the big deal man?" asked Alwyn.

"Well, it would be a big deal if we were out there and had no food to eat, no", I said.

"Why would I be out there at first place?" asked Alwyn.

"For a lot of reasons", I said.

"Like what?" asked Alwyn.

"Like not able to find a job", I said.

"I won't need a job, my dad is a very successful businessman", said Alwyn.

"Have you never heard how companies fail? Did you not know that our country is still struggling to get out of economic depression?" I asked.

"I heard about the depression but guess what we are fine ha ha ha", laughed Alwyn.

"Ok, fine then, you keep on throwing the bread", I said. I started to walk away from Alwyn. He threw a piece of bread at me. I picked up the bread and walked towards my table.

"I told you, he is a moron", said Sarah.

"Don't worry, he will realize some day", I said.

Alwyn threw another piece of bread at us.

"Hey you", said Jatin in an angry mood.

"No, Jatin no", I said.

"Stop throwing the bread at us or", said Justin.

"Or what?" asked Alwyn as he walked towards us. I stood up and looked Alwyn straight in the eye.

"What do you want?" asked Alwyn.

"Why don't you get all your frustration out on us in one day rather than doing this every day?" I asked.

"Ok", said Alwyn and punched me on the right side of the face.

"Hey", said Jatin while holding Alwyn.

"Jatin no, let him", I said. Jatin let Alwyn loose.

"Ok, that's it, or you have more frustration inside you?" I asked. Alwyn punched me in my stomach.

"No, you son of a bitch", said Justin as he held Alwyn from his hand.

"No, leave him, let him get all of it out today. I can't handle this everyday", I said.

"You want more", said Alwyn.

"If you want to give more", I said. Alwyn punched me 4-5 times on my face. I fell on the floor. I started to bleed from my face.

"Stop Alwyn, I am going to the principal's office", said Sarah.

"No Sarah", I said. Sarah did not listen to me. She kept on walking.

"Jatin please go and stop him", I said.

"Alwyn, you have more frustration or are you done?" I asked. Alwyn looked at me. I was bleeding from the face at 2-3 places.

"Hit him back Jake", said Justin.

"No. Alwyn come on buddy, hit me, I want you to get everything out of you today", I said. Alwyn hit me 3-4 times in my stomach again. I fell on the ground. I could hardly get up.

"Alwyn stop for God's sake", said Jatin. I stood up again.

"Ok, you have more", I said while I was taking deep breaths.

"He is going to kill you Jake", said Justin. Some members of the staff came and stopped Alwyn.

"No leave him", I said.

"What? He has beaten you so badly, you want us to leave him?" asked a staff member of the cafeteria.

"Yes, please, ahhh, let him go", I said. Justin and Jatin held me through my arms. Alwyn with other friends ran out of the cafeteria. A staff member brought a first aid box. He cleaned my face which had blood all over. He also tried cleaning my shirt but it was badly filled with blood.

"We need to take him to the hospital", said Jatin.

I fell to the ground and was unconscious.

"Jake", I heard.

"Jake", I heard and saw a nurse.

"What? Where am I?" I asked.

"You are in an emergency room", said nurse.

"Wait, but I was in school. How did I get here?" I asked.

"You collapsed in school. You had a lot of bleeding. We brought you here in ambulance", said nurse.

"Does my mom know about this?" I asked.

"Yes, she has been informed", the nurse said.

"What happened to me?" I asked.

"You have two broken ribs", said nurse.

"No, not again", I said.

"What? What do you mean by not again?" the nurse asked.

"My arm was broken few days back", I said.

"Really, how?" the nurse asked.

"I fell from a swing", I said.

"Oh no, so sorry to hear that", the nurse said.

"So, where are my friends?" I asked.

"They should be in their homes. We brought you here in the ambulance", the nurse said.

"I am going to miss school again", I said.

"Don't worry about the school right now", said nurse.

"Jake", my mom said as she entered the room.

"Hello ma", I said.

"Oh no, not again", my mom said while hugging me. She started to cry.

"What happened?" my mom asked.

"Nothing, I fell from the stairs in school", I said.

"Hello", my mom said to the nurse.

"Hello ma'am, he has two fractured ribs. This type of injury usually heals in 4-6 weeks on its own. Doctor will be here shortly", I said.

"Oh baby", my mom said.

A tall man with beard entered the room.

"Hello ma'am, hey buddy, my name is Doctor Smith", said doctor.

"Hello", my mom said.

"Hello ma'am, sorry about all this", said Smith.

"He was injured few days back and now this. I can't believe this", my mom said.

"Yes, I checked his medical records. It is very un-fortunate. We will have to secure his chest area for a little while. I am going to prescribe him some medicines including pain-killers. Please administer pain-killers only if you deem absolutely necessary", the doctor said while handing over a small paper to my mom.

"So, can I take him home?" my mom asked.

"Yes, absolutely, just make sure he gets ample rest. We have given him strong pain-killers right now, but he will feel pain while breathing once the effect of pain-killer subsides. I suggest you to give him a pill of this pain-killer in about 4 hours from now", said Doctor.

"Sure, I will", my mom said.

"Oh, some police officers are here. They wanted to ask some questions from Jake", said doctor.

"What? Police officer, but why?" my mom asked.

"I have no idea, I guess they would be able to explain. Are you Ok talking to them?" asked doctor.

"No, I feel a lot of pain while talking. May be they can talk to me some other time", I said.

"Ok, fine. I will let them know that the patient is not in a position to give any statement at this time", said doctor.

"Thanks doctor", my mom said.

"You are very welcome. Good luck to you young man", said doctor.

"Thank you Sir", I said.

"You are very welcome", said doctor as he left the room.

"Are you telling the truth about you falling off the stairs in school?" my mom asked.

"Yes, ma, I am ahh..it hurts", I said.

"Ok, sorry sweetie, don't speak", my mom said.

My mom drove me home. She cooked me a light meal. I ate the meal and medicines. The medicines had a lot of sedation in them.

"Jake, I will be staying home tomorrow with you. I have also e-mailed your school that you are injured, although they may already know it", my mom said.

"I am feeling sleepy", I said.

"Ok, you can go and sleep now. Try to sleep straight, don't sleep on the side as it may hurt", my mom said. She took me inside my room. She changed my clothes and then laid me on the bed. She placed two pillows, one on the right and one on the left side.

"Ok, that should make sure that you sleep straight. I am going to sleep right in this room on the carpet", my mom said.

"Why? You should go and sleep in your room", I said.

"No, I will sleep in this room tonight", my mom said as she left the room. The medicines were making me dizzy and I have no idea when I felt asleep.

I woke up in the morning and was given a nice breakfast by my mom. My mom received a call from the school. She was told about the whole incidence.

"Jake, so you lied to me", my mom said while I was sitting on couch and watching TV after breakfast.

"About what?" I asked.

"You had a fight with Alwyn and he did all this to you, hmmm. Who do you think you are?" my mom asked as she looked a little angry.

"Ma, take it easy", I said.

"Take it easy, he broke your ribs. I am calling the police", my mom said.

"It's Ok ma, he had no power to break my ribs", I said.

"Really, then how did he manage to do it?" my mom asked.

"Because I let him", I said.

"Why would you let him beat you and where the hell was everybody else in the school at that time?" my mom asked.

"I allowed Alwyn to hit me. I am practicing non-violence", I said.

"Non-violence, but why?" my mom asked.

"Come on ma, last time when I punched Jake, you scolded me. Now this time, I did not punch him and you are still scolding me. What do you expect me to do?" I asked.

"Someone could have at least, I am going to complain about this to school's administration", my mom said.

"No one is to be blamed for all this ma. It is all karma, what I did came back to me. I have learned my lesson", I said.

"I never encourage you to hit someone but I never said that you should not defend yourself", my mom said.

"You see ma, Jesus made blind man see. He walked on water. He cured sick. He turned water into wine. I mean these are very small things what he was capable of doing. No one had the power to crucify Jesus. He wanted himself to be crucified and that is what happened. If he wanted, he could have just killed everyone with his mere thoughts. I mean come on, he had the powers way beyond a normal human being", I said.

"So, you are saying that you had the power to beat Alwyn but you did not do to it just to be like Jesus", my mom said.

"Yes, ha ha", I laughed. "Ahh, it hurts", I said.

"Ok, I want you to self-defend yourself next time. I am going to call the police anyways", my mom said.

"Come on ma, they did not file a police report against me when I punched Alwyn. Why should we file a report now? It is Ok, I am sure principal will take care of the rest", I said.

"Ok, but I still need to see him and make sure that no one hits you next time", my mom said.

"I told you ma, no one can beat me until I allow it", I said.

"Don't be over confident Jake, you have already met your match", my mom said.

"Match, come on ma, I can beat Alwyn in 30 seconds", I said.

"Ok, I don't want any more issues between you and him", my mom said as she picked up her phone and went to the bed room.

I kept watching the TV and felt asleep on the couch. My mom woke me up for the lunch and I went back into my room and slept on the bed throughout the afternoon. The painkillers made me dizzy.

I rested at home for 2 more days and was back in the school. My mom had met with the principal. I came to know that Alwyn was dismissed from the school. My mom asked me to talk to the police, but I refused. Alwyn's father met with my mother and apologized. Things were getting back to normal. I came to know that Alwyn's father was going to send Alwyn to a boarding school in North Carolina.

There were rumors that Alwyn's father was not going to run for president anymore.

This conversation is from another lunch period at school café.

"It is so nice in here after he is gone", said Sarah.

"Yep", said Justin.

"I wonder what he would do in the boarding school", said Jatin.

"He will beat them all, over there", said Sarah while laughing.

"Why aren't you saying anything?" asked Jatin from me.

"About what?" I asked.

"About Alwyn not being in this school anymore", said Sarah.

"I mean, that's not a solution", I said.

"What do you mean?" asked Sarah.

"Punishment is not a solution to fix the problem. It is just a way to make problem go away, that's it", I said.

"So what are you suggesting, should he be right here right now, beating us, you know", said Justin.

"No, that's not what I am saying", I said.

"Then what is it Jake?" asked Jatin.

"We should hate the crime, not the criminal", I said.

"But crime is committed by criminal, no?" asked Jatin.

"Yes, but that person may become a better person, if he or she is given an opportunity", I said.

"Opportunity for boys like Alwyn, come on", said Sarah.

"Yes, that is the whole point. We have to give second chances", I said.

"The school already gave him a second chance. He was suspended and then re-instated. He did the same thing of bullying again. I bet if we bring him here right now, he will be using his same big mouth to insult us all", said Justin.

"Yes, that is true. He got what he deserved. If I was in your shoe, I would have not let me him get away with this", said Jatin.

"How could say that? Your ancestors are from India and Gandhi followed non-violence policy", I said.

"Yes, that was true but not anymore. India is a nuclear power now. It has one of the strongest militaries in the world after US, Russia and China. What does that tell you? Non-violence is no excuse for not defending yourself", said Jatin.

"Yes, Jatin has a point", said Sarah.

"Yes, but punishing someone is not a solution either. We punish people who commit crime by adding criminal records on their background histories. What purpose does it solve? It is good only for those who are hiring, but for those seeking jobs it is no less than a death sentence. You would either become a criminal or a homeless this way", I said.

"One could always run one's own business", said Justin.

"You have no idea what you are talking about. Our country is all about credit check, background check, rental history check and so much of other bull-shit", I said.

"So, what are you suggesting?" asked Sarah.

"All these things are necessary for a good society", said Jatin.

"Necessary for a good society? Come on buddy, give me a break. You call a society with hundreds of people committing suicide and sleeping on the sidewalks sick, a good society. I say, fuck this type of society", I said.

"Oops", said Sarah.

"Sorry guys, ha ha", I laughed.

"You need to keep those words out of the school. Thank god no teacher is around", said Justin.

"Ya, I know. Anyways, the point is not to screw people further, who are already screwed", I said.

"It is very hard to say, I mean society has to be kept safe", said Justin.

"We are part of the society. If I get a criminal record on my background history then I will suffer throughout my life. I shouldn't have to go through all that", I said.

"Yes, you are right. Others will benefit but you will keep on getting screwed", said Sarah.

"Yep, one should not be punished throughout life for one crime", I said.

"But, I have heard that some employers do hire people who have prior criminal records", said Jatin.

"Yes, some people are generous and believe in giving second chances. But those people are very few", I said.

"I bet", said Justin.

We talked about these issues for another 5 minutes or so.

Chapter 12

The Sensitive Bird

The following day my mom received a call from the news reporter who interviewed me. She asked if I would be available to give another interview in their studio. I accepted the offer. Of course, I had to convince my mom, which was a pain, but she agreed eventually. The interview was scheduled for Saturday, in the evening. Susan, the reporter who interviewed me previously was the one who was going to interview me again but this time on live TV.

Just before the interview.

Susan told me how to sit, respond to her questions etc. My mom was in another room. The studio had two very nice chairs with a table placed in between.

"Ok, Jake, we are almost ready to start. Don't be nervous. I know you are a very confident boy", said Susan.

"I am fine. You can start anytime", I said as I sat comfortably on the chair.

There was huge camera in the front with 3-4 individuals around the camera. There were 4-5 other individuals inside the room and everyone was doing something. One person had a microphone held in our direction with a huge iron rod. I had a small microphone on my shirt and so did Susan.

"Jake, we are going to start. I will count from 5 backwards. Ok, 5, 4, 3, 2, 1, go", said the man.

"Good evening. My name is Susan. I am here to interview a very special boy. His name is Jake. This is the second time I am going to interview him. The first time was a little informal and I am glad we could get Jake here today for a more formal one. You all know that his previous interview was seen by millions across the country and not just in New York. We got numerous requests to get Jake's one more interview. We have also received hundreds of questions that the viewers want to be answered by Jake. We will take some of those questions. Welcome Jake", said Susan.

"Thanks", I said.

"So, how come you have so much knowledge at such a young age?" asked Susan.

"Well, TV is great source for knowledge and I must confess that I do watch a lot of it", I said.

"Ha ha, Ok, so in your previous interview you criticized our leaders, do you hate them?" asked.

"There are no leaders, just politicians. I hate their actions, not them", I said.

"What actions?" asked Susan.

"The actions of inactions", I said.

"Sorry", said Susan.

"Well, their actions of not acting on things that need to be addressed most", I said.

"What are those things?" asked Susan.

"I addressed all those in my previous interview. It would be just repetitious to go over it again and again", I said.

"So, how could we make our leaders, sorry politicians to take actions on things that need most attention?" asked Susan.

"By penalizing them", I said.

"Penalizing, how?" asked Susan.

"I guess, I said this in my previous interview, until and unless the politicians don't face punishment for not doing their jobs effectively, we can't have an efficiently working system. We would just be on their mercy to provide us with what we need", I said.

"But isn't that the whole purpose of having a democratic nation? I mean, different parties, so that they can find each other's faults", said Susan.

"Negative campaigning has become toxic these days. People would say so many bad things. I know one time they literally placed horns on one candidate to look like a devil. I mean, seriously", I said.

"No, we all know, negative campaigning could be really repulsive sometimes", said Susan.

"Exactly, it serves no good purpose. To a man living on the street, these things do not matter. That person sees one politician after another but he is still staying out there on the street", I said.

"Yes, but what is the solution to all this?" asked Susan.

"Accountability", I said.

"Ok, what in accountability?" asked Susan.

"The courage to take the responsibility", I said.

"I don't understand", said Susan.

"If a single man goes without food or health care then the President will have to go without food and healthcare", I said.

"That is impossible", said Susan.

"Nothing is impossible, even impossible says I, m possible, ha ha", I laughed.

"So why do you hate the system of our country so much?" asked Susan.

"Would you like a black cop to shoot you, just because you are white?" I asked.

"Why would I like that?" asked Susan.

"That is just a way of putting it. I did not mean to insult you but just wanted you to know the severity of the situation", I said.

"So, you are referring to police killing black folks around the country, right?" asked Susan.

"Yes, I am sick of those news. I am happy at least those news are covered by the media extensively. So, I must appreciate you guys for getting the facts in front of the world", I said.

"Thanks Jake, we will take a small break and will be back for more with this interview", said Susan.

"Jake, do you need something?" asked a lady who was standing next to the camera.

"No, I am good", I said.

"Ok, we will start again in about 2 minutes", said Susan while she got up from her seat and got close to the camera and started looking up something.

"Everything is alright?" I asked.

"Yes, everything seems to be alright", said Susan.

"Susan", said a man while entering the room.

"Yes, Sir", said Susan.

"We need to stop this interview right now", the man said.

"Stop the interview, now", said Susan as she looked extremely surprised.

"Yes, Susan, it has to be stopped. Jake is offending too many people", he said.

"Which people?" asked Susan.

"Politicians", he said.

"But, we have less than one minute to start the interview again", said Susan.

"Shit, ok, continue, but no politics; ask him about school or something else. There is so much pressure on me. I will lose my job", said the man.

Susan came back and sat on the chair. She looked very sad. The cameraman waived at her. She retained her composure.

"Welcome back, we are back again to talk to Jake. Alright Jake, enough of politics, tell us about your school?" asked Susan.

"School, what about school. My school is just like any other school", I said.

"No, I mean, what do you do in school? Any special activities?" asked Susan.

"Nothing special Susan, except for the lunch sessions", I said.

"What's special about lunch sessions?" asked Susan.

"Me and my friends chat about social problems in every lunch session", I said.

"What do you talk about?" asked Susan.

"About how poorly this city and this country was run", I said.

"So, you play any game?" asked Susan.

"Yes, I play some games sometimes. Na, I am just kidding", I said.

"Tell us about you hobbies", said Susan.

"My hobby is to find problems, I guess", I said.

"Problems, really what kind?" asked Susan.

"All kinds", I said.

"Any example?" asked Susan.

"Yes, look at this room, there are so many lights, I bet you can do this interview with even half", I said.

"Ahmm, oo hoo oo hoo, I am sorry", said Susan as she picked up a glass of water in front of her and took a sip from it.

"That was just a suggestion Susan", I said.

"No, that's a great suggestion, we will try to see if that works", said Susan.

"I was saying that because thousands in this city can't afford to pay electric bill and as a smart citizen we should save power. If the demand is less, the prices would drop and everyone would be able to afford it", I said.

"Completely agree with you Jake", said Susan while smiling.

"We all need to change our habits. We all have to learn to give second chances. I know, it is tough to fix the system, but not tough to change our attitude", I said.

"Attitude, what about it?" asked Susan.

"We need to think that we could be in a person's shoe with whom we are dealing", I said.

"Ok, no that's a good thing to do", said Susan.

"Would you give a job to a person who has murdered someone in the past but has undergone full punishment for it?" I asked.

"I am not sure but I guess it would depend on a lot of things", said Susan.

"Like what?" I asked.

"Well, whether the person has undergone enough transition", said Susan.

"How would we know that?" I asked.

"I have no idea Jake", said Susan.

"Second chance", I said.

"Yes, but many people would be scared to hire or give a second to such a person", said Susan.

"That is what we need to work on", I said.

"Yes, I guess so", said Susan.

"You see, the charity begins from home", I said.

"Of course, but it should not stop there", said Susan.

"I guess everyone is doing everything to the best of their ability but we still have these issues", I said.

"Oh, you are being sarcastic now", said Susan.

"No, seriously we all are doing everything and therefore we have these problems, come on Susan. The problems would vanish overnight if everyone takes a step", I said.

"Ok, then how could you put all the blame on politicians then? Are they not the scape goat?" asked Susan.

"Politicians have to run this country like parents have to run a family. It is up to a father and mother to teach values to its kids. It is up to politicians to teach moral values to our citizens, although some already have it", I said.

"So you are saying that politicians should teach us how to act in a society, how?" asked Susan.

"By setting an example", I said.

"What example?" asked Susan.

"When India was seeking independence from British empire, Mahatma Gandhi started what is called as a boycott moment. In this moment they boycotted everything made in British factories for which Indians had to pay hefty amount. He himself started to wear a dhoti and stopped wearing all foreign made clothes. He set an example and everyone followed", I said.

"Hmmm, so what are you suggesting here?" asked Susan.

"Leaders should lead by example. To end homelessness, they should live like a homeless, till everyone gets on their feet. To end hunger, they should go hungry. To make healthcare accessible to everyone, they should go without healthcare, even if a single citizen is without it. We need leaders not politicians", I said.

Susan was quite for a while.

"Who would make sure that the next politicians are like such?" asked Susan.

"No one can make that sure. We need lions and tigers as leaders, not sheeps who just follow the previous individuals", I said.

"Gandhi was not like a lion or a tiger, he was a very simple man", said Susan.

"Yes, a very simple man with tons of strong will", I said.

"Same applies to Martin Luther and Nelson Mandela, no?" asked Susan.

"There are many more who did not reach that level of fame. Do not forget Rosa Parks", I said.

"Oh yes, who could underestimate what she did being a woman", said Susan.

"So, we need leaders, strong ones. That's the gist of this whole talk", I said.

"Absolutely, thank you so much for coming to this show Jake", said Susan.

"Thank you for the privilege", I said.

Susan shook my hand.

"Thanks to all the viewers for watching this interview, we will see you next week", said Susan.

The cameraman asked us to be seated by making a hand gesture. I went to the other room where my mom was waiting.

"I watched your interview from right here. I am impressed with your knowledge", my mom said.

"Really, thanks ma", I said.

Susan entered the room and said, "Thank you ma'am for letting us interview him. I am getting more and more impressed with his knowledge. You have got a special soul here", said Susan.

"Thanks", my mom said and smiled.

"Ok Susan, I guess we should be going now", my mom said.

"Sure, absolutely, oh here is a CD of the whole interview", said Susan while handing me over the CD.

"Thanks, see you in the future sometimes", I said.

"Sure, bye", said Susan.

"Bye Susan", I said.

I and my mom went to a restaurant for dinner. After dinner we went home. I went to bed a little earlier because I was feeling very tired.

It was Sunday. I got up a little late. My mom was watching TV.

"Jake, good morning, how are you?" my mom asked.

"Yep, getting better every day, seems like it is healing pretty fast", I said.

"I was watching news and they are calling you, ha ha, guess what?" my mom asked.

"What ma?" I asked while rubbing my eyes. I went and sat on the couch.

"See", my mom said.

I looked at the TV. The bottom of the screen read, interview with little Mahatma of New York City.

"They are calling me Mahatma of New York city. Isn't that utterly non-sense?" I asked.

"Can't say why they are doing that", my mom said while smiling.

"What have I done to deserve that kind of title ma? Nothing, I have not done anything great. Come on, just few thoughts", I said.

"I don't know Jake; these reporters can throw someone to the ground or raise them to the level of Mahatma. They possess these powers", my mom said.

"Yes, but we need to call them and tell them that I don't wanna be called a Mahatma, I don't deserve that, end of story. I mean come on ma, think for yourself, I am too young for that kind of title too", I said.

"Ok, you can call them. I mean you can call Susan", my mom said.

I talked to Susan on her cell phone and requested that I should not be referred to as Mahatma. She told me that she was unaware of such a thing and it was probably some other reporter using that title to describe me.

"Ma, Susan says she has no idea who is doing this. I mean, what if they start calling me moron of New York City", I said. My mom laughed and so did I.

"There must be something that one could do about it", I said.

"Sure, but it would be too late. Remember how they start news and even if they retract it, the damage is already done", my mom said.

"Yes ma, should we talk to a lawyer?" I asked.

"Na, I don't think it is such a big deal. I mean, they can call you whatever they want but you would stay my sweet little boy", my mom said.

"Ma, so should we just sit like that, I mean someone has to stop them", I said.

"So my baby is getting more popular now, hmmm", my mom said while smiling.

"Ma, come one now. You see, popularity brings pride, pride brings ego and ego brings disaster", I said.

"Well, you could control ego", my mom said.

"Ego comes automatically, when people run after movie stars for a mere glimpse, their ego level automatically rises", I said.

"Hmm, true", my mom said.

"Being popular is a recipe for disaster", I said.

"Not always true, look at Mother Teresa, she was popular but humble too", my mom said.

"Yep, that is one very good example", I said.

"I guess, it depends, ok enough talk, come and eat something now", my mom said.

"Sure ma, let me call Clay", I said.

"Clay, right now?" my mom asked.

"Ya, let me see what he is up to", I said.

"Ok, but after eating something", my mom said.

"Ma please", I said.

"No, stop behaving like a kid, you are mahatma of this city, ha ha", my mom laughed.

"Mahatma, ha for sure come on ma, just one phone", I said.

"After you eat something", my mom said. I moved towards the dining table reluctantly. I sat there and watched TV from a distance. They were still playing the same news over and over again. Many experts were analyzing my interview. Some were criticizing and calling me a hypocrite kid from a rich family and some were appreciating me.

"Look at them ma", I said while pointing towards the TV.

"That is why I told you to stay away from these guys, but you never listened", my mom said while placing a plate of food in front of me.

"But why are they calling me hypocrite? Is it my fault that I am born in a rich family", I said.

"Of course not, they have to find a reason for criticizing someone. Of course, they have to keep running their channel with interesting stuff", my mom said.

"Yes, but, don't they have any ethics. I mean, they are accusing me of something which I am not. I genuinely feel for people who are suffering. What motive would I have for all this?" I asked.

"They try to co-relate everything, whether true or not. They are certainly going to use the fact that you live here in this nice house and worry about people with no home", my mom said.

"So, what should I do? Sleep on the street?" I asked.

"No, but isn't that what you were suggesting about the mayor or the president", my mom said.

"Yes, but I am not the mayor or the president. How could someone expect me to be out there, although I won't mind if I hold those offices", I said.

"Yes, but they expect you to be out there with them, if you are fighting for their rights", my mom said.

"So, you are suggesting that I should add to the problem?" I asked.

"Won't mayor or president add to the problem if they are out there too?" my mom asked.

"That would be their punishment", I said.

"Come on Jake, the world does not work that way. The mayor, especially president need super security. They can't be out there on the streets. It is just not possible", my mom said.

"How much security Gandhi had?" I asked.

"I bet, he must have had some security", my mom said.

"No ma, he had no security. His followers were his only security. I mean, he did not have security carrying automatic weapons", I said.

"I know, but at later stages, when he got very popular, he was accompanied by security", my mom said.

"So, you are saying that the system should keep on going the way it is going now", I said.

"No, that's not what I am saying", my mom said.

"You see ma, we need initiative from leaders, not people. Leaders have to step up their game. They have to lead by example", I said.

"Yes, but no one takes that kind of initiative", my mom said.

"That is the root of the problem", I said.

"Ok, eat the food now, you are giving too much strain to your little mind", my mom said.

I saw that the news folks were interviewing a politician and asking for his view point on my thoughts.

"Yes, he is too small for all this, come on, he is just a kid", said a politician.

"Many individuals achieved a lot at young age. I think the boy had a lot of good points. Would you be willing to live on the street if you fail to provide basic amenities to everyone?" asked the lady interviewing the politician.

"That is just not possible because of the security reasons", said the politician.

"No, we totally understand that. So, the answer is no then?" asked the lady.

"I never said no, it is just not feasible", said the politician.

"This little boy claims that everything is feasible", said the lady.

"Why doesn't he come out of his luxury house and sleep on the streets rather than throwing mud on our faces", said the politician.

"He is just a kid. How is he supposed to survive on streets?" asked the lady.

"So how are we supposed to survive on the streets? Aren't we humans too? Why should we face punishment for others negligence?" asked the politician.

"But he is claiming that they are there because of the screwed up system? Are you going to get the system fixed?" asked the lady.

"System is already running efficiently. People need to know, who the criminals are, where they live, what kind of crimes they commit. Would you like to go and live in a neighborhood where rapists live? I bet you won't. Also, people are made aware as to where the child predators live, only because we have this system setup. Just imagine what would happen if we have no such information available to the public. You could be living next to a serial killer", said the politician.

"No, we completely understand that. So, that would mean that we should let the system go as it is now", said the lady.

"Yes, there is nothing we can do about it. There are pros and cons to everything. Knowing someone's criminal history is extremely important. Without it, the people would be more vulnerable to crime", said the politician.

"But what if someone has been punished for their crime? Why should they carry the badge of a criminal for rest of their lives?" asked the lady.

"There is no other way around it", said the politician.

"Shouldn't the criminal record be removed once a person has paid for it in some way. Think about the traffic ticket. Once someone pays the fine in full, the ticket is removed off of your record. This prevents your insurance rates from going up and it does not affect your driving record", said the lady.

"Of course, I mean the individuals with previous criminal records get jobs too", said the politician.

"I guess, this whole talk was about politicians acting as leaders, but I guess from your prospective they can't do much", said the lady.

"Politicians are leaders too. They run this country and it is not an easy task to run a huge nation", said the politician.

"Sure, well, thank you for coming on our show", said the lady.

"Thanks for having me", said the politician.

The interview was over. My mom also watched the whole interview.

"There are two sides of a coin", my mom said.

"Ya, I guess, what he was saying is right too", I said.

"Yep, I guess, they are doing the best they could", she said.

"I would have to concede on that, ma", I said.

"Good, the world is as it is now. You were trying way too hard", my mom said.

I rested for rest of the day.

The following Sunday, Clay took me out to visit the city.

"So, where to Sir?" asked Clay while I took a seat in his truck.

"How have you been?" I asked.

"Alive, ha ha", laughed Clay.

"Me too, ha ha", I laughed.

"Hey, I was reading about these artists in the town", I said.

"Artists, what artists?" asked Clay.

"Ok, there are artists in the city, who are starving; I mean I read about them. They are great in what they do but they don't have big names to back them up", I said.

"Are you referring to guys who make arts etc?" asked Clay.

"Yep, that's right. I have the address, right here", I said.

"Ok, so what are you planning to do by going there?" asked Clay.

"We will see and appreciate their art", I said.

"Would you buy something too?" asked Clay.

"Sure, mom gave me few bucks for it", I said.

"Few bucks, ok", said Clay as he entered the address into his GPS.

We drove towards the destination. Along way, I saw the same scene of homeless folks on the streets. This time I closed my eyes as I couldn't handle this anymore.

"What happened? Why did you close your eyes?" asked Clay.

"Why see, if I can't do anything about it", I said.

"Oh yes, I know what you are talking about. Hey, we tried, what if we failed", said Clay.

"I think you should have accepted the opportunity to run for president", I said.

"Yes, just run, not be", said Clay.

"You can always run independent", I said.

"Yes, I could get approximately 10 votes", said Clay.

"Ha ha, no 20", I said.

"A lot of candidates join the race and then drop every year", said Clay.

"Yes", I said while my eyes were still closed.

"Come on, open the eyes now, see the city. Don't see them", said Clay.

"When I open my eyes, all I see is them", I said.

"You could see the glass half empty or half full", said Clay.

"I want a full glass", I said.

"Everyone does", said Clay.

We arrived at our destination in about 20 minutes. There were few artists standing outside a building. We parked the truck in a parking lot close by. Clay and I walked towards them.

"Hello", said a man.

"Hi there, are you an artist?" I asked.

"Yes, I am", he said.

"Wow" said Clay while looking at a painting.

"You painted this?" asked Clay from the man.

"Yes Sir, I did", said the man.

"Nice work", said Clay.

"How much for the painting?" I asked.

"I will take 20 bucks for it", said the man.

I took out 20 dollars from my pocket and gave it to the man.

"Thank you so much", said the man.

We moved on. There were 8-10 artists in that area. They looked poor. They all placed their paintings outside on the sidewalk.

I bought all of their paintings. They were very happy.

"What are you going to do with these paintings?" asked Clay.

"Give them the right price for their art", I said.

"Right price? You already gave them what they asked for, you did not even haggle", said Clay.

"You will know what I mean", I said.

"Ok, no more mysteries, what is it Jake?" asked Clay.

"My mom knows an agent who presents work of top artists in the best galleries of the city. I am going to ask mom to talk to her to present these guys work in the gallery", I said.

"But why? I mean, it is really nice of you to think that way but, you need to think something about yourself. I always see you being worried about others. It is getting to extreme levels, don't you think?" asked Clay.

"We are not going to lose anything if their work is seen by a lot of people. Who comes to this part of the city? People go to nice areas to look at art and these guys would never make it there", I said.

"Ok grandpa, you are the boss", said Clay.

"Ha ha", I laughed.

We drove the truck towards the artists. They loaded their paintings in the back of the truck. All we heard was a ton of thanks from them.

"See Clay, people in those big name galleries pay millions for a painting and even then the artists' complain that their art deserved more and these guys are content with 20 bucks a piece. This is called life", I said.

"So, where next boss?" asked Clay.

"Come on Clay, I am not your boss", I said.

"No, I mean boss like boss, you know, not an office boss", said Clay.

"Ok, that's fine then. I guess we should keep these paintings at home first", I said.

"Sure", said Clay as we drove back towards the home.

We reached home. I rang the bell and my mom came out.

"What have you got there?" my mom asked.

"Paintings", I said.

"Paintings, from where?" she asked.

"It's a long story. Anyways, these paintings are made by very good and least known artists", I said.

"Where did you find them?" my mom asked as I placed a painting in the living room.

"We found them", I said.

"Wow that looks good", my mom said while looking at a painting.

"You think so, wait for more", I said.

"What? How many did you buy?" my mom asked.

Clay entered the house with 2 paintings in his hands.

"Hello ma'am", said Clay.

"Hello Clay, how many did you guys buy?" asked my mom.

"Not me ma'am, I am just following the orders of the boss", said Clay.

"Jake, where did you get the money to buy all these? How much did you pay for these?" my mom asked.

"Wait ma, let me get all in", I said while moving out towards the truck. My mom followed me.

"Did you buy the whole shop?" my mom asked.

"No ma, I did not", I said while picking up 2 paintings in my hands. My mom also picked 2 paintings and took it inside.

"How much did you pay for these and what are we going to do with all these paintings?" my mom asked.

"I paid like 20 bucks a piece and I will tell you what to do with these", I said.

Clay brought rest of the paintings inside.

"20 bucks a piece, so it would like 200 dollars. Where did you get that kind of money? Clay did you help him buy these?" my mom asked as she looked a little angry.

"No ma'am", said Clay.

"Ma, this is my pocket money. I saved it", I said.

"What? So, all the little money that I gave, sorry sweetie, I misunderstood you", my mom said while hugging me.

"Ma, don't worry", I said.

"These are amazing paintings, wow", my mom said while looking at them one by one.

"Clay, please have a seat", my mom said.

Clay sat on the couch while my mom kept staring at paintings one by one.

"Amazing", she said.

"You like them ma?" I asked.

"I love them. Where are we going to hang them all?" she asked.

"We are not going to hang them here", I said.

"What?" she asked.

"I want you to ask your friend, you know the one who arranges artist exhibitions in top galleries to present these paintings there", I said.

"Wait, what?" she asked as she looked completely confused.

"Ha ha", clay laughed.

"Ok, Jake, listen to me very carefully. From now on, I want you to focus on your studies. I have given you way too much rope", my mom said.

"I already did my homework ma. My grades are good too. You can check. It is my extra time", I said.

"What makes you think that I will talk to my friend about this?" my mom asked.

"Because you are my ma and you love me and you won't disappoint me", I said.

"No baby, not this time. I am not going to ask for someone's favor", my mom said.

"Who is asking for favor ma? Show her these paintings and let her make up her mind", I said.

"No, I am not going to show her these paintings. You bought these paintings and that should be sufficient encouragement for them", my mom aid.

"Come on ma, what if one of these guys has the talent of Picasso or da vinci", I said.

"I have cooked food, I bet you did not eat anything out, right?" my mom asked.

I and Clay looked at each other and smiled.

"I love food made by you ma", I said.

"Very clever", my mom said.

She brought food for both of us. We ate the food together. Clay left in about 30 minutes. I studied for a little while and then slept on time after dinner. I was back in school the next day.

During lunch session.

"So mahatma", said Jatin while smiling.

"Mahatma, ya sure, don't use that word again", I said.

"Why? A lot of kids know about this", said Jatin as we stood in the line to get the food.

"Ya, come on Jake, we saw it on TV", said Sarah.

"Sarah, do you even know what that means? I mean, they would call someone Buddha tomorrow, but that won't make someone Buddha", I said.

"Come on Jake, take it easy, they are just trying to be a little, you know", said Jatin.

"If you don't wanna be popular then why go and give interviews. Aren't you trying to be hypocrytic?" asked Sarah.

"I guess you are right, I am hypocrite, just like all", I said.

"No, I am sorry, this is not what I meant", said Sarah.

"Come on Sarah", said Jatin.

"I am sorry, ok, I know why people avoid these media people. They call a sheep a lion, a fly an elephant and a snake a dog", said Sarah.

"Wait, what?" asked Justin.

"She meant, they modify things way too much", said Justin.

"What a boring thing you said there Sarah", said Jatin.

"Boring, how about you tell something interesting", said Sarah.

"Quit it guys", I said.

"So, I bet you will avoid these media guys in the future", said Justin.

"Yep, now I understand why movie stars cover their faces and run away, whenever they see news reporters", I said.

"Mahatma ha ha", laughed Sarah.

"Sarah, no", said Jatin.

"Come on now, you really wanna start this teasing game now?" I asked.

"You, yourself went to the media, we did not ask you to go", said Sarah.

"Come on Sarah, cut it now", I said.

I stood up from the table and went back to the class.

In the evening, I was finishing my homework. My mom came to my room.

"Jake, I talked to Linda about those paintings", my mom said.

"Really, is she coming to see the paintings?" I asked.

"Yes, she will be here any time", my mom said.

"Awesome ma, you are the best", I said.

"No problem, I see that you are finishing your homework on your own", my mom said.

"I will have to do it, there is no getting around it, so why not do it first and then have fun", I said.

"Good approach Jake, you are making my life easier", my mom said.

My mom left the room. I heard the doorbell in about 15 minutes. I went out of my room towards the front door.

"Hello", said Linda while entering the house.

"Hey Linda", my mom said.

"Hello there", said Linda while looking at me.

"Hello ma'am", I said.

"Come on in", my mom said to Linda.

We all walked into the living room. Linda sat on the couch. I sat on the sofa next to the couch. My mom went to the kitchen and came back with 3 glasses of ice tea.

"Ok", said Linda as she looked at the painting behind the couch. She stood up and started walking while looking at each painting.

"You like them?" I asked.

"Where did you get these Sheela?" asked Linda.

"Jake got them", my mom said.

"I got them from the city", I said.

"Where in city?" asked Linda.

I told Linda from where I got the paintings.

"What do you think?" asked my mom.

"Hmmm, not sure Sheela, these are good paintings but people buy from someone who has established name", said Linda.

"Established name", I said.

"Yes Jake, a lot of things go into this. The name of the artist, how many paintings he has sold before, for how much, whether the artist is well recognized and the list goes on", said Linda.

"So these guys would never be able to make it big?" I asked.

"Think of this as movies. People want to see movies of well-known actors. Movies sell because of their names, not because they are all awesome, although some are. The same holds true for art. When a well-known painter makes absolutely crap painting, people say that the artist did it intentionally. They find a reason to praise them", said Linda.

"So how do these artists become famous?" I asked.

"Years and years of work", said Linda.

"So, there is no way these paintings could be shown at a gallery?" my mom asked.

"No, I am not saying that these could not be shown. The competition for slots is extreme. There are hundreds of artists competing for a single slot. It is just not possible to accommodate all. Sometimes we have to turn down very talented artists", said Linda.

"So these paintings could be shown at a gallery?" I asked.

"We can't just show these paintings. We need to do the legal paperwork with the artists before proceeding, if we are to even proceed", said Linda.

"Do you like the paintings or not?" I asked.

"It is not for me to like the paintings, it is up to the art lovers to make such a decision", said Linda.

"No, you are experienced, you know how these things work", my mom said.

"What if you make a special day of exhibition for un-known and new artists?" I asked.

"If you don't mind me asking, why are you so much interested in getting these to exhibition?" asked Linda.

"Well, he is, never mind", my mom said.

"Linda, someone must have given a chance to popular artists for the first time, otherwise they would have never made it to the top", I said.

"Of course, someone may have given them this opportunity, but no one is willing to take a risk these days", said Linda.

"What risk?" I asked.

"You know, paying for gallery space, paying for advertisement and countless other things. It takes a lot to get people to the gallery, they don't just show up", said Linda.

"How much money it takes?" I asked.

"Oh, thousands of dollars for arranging one event", said Linda.

"Thousands of dollars", I said with surprise.

"Yep, we have to be sure that event must be profitable", said Linda.

"What if we make the event right where these poor artists are, I mean where they present their art? Wouldn't that save us a lot of money?" I asked.

"It all comes down to one thing, people are not willing to spend time and money on un-known artists", said Linda.

"No, I understand", I said.

Linda stayed for another 15-20 minutes. She chatted with mom for a while and then left. I went back into my room.

My mom came to my room after a while.

"Disappointed?" my mom asked.

"What can we do? I mean, she is right from her point of view", I said.

"Yes, they got to make money, not lose it. So, what are you doing?" my mom asked.

"Nothing ma, just something", I said while using my computer.

"Ok, I am gonna be going to the market to get some stuff. You wanna come?" my mom asked.

"Na, you go on, I will spend some time here", I said.

"Ok, bye and enjoy", my mom said as she left the room.

I kept looking at various avenues of art exhibitions but nothing was encouraging. I turned the computer off in about 20-30 minutes and went to see TV in the living room.

To my surprise, they were still extracting news from my interview. Some news channels were criticizing and some were appreciating. I was getting fed up with how news channel twisted things around. I always used to think that news channels tell everything that is true, I could not have been more wrong.

"Can you believe this kid? I mean, isn't the media just trying to hype him, just like Justin Bieber", said a man giving his views on the news channel.

"Justin Bieber, you are referring to two entirely different personalities here", said the host.

"What difference does it make, it is all hype, nothing more", said the man.

I changed the channel. On another channel they were showing a candidate for president who was claiming that he was willing to sleep on the streets, if he failed to provide home to all.

"So, you are saying that you would take your security with you, in the streets and sleep on the streets where the poor live", said the host of the show.

"Yes, I would", said the candidate. His name was Donald Grey.

"Don't you think it would be an un-necessary burden on presidential security and wouldn't it be a big risk on your life too?" asked the host.

"No, I don't think so", said Donald.

"Why not? Where would your security sleep?" asked the host.

"They would sleep in the recreational vehicles", said Donald.

"RV's", said the host with surprise.

"Yes, why not?" asked Donald.

"Don't you think that would be an un-necessary constraint on tax-payers money?" asked the host.

"Security would be there, no matter where I go", said Donald.

"So, basically you would get all the amenities, even if you are on the street. Amenities like food, water, medicines, security. I mean, does it make any difference?" asked the host.

"See, you have yourself answered your own question. For a president to sleep on the streets is not the solution, it is in fact adding to the problem", said Donald.

"So, I guess we will have to rely on the promises that politicians make, that's all", said the host.

"No, one should look at the track record and how that individual has performed in the past", said Donald.

"We see that once a person gets into that powerful position, they usually forget their promises. They make these promises to win the elections, that's all, that is the whole purpose", said the host.

"I don't make fake promises. I will do the best that I could do. It is very important that we get the right person in the white house this time", said Donald.

"Well, thank you so much for coming to the show Mr. Grey", said the host.

"We will now interview the next candidate for the presidential race, his name is Julian Hayes. Welcome to the show Julian", said the host.

"Thanks for having me", said Julian.

"So, you must have heard what Mr. Grey had to say about accountability", said the host.

"Accountability, yes, we need to be held accountable for our actions", said Julian.

"But so far, I mean historically, we have not held presidential candidates accountable to the point what we heard from this boy named Jake. What do you have to say about his viewpoint? Do you think it is hypocritical for a rich boy to say this or he has some point in that?" asked the host.

"Yes, I have heard about that boy. I can't really say for sure. His point of accountability is correct but for a president to be sleeping on the streets is just not possible", said Julian.

"So, how do we hold politicians accountable?" asked the host.

"There is no clear answer", said Julian.

"Mr. Grey said that he will sleep on the street, if he can't get shelter for all the homeless", said the host.

"That's just not possible. Just imagine about the security, it would be a chaos", said Julian.

"What are you suggesting? What different would you do?" asked the host.

"Well, we could ask the, hmmm, I am not really sure", said Julian.

"So, you are saying that there is practically nothing we can do to make them accountable", said the host.

"No, I am not saying that, all I am saying is that what that boy suggested is completely preposterous", said Julian.

"But, there is no other way, is there?" asked the host.

"We could pass a law that a politician would have to pay fine or be put in jail for not performing the duties which he or she was meant to perform", said Julian.

"Do you really think that a law like that would ever be passed by the congress?" asked the host.

"I don't know", said Julian.

"So, we come back to the original topic of accountability", said the host.

"We need to look at the track-records, like Donald suggested earlier. That is the only way to choose the right candidate", said Julian.

"Are you suggesting something different or the same thing?" asked the host.

"There is no different thing here. We have a good system set up", said Julian.

"What about leadership, what about candidates themselves offering them as sheeps of sacrifice?" asked the host.

"Sheeps of sacrifice, what do you mean?" asked Julian.

"I mean they should give away the luxurious lifestyle and adapt to a more simplistic lifestyle like that of Gandhi", said the host.

"Aaa, simplistic lifestyle, I am not sure what goal would that achieve", said the host.

"That would set an example and make people help others more and more by decreasing one's expenses", said the host.

"Do you expect the president of US to be riding on a Pedi cab?" asked Julian.

"I understand the security reasons but my point was about making a simple lifestyle, decreasing your luxuries, not necessities", said the host.

"So, should the president stop flying in air force one?" asked Julian.

"I said, what is necessary should stay, it is not about that, anyways never mind", said the host.

"No, go ahead, what is it about?" asked Julian.

"If you are the leader of the nation and your citizens are eating food from trash then you should not be drinking a $5000 wine, right?" asked the host.

"So, what are you suggesting? By drinking a cheap wine, all the problems would vanish", said Julian.

"It is about the attitude, not about the expenses on the whole", said the host.

"I am confused, what is your point here?" asked Julian.

"If your kid needs money, would you go and buy a luxurious car or you would buy a little cheaper car and give rest of the money to your kid, who is in need?" asked the host.

"Good going lady", I said while watching this interview.

"I guess, you are getting a little obsessed with that boy's ideas", said Julian.

"Julian, I am not getting obsessed with anyone. These are my thoughts", said the host.

"Your thoughts, he is trying to get everyone against good politicians", said Julian.

"These are simple questions; I mean as a father of the nation, you should not be eating in a five star hotel if your kids are eating trash. It is common sense which anyone would understand. We are not saying them not to eat food; we are saying that they should at least show some concern. As I said before, the problem is with the attitude", said the host.

"I don't agree with you. President has to meet with top leaders and they are given the best welcome, usually in five star hotels", said Julian.

"So, you are saying that Gandhi never met with top leaders of the world. He did, but not in five star hotels", said the host.

"Why are you so obsessed with Gandhi? He lived on his terms and present politicians on theirs. We can't say one's lifestyle is better than the other", said Julian.

"You are missing the point here", said the host.

"What is the point?" asked Julian.

"To show concern, that's all. The politicians seem absolutely carefree about the common person", said host.

"I don't agree with that", said Julian.

"Why not?" asked the host.

"Look at Utah State, they have given homes to the homeless, if homelessness is the only issue we are referring to here. There is a decline of 91% in homeless individuals. What do you have to say about that?" asked Julian.

"Why can't we do that in every state?" asked the host.

"At least there is a start, I bet others will follow", said Julian.

"I guess, no matter what we do problems will stay", said the host.

"No, that is not true. Problems are resolved by a cumulative effort. If we think that one politician will remove all the problems of the country then we are wrong. Every individual has to step up their game", said Julian.

"What have you done to step up your game?" asked the host.

"In my region we have increased the federal funding by 10%. We have also opened 2 new schools, made roads, opened a new emergency facility and the list goes on", said Julian.

"Yes, but aren't those things already been done by one individual or another?" asked the host.

"I can only talk about my administration which has done much more than the others have accomplished in years", said Julian.

"Ok, I guess you are right in many things you have said here. We can't agree with a lot of individuals who say things about the government. I personally feel that Jake, the boy who received so much media attention was nothing more than media hype. You are doing an awesome job in what you are doing. He must be sitting on his couch doing nothing and just watching this show right now. Thank you so much Julian for coming to our show", said the host.

I was extremely angry. I slammed TV's remote on the wall. The batteries from the remote came out. I started to cry. There was no one to console me during that brief period of 5 minutes. I learned my lesson of making myself available to the media. My mom warned me against all this and it was back firing now. I went inside bedroom and laid on the bed while staring at the roof.

My mom came back in about 20 minutes. She came to my room.

"Jake", she said.

I did not reply.

"Jake, why are you not replying?" she asked as she held me from the side.

I started to cry again and while crying I said, "They are calling me a hypocrite".

"Who is calling you that?" my mom asked while placing my head on her chest and moving her hand over my head gently.

"The TV guys", I said.

"What did they say?" she asked again.

"They call me a hypocrite", I said.

"Oh no, that's why I always told you to not get involved with the media. I guess, you would be careful in the future", my mom said.

"Now everyone in the school would tease me", I said.

"Well, it is up to you, whether you care about what others say or not", my mom said.

"What do you mean?" I asked.

"People are always going to say one thing or another", my mom said.

"I know, but what should one do if they laugh at you?" I asked.

"Just ignore them", my mom said.

"But how?" I asked.

"Ok, I am going to tell you a small story. I am not sure if you have already heard this because it is a very common story. A father and a son bought a donkey. They passed through a village. People started laughing at them by saying that, look at these foolish people, despite a donkey, they are walking. The father asked son to ride the donkey. They reached a second village. There also people started saying negative things. This time they said, look at this selfish son who is riding on a donkey while his old father is walking. The son asked his father to ride the donkey and he himself started to walk.

They then approached a third village. There also people started saying things and this time they cursed the father by saying that look at this mean father who rides on a donkey while his son is walking. This time both father and son got on to the donkey. They approached another village and people cursed them both by saying that look at these selfish people, both are riding on this poor weak donkey. The father and son got so frustrated that they picked up the donkey.

They approached another village. This time people could not stop laughing. They said that they have seen many fools in their lives but not anyone carrying a donkey on their backs. The father and son had no option but to sell the donkey. Moral of the story, people would say one thing or another, no matter what you do. It is up to you whether you listen to them or not", my mom said.

"Wow, that is an awesome story ma", I said.

"Wait, let me tell you one more story", my mom said.

"Ok", I said.

"There was an old lady who lived in a village. One day a man came to her and said that no one in the village knew her. The old lady said, what the hell are you talking about, I don't know the whole village", my mom said.

"Ha ha ha, that was good one ma".

"You got that one?" my mom asked.

"Of course", I said.

"I asked because many people don't understand that joke", my mom said.

"Very uplifting ma. Thank you so much. I would not care what others say from now on", I said.

"Good, that is what I want", my mom said.

"I am feeling hungry now", I said.

"No problem, come let me prepare dinner for you", my mom said.

The following day during the lunch session at school.

"Jake, I saw on TV, the news reporters calling you a hypocrite", said Justin.

"Yes, that's what I am, a hypocrite", I said.

"What?" asked Sarah.

"Yes, that's what we all are, we just sit here and criticize all, without taking any initiative on our own", I said.

"No, we are too young to do anything", said Sarah.

"Ants are too small but they are still able to carry a huge insect to their homes", I said.

"Ok, so what are you suggesting here?" asked Jatin.

"I am saying no one is too small or weak for anything. We need to learn to stand up and act with unity, that's all", I said.

"We need to do what Jake?" asked Justin.

"Unite", I said.

"Aren't we already united?" asked Sarah.

"No, we are not", I said.

"You are insulting us now", said Justin.

"Listen Justin, we are not small for anything. If we unite, we can do a lot", I said.

"Yes, but what do you want to do?" asked Sarah.

"Force the politicians to act like leaders", I said.

"Oh come on Jake, you are starting with the same boring crap again", said Jatin.

"Yes, don't you have anything else to talk? My ears are literally hurting now", said Sarah.

"This weekend, I am going to stand in front of the mayor's office and demand shelter, healthcare for every person in this city", I said.

"What, you are going to protest?" asked Jatin.

"Yes, peacefully", I said.

"Are you guys with me? I mean, would you stand there with me?" I asked.

"Our parents would never allow that Jake", said Sarah.

"You can protest online, through social media", said Jatin.

"Yes, that's a brilliant idea", said Sarah.

"Na, let's call it quit. I am not going to do anything, just behave like all others", I said.

"Really?" asked Sarah.

"Yes, I don't think we can change the whole system. I guess we can change ourselves. We could be kind to people, we could use our own common sense and that's pretty much what we can do. We can fix ourselves, rather than fixing other", I said.

"That's a great point Jake, we can change ourselves. If everyone changes one's attitude then problems won't even arise", said Justin.

"I agree", said Jatin.

"I guess, I can start a social media post with the title of change oneself", said Jatin.

"Ya, that would be a good idea. Let us see how many people like or follow", I said.

"Change oneself, really good Jake", said Sarah.

Jatin posted on social media. He wrote to change oneself. In the post, he also wrote to help people, not ignore them. Hire people with criminal history, give them second chances. Donate to charities in our own country more than charities abroad. Elect a president who is a leader, not a politician.

The following day during lunch.

"One million like guys", said Jatin.

"One million, no kidding", I said.

"Yes, one million in just one day. The message is spreading fast", said Jatin.

"Good job Jatin", said Justin.

"No, good job to us all", said Jatin.

"I bet it is spreading fast enough because of you Jake", said Sarah.

"Me how?" I asked.

"Because you have been on TV few times", said Sarah.

"We all were on TV, remember the first time during mayor's speech", I said.

"Did you hear the news that the ex-governor of Texas is running for president. He is saying that he will provide healthcare to everyone and he will live the life of a cowboy, even as a president", said Jatin.

"What purpose would that solve? Also, it is absurd, no?" I asked.

"Living like a cowboy, come on, what is wrong with people in this country?" asked Justin.

"I guess, he is trying to say that he will live a simple life, that's all", I said.

"Simple life, being a cowboy is a simple life. It is a tough life", said Jatin.

"Yes, that's right. Maybe he is trying to say that he will live a tough life, even as a president, who knows", said Justin.

"Anyways, whatever the reason, I don't see that solving any purpose. I mean, you could live like a cowboy or a coal mine worker. Hold on, how would he be able to perform his duties?" I asked.

"From a horseback, ha ha ha", laughed Justin.

Everyone laughed.

"If there is a specific reason for that type of lifestyle, then it is fine but just for the purpose of showing to live a common man's life would not achieve anything", I said.

"Listen to this, another candidate from Alabama says that he will sell all of his land to help the homeless folks", said Jatin.

"They don't get it, do they? The solution is in fixing the cause, not the effect", I said.

"That's a great point and one candidate is actually addressing that", said Justin.

"Who?" I asked.

"Clay", said Justin.

"Clay, our Clay?" I asked.

"Yep, our Clay, he is running independently", said Justin.

"I can't believe this", I said.

"Yes, I saw it in the news online", said Justin.

"That is awesome news, I need to talk to Clay. He did not even tell me, I wonder why?" I said.

It was evening and I was at home. I called Clay.

"Clay", I said.

"Hey there buddy", said Clay.

"You are not a good man. You did not tell me", I said.

"Surprise, isn't that sweet", said Clay.

"So, what made you change your mind?" I asked.

"All the bull-shit that they said about you in TV made me very angry. I guess it is time for revenge", said Clay.

"Revenge?" I asked.

"Yes, what would be better than these politicians to see getting defeated by an ex-homeless", I said.

"That would be sweet Clay", I said.

"Ok, so we need to get to work. We need votes. I also need to participate in the debates", said Clay.

"Yes Clay, don't worry, I will get all of my friends overboard. Mom will tell all her friends and we would do best to win this by all means", I said.

"I am doing this for you, I hope you understand this", said Clay.

"I can't be more happier Clay, thank you so much", I said.

"Come and see me over the weekend", said Clay.

"No need to say that, I will be there", I said.

"Alright, have fun. I need to learn a million things on how to be the president", said Clay.

"Yes Sir, ha ha", I laughed.

"Sir, ha ha, I have not won yet, in either case, nothing to lose in trying", said Clay.

"Absolutely, that's a positive way of looking at things", I said.

"Bye for now", said Clay.

"Bye Clay, I will see you soon", I said and hung up the phone.

Chapter 13

Wings of a Great Soul

After 7 months, hours and hours of hard work, campaigning and thousands of dollars, Clay lost the elections. It was a very sad day for all of us. I and Clay were in the barn.

"At least we tried", said Clay.

"Yes we did try Clay and life does not stop here. If this country wants to elect people who give nice speeches and do little, then let it be", I said.

"I am getting very tired of this life. I guess, I will like to go back to my real home", said Clay.

"Real home?" I asked.

"Yes, where our father, the lord lives", said Clay.

"No Clay, if he wanted you back, you would have died on the streets. He kept you alive for a reason", I said.

"Maybe", said Clay.

"Clay, I was thinking that we have so much land here. Why don't we make a shelter of our own, you know for people who have no place to go", I said.

"Jake, Oh Jake, you have no idea how happy you have made me by saying that", said Clay.

I and Clay talked to my mom about this idea, to which she agreed. We went to the city and circulated brochures for donations and volunteers. We had gained enough public recognition to attract people to our project.

Soon, donations started pouring in; highly skilled volunteers started to come and build the structures. A huge shelter had started to come into shape. Months passed. People from other states also came to help. We made a small hospital, a huge shelter and a big kitchen. Despite building these structures, we still had a lot of free land.

We had two buses donated to us by a millionaire. The buses went to the city every day to pick sick people from the streets. They were treated at the hospital and given free food till they felt better. Doctors and nurses volunteered at the hospital. Once their health improved, they were asked to volunteer and help others in need.

Some were completely cured of their disease and addiction. They left the shelter and found good jobs. They regularly donated to the shelter from their paycheck. Many of them came to the shelter over weekends or even weekdays to volunteer.

After 5 years.

"Jake", said Clay as he was lying on the bed sick.

"Yes Clay", I said.

"I guess, I have to go back to my true home. He kept me alive for a reason and I guess he made full use of me", said Clay.

"You are not done yet. We have a lot of work to do. We are taking care of one city only. Many people need our help in other cities also", I said.

"I know, I guess you will have to take it from here", said Clay.

Doctors and nurses took full care of Clay. His condition improved for a while and then deteriorated again.

After about 3 months, Clay passed away peacefully in his sleep. We buried him close to grandpa. It was a very sad day for the whole shelter. Everyone loved Clay. The way Clay worked tirelessly to help those in need could not be described in words.

During these years my mom also worked tirelessly. She was extremely sad when Clay passed away. She left her job 3 years back and worked at the shelter day and night. I also quit the school and moved to the farm 3 years back. I used to study from home.

The whole responsibility of running the shelter came on me and my mom's shoulders. Years passed, donations increased, volunteers increased. New shelters on the same principal of love and respect for the destitute were opened in other cities.

I kept studying alongside taking care of shelters. The system of this country did not change, despite numerous efforts. More and more people used to hit the streets. Our job was to take care of them. Some, we were able to treat; those we could not treat were send to other countries for treatment, since it was much cheaper abroad to get the treatment for them. We partnered with charities abroad.

I went to Pingalwara in Punjab state of India. This was a facility started by one man without parents. There was a time when he had no shelter to take care of people with severe diseases and now this facility took care of hundreds of individuals all because of one man's vision. His name was Ramji Das who later became popular by the name of Bahagat Puran Singh.

Pingalwara housed around 1100 destitute individuals with more facilities opened in other cities of India. This facility took care of individuals who had severe diseases and were deserted by their family members. I guess, we all know about Mother Teresa's efforts but Bhagat Puran Singh's efforts were no less than hers. He passed away in 1992. I was able to meet with other individuals who were taking care of this facility. I learned a lot during my visit to this place. I also wanted to reach that number for each of our facility.

I returned to United States in about 2 months. It was a life changing experience for me to be in India and experience love and compassion for humanity.

Nothing had changed in our country. Same politicians and no leaders. Many politicians approached me and asked me to support them in their campaigns, to which I always declined.

My school friends, Jatin, Sarah and Justin had grown up by now. They all got married. I guess; I was the only one who did not marry. All three came to meet me once in a while. They volunteered and also made huge donations to the facility.

There were talks that the government was going to pass a law to remove criminal history from background checks of those who had served time. There were also talks of universal healthcare, but these were mere talks.

I was called to white house by the President to give me an award of service to the nation, to which I declined. I don't think I deserved such an award, since a lot was still required to be done.

After about 15 more years.

We now have 5 facilities in major cities of our country. I think it is just a starting. They call me Mahatma of New York City because that is where this work began. I still think that I don't deserve any title like such. I have been called by media several times for interviews to which I have always declined.

I thank you all for reading my story and I hope that you would also do something for others, starting from our own country. As the old saying goes, 'Charity begins from home, but it should not stop there'.

www.ingramcontent.com/pod-product-compliance
Lightning Source LLC
Chambersburg PA
CBHW022341290526
45786CB00014B/2018